GAME BIRD SHOOTING

By

CAPTAIN CHARLES ASKINS

THE AMERICAN SHOTGUN
MODERN SHOTGUNS AND LOADS
WING AND TRAP SHOOTING
RIFLES AND RIFLE SHOOTING
SHOTGUNOLOGY

MALLARD DUCK, HEN (*lower*) AND DRAKE (*upper*)

ERRATA: *Anas Platyrhyncha Lin.*

GAME BIRD SHOOTING

BY

CAPTAIN CHARLES ASKINS

SHOTGUN EDITOR OF "OUTDOOR LIFE"
AND "THE AMERICAN RIFLEMAN"

Edited by

EDWARD CAVE

NEW YORK
THE MACMILLAN COMPANY
1931

NORWOOD PRESS LINOTYPE, INC.
NORWOOD, MASS., U. S. A.

INTRODUCTION

SPORT that involves killing has no more today to be honestly said for or against it than when primitive man cast the first stone at another animal not of his kind. The whole incalculably vast subject, and all its world-mist of controversy, detonates of its own expansive gases when touched with the fire of one imperishable truth.

Let the humanitarians say their worst. Likewise the holy and the unholy among us who shoot. If finally the argument has generated enough pressure to warrant blowing it up, five honest English words will suffice. They belong to old Dr. Samuel Johnson, known in his day and ever since as a great exploder.

"Mankind is a damned scoundrel!" roared the old lion of the eighteenth century. Maybe he said "rascal."

Having actually a very large and tender regard for all humanity, he did not overstate the fact. If you happen to know or find out that he was not talking about shooting, for sport or otherwise, that is neither here nor there.

There is no honest palliation under the sun, never has been or will be, for the day-by-day monstrous crimes of the human race against helpless and harmless animal species—especially captive species.

Let therefore nobody carp who finds this book lacking in the sophistry of the modern school of sportsmen-conservationists. Were it devoted to the subject of game conservation, I seriously doubt if any other man could be found to give sounder views than Charles Askins has expressed at various times for years. Instead, it is an honest book on hunting, written out of a half-century's experience, by a man who during all that time has been an unequivocal and law-abiding, if moderately assiduous, shooter of American game birds. If at times the reader shares the feeling which has come to me now and then in editing Mr. Askins' chapters, that on this or that occasion he might have been satisfied with a lighter bag of game, there is an answer for that too. But we'll come to it later.

I first heard of Charles Askins as a dog handler. Jesse Sherwood, prominent Chicago sportsman and field dog fancier, told me there was a handler out in Nebraska who was a wonder with dogs but too skilful with a gun and too interested in shooting to make for himself a secure place among the country's top field trial handlers. So too said Joseph A. Graham, Philadelphia newspaper editor, sportsman and authority on field dogs. Another common friend who spoke well of the Nebraskan was Horace Kephart.

First as editor of "Field and Stream," then as editor of "Recreation," I had been looking for a professional field dog handler who could write. I wanted to find one who could develop into another C. B. Whitford—in which, however, I never succeeded. Mr. Whitford, then in the sunset of his activity, was too occupied in writing his book, "Training the Bird Dog," to do much magazine work. His last article for me appeared in "Recreation" for January, 1908. Mr. Askins' first article, in "Recreation" for April of that year, was not a "dog" article. In fact he never did write so much as a single line of copy for me about dogs. His first article, written upon my invitation following some correspondence, was a very thorough and ably put together essay on selecting a shotgun.

So far as I know, this was Mr. Askins' first ambitious magazine article. It was the means of his becoming one of my department editors, and a regular contributor to "Recreation" during the eight years that I subsequently put in as its editor.

I found him like Mr. Whitford, possessed of more brains and writing ability than were to be expected in those even then decadent times for sportsmen's magazines. And it is a happy sequel, to me, that I have so long afterward had the privilege of editing both the revised edition of Mr. Whitford's book above referred to and the present volume.

These two men were both natives of Illinois. And just as Whitford all his days was a quail man, so too is this true of Askins. For although I am morally certain that the Oklahoman (he has lived there for the last twenty-three years) is a better shot at doves and ducks, he still declares a preference for hunting Bob White over the pursuit of any other game bird. In this is found a trail that leads to interesting speculation and reflection concerning shooting men, and this one in particular.

Thirty years ago, one day out alone with a pointer pup and the quail and the Iowa hazel brush, I brought down a hen bird with a broken wing. Caught by the pup, her neck twisted, she was put in the side game pocket of my hunting coat. But upon getting another quail to put in the same pocket, I found my first victim very much alive. Whereupon, feeling immediately sorry, I brought her carefully home. All that fall and winter that little hen quail lived in a big cage in my bedroom. And many a time was I wakened by her plaintive rallying call at daybreak. When spring came, although she could never again take wing, she was liberated in a field where other quail used. Never since have I been keen about shooting quail.

A personal matter, purely, among hunters. Charles Askins, let us say, would have wrung the bird's neck properly. Perhaps thirty years ago— But one must not be too sure.

"All that is tenderest, sweetest, most appealing in American sporting literature has been written of the quail," says Mr. Askins, in his first chapter on the quail. And this prompts even more strongly the pertinent and interesting question: What kind of man actually is this, who has been a shooting man so long and, save the mark, in the course of becoming an authority on American game bird shooting has shot so much game? The answer, to which I cannot do proper justice, is the only excuse for this preface.

One suspects that a shooting man who never does any real work but puts in his time fooling with guns, shooting, and running a typewriter, gets small encouragement in a farming community to love his fellow man. Less when he is independent of local affairs, weather conditions and the usual neighborhood give-and-take—he wears "shorts" in summer, baring his knees to the Oklahoma breezes with the satisfaction of a true Erskine,—and on top of that is deaf from years of shooting. Indeed, if being "not very fond of people," as he confesses, has helped to keep him away from crowds all his life, it nevertheless and despite the conditions hinted at has not prevented people from being fond of Charles Askins— the home folks anywhere he stays, especially the boys, and many hunting companions,

This man who has shot so much game, and whose natural reticence to boot might make him seem cold-blooded, has a little graveyard for his pets in a grove on the farm where he lives. There is buried Monty, the wolf-dog which is told of in Chapter XXVII. There too is Jimmy Cat, a Persian that died one spring day this year.

"I made him a coffin out of an ammunition box, curled him in it with his bushy tail over his nose the way he slept, and buried him beside Monty, the sheep dog.

"This is all a waste of sentiment, of course, but I have always been the same since a boy. I have killed a lot of game, but never shoot anything that hasn't a chance to escape, and can't bring myself to shoot anything about the farm—chickens, pigs, cattle. Won't raise pigs, because they always become pets and then have to be killed."

His father, a farmer "but not a good farmer," was interested in breeding thoroughbred horses—which never paid him. Still, he had fine horses, and, along with learning to shoot, young Charley learned to ride. Learned to ride as well as a cow man—better than many, because he had higher-spirited horses and that inherited fondness for animals.

He was sent to school to be a lawyer. When his father died, finding he had to make his own way he taught school in the winter and played "summer" baseball. On the highroad to becoming a professional ballplayer, he hurt his throwing arm permanently.

Meanwhile there had been shooting and dog training, in plenty. The Askins farm was in St. Clair County (Illinois), six miles west of Belleville. His first winged game, undoubtedly shot sitting, was wild pigeons. At seven acquiring a rifle—which he shot with a rest and then carried home to be reloaded—by ten or eleven he was sharing a light shotgun with his brothers. This was duck country, and about one farmer out of every five became a market hunter as soon as the fall crops were in the ground.

"About the middle of October the market hunters would leave home, to go up on the Illinois River for a month. Then after a brief visit at home they would drift off south, spending most of the winter in the New Madrid marshes, across the Mississippi in Arkansas, and coming home about the first of May. My first winter and spring in the New Madrid marshes gave me so much malaria and rheumatism that I got permission from my father to go to Minnesota to get rid of them. Up there I went to work for George Gray, of Appleton. He was a market hunter as well as having a kennel of dogs. My work was to train his duck dogs. In doing this I took out just fifty shells a day. These were brass shells loaded with black powder; loaded the shells myself. George would have been pleased if I'd killed fifty ducks a day, but I never did. I think I averaged about three dozen a day, which he sold.

"The next year I spent in the old Indian Territory, which was then full of game. I never had sold any game, having worked for somebody else. Down there I made my expenses training a bunch of bird dogs."

In 1890 the dog handler married and settled down, to live at Marion, Ill., farming. There he had more quail to shoot than he ever has had elsewhere—shot quail better, too. About 1893, he undertook to break the record made some years before by Hiram Stotlar, a market hunter—72 quail in a day. He didn't do it, being short 11 birds; but there was one run of 23 straight. Quail shooting with a shotgun, in that country where the birds were plentiful and easy, became monotonous.

The death of his wife ended ten years of farming and spoiled him forever for that.

"From 1900 to 1906 I handled a string of field trial dogs and shot a great deal, shooting in every state in the South except Louisiana and South Carolina. Never was a very good trainer, because I liked to shoot too well. Shooting and dog training don't work well together, but I won sometimes. What really caused me to quit field trials was my loss of a setter that I had trained. He was called Doc Hick, a great field trial dog, the most highly trained dog that I ever have seen, and the most lovable and biddable. I had him from the time he was a puppy until he won the United States Subscription Stake at four years old. He was with me day and night, slept under my bed, never out of doors in his whole life, and he ate whatever I had to eat. Having won extensively, he was sold to John Considine, and had to be sent from Mississippi to Seattle, Wash. I put him in his crate, and he certainly thought that we were going together. And the next I heard of Doc Hick he was dead.

"I never since have had any heart for dog training. My dogs now are just about the least trained bird dogs that ever went afield, because I never punish them. I let them do what pleases them best, they do the best they know how, and we have a grand time together; but it is scandalous handling in the eyes of a stranger."

Thus we learn an ample reason why the dog handler of Valentine, Nebr., never wrote about dog training. There was at the time, I recall, another. Together they reflect the sensitive nature of the man, whose defection has become so conspicuous a loss to the fraternity of field dog fanciers. The absence from this book of the logical chapter on dog handling, if regrettable, is accounted for, with amends, in the author's own way. A most charming revelation to all who may deplore his resolution in forever turning his back to the subject.

There came the time, starting after he went to live in Oklahoma, when the former dogman, farmer and market shooter not only turned to writing articles on guns and shooting, but also to doing juvenile fiction. Five years of this and he was well in the saddle.

Since the publication of his first book, "The American Shotgun," except for a period of service as a captain in the Ordnance Department during the World War Mr. Askins has devoted all of his time to writing on shotguns and shotgun ammunition, wing shooting, game birds and game bird conservation.

"Here in Oklahoma, wheat farming and the one-way plow, which follows hard after the combine, is getting the nesting birds, breaking up the nests and killing the young before they can fly. Of the doves we had ten years ago, not more than one in ten remains. They breed around the house and I have only three pairs where I used to have from twenty to thirty. It is the same way with the quail. Last year there were practically no quail here. In the summer I had two bevies on my place. I used to warn the shooters. Nobody could shoot those quail. Yet they were killed anyhow—potshot by hoodlums in automobiles."

Another come-down which I am privileged to mention concerns crippled quail. "You must not think you are unusual because you turned loose a cripple," Mr. Askins reproved me recently, on my mentioning it. "I do it myself, if no one is with me to catch me at it—and the bird is not badly body shot. Vermin gets them, of course, but I don't like to kill them in my hands."

I have said that one might wish the shooting man had been sometimes less keen. But those times are long gone by. And surely the man who so loved Doc Hick, and Monty, and Jimmy Cat, who turns loose crippled quail, keeps a gang of pet squirrels supplied with corn on the cob, but won't keep pigs because they would become his pets and then have to be killed —surely he has actually never been less generous toward his game than any of us others, who profess honest fondness of the gun. For such a shooting man to have to put up his gun on a good day, when game was there in plenty, would have been as inexcusable as it would be today for Lindbergh to be seen on a train or for Bobby Jones to be caught playing croquet. There are indeed, we may be sure, some sticklers for consistency who will now aver that Mr. Askins is getting chicken-hearted. To which we can agree with satisfaction. For surely if there is any compassion whatsoever in mankind, then truly it is most becoming where it is least expected.

As Mr. Askins well puts it in his conclusion, there is merit in privation. Always remembering that to the true disciple of wing shooting there must still be some shooting, it may be hoped that this book will achieve its best purpose in pointing out the contrast between wing shooting that was and wing shooting that is. Having eaten our cake, perhaps with such inspiration we may the better appreciate the crumbs that remain, hoarding them over to a new and better day of actual game restoration.

EDWARD CAVE.

Mt. Vernon, N. Y.
June 22, 1931.

FOREWORD

THIS book is written entirely from the point of view of the shooting man. No serious attempt has been made to describe the various game birds according to the standards of ornithologists. They are instead described by an oldtime bird hunter. Added to the chapters about game birds are a few others that deal with equipment and wing shooting. Supplementing the information about game, these are intended to aid the man who does not have a book especially devoted to the gun.

While making no pretense of containing the wisdom of Solomon or the authority of Wilson, Audubon and Coues, what is presented does represent knowledge, largely gained by many years of shooting small game. Here and there some attempt is made to add variation to the descriptions of birds and their habits and habitat, by relating hunting incidents. Again, there are a few narratives of hunting trips. Like the rest of the volume, this material is drawn from the writer's own experience.

Whatever the reader may gain in information, it is intended that first of all he shall be entertained. If there is here to be found some worth-while inspiration, some firm encouragement to follow the gun, if pleasant memories are called up and the reader is helped to while away an occasional happy hour in the off season, this is all the author asks.

A part of the book has been published before, in magazine articles. However, except for two revised chapters all such material has been completely rewritten. For the privilege of using that which was published serially some years ago in "Field and Stream," and that which appeared more recently in "Outdoor Life," I acknowledge the courtesy of the publishers. For the illustrations by the Wright brothers, my thanks are tendered to Mr. Lors E. Krogius and to Dr. E. H. Ekman, of Finland. For opportunity to use many of the photographs reproduced, I am similarly indebted to the National Association of Audubon Societies, and to Mr. Charles B. Morss, Mr. Edward Cave, and a number of other sportsmen photographers whose pictures used to beautify "Recreation" under Mr. Cave's editorship.

CHARLES ASKINS.

Ames, Okla.
1931.

CONTENTS

Part II

WATERFOWL SHOOTING

ILLUSTRATIONS

Part I

UPLAND GAME BIRD SHOOTING

Chapter I

THE PRAIRIE CHICKEN

The Pinnated Grouse. The Sharp-tailed Grouse

MY first real chicken hunt occurred in the Osage Nation of the Indian Territory in the late eighties. There were three of us, with a team, a wagon and a pair of dogs.

The dogs were ranging ahead and we followed in the wagon. Nothing had stirred from the tall prairie grass.

I noticed that some dwarf postoaks well ahead of us seemed to be conspicuously filled with birds' nests, fifty to the tree and many trees loaded. "What are they?" I asked.

The driver said "Chickens," and I whipped out and on ahead with my dogs. Soon the chickens flew out of the trees, hundreds of them; but there were others on the ground that didn't fly. The dog pointed, and I shot at a chicken, missing with both barrels at about thirty yards.

All around me the chickens climbed out, cackling. They didn't fly far, and they put up three bevies of quail in their flight.

Getting out the empty brass shells and reloading as fast as I could, I was interrupted by a shout from the wagon. Looking back, I saw eleven deer, coming from the timber, crossing an opening within a hundred yards of me, the does in front, bucks behind, galloping slowly, unafraid.

1

The driver grabbed his old Sharps rifle, but couldn't find his cartridges in time. He finally shot and missed.

As the deer entered the next clump of oaks, a great flock of large black colored birds, looking not unlike crows in the distance, took wing and went into the timber with the deer.

We estimated that bunch of wild turkeys as containing three hundred birds, and I never since have seen another such flock.

The driver tied his team and followed the deer. The old-timer took his shotgun and followed the turkeys. Taking the dogs, I went on down into a lush grassy valley, along a branch, where the chickens and the quail had gone.

The dogs pointed, now chickens, now quail, and along with what I bagged of them I killed one turkey and five mallard ducks. I couldn't carry all the birds; they were piled under a tree until the wagon came up.

The driver got no deer, the oldtimer killed two turkeys, and I emptied all the shells I had.

The Osage Indian has become rich since that day, his race is the richest people in the world; but if he had only known it he was nearer to Indian heaven in those days than he ever will be again.

That night I myself felt that I was surely in a hunters' paradise as I loaded shells by lantern light and listened to the coyotes howling as they ringed the camp. Today I know all too well that it was nothing less.

ALL CHICKENS ARE CHICKENS

WE are classing all the birds in this chapter as prairie chickens, though there are minor differences or varieties of the true chicken, besides the sharptail, quite a different bird. All prairie chickens look alike, from those found on the Atlantic Coast to the chicken of the Panhandle of Texas, though they bear different Latin names. The Eastern variety is practically extinct.

The pinnated grouse is strictly a prairie bird, though sometimes driven to the woods by stress of weather or for forage. He is the only prairie grouse in this country, or perhaps in any other country, grouse in general being "woods Indians." The willow grouse is more or less a bird of the open, but he is really a ptarmigan, with a range extending across British America and the North of Europe.

Our pinnated grouse is said to have an unconquerable aversion to civilization, refusing to nest in a cultivated field or anywhere except the unbroken sod. This may be only relatively true; possibly we have accepted a conclusion without testing it. No game bird was wilder than the turkey, yet he was domesticated; because there was real need of him—he fitted splendidly into a domestic niche not previously occupied.

The prairie chicken cannot replace or displace the universal domestic hen—man can live without him, have as much to eat, make as much money. He is of interest only to the sportsman, who should have protected him and perpetuated his race. If it had been the business of the poultryman to breed prairie chickens, we should have had them by the millions; but it being the business of the shooting man, our finest grouse may become extinct.

When the Cherokee Strip of the Indian Territory was opened to settlement, in 1893, the land was alive with prairie chickens. They came in from the prairie to feed with the tame hens, alighted on the roof of the shack before daylight, followed the plow and dusted in the furrow, watered at the horse-trough, and scratched in the garden like veritable brown leghorns.   In six years they were all gone, not a bird left east of the Cimarron River.

People said the chicken had gone west, migrated through dislike of civilization, of the plow and the reaper.   As a matter of fact they were all dead.

It was difficult for the settler to understand that.   Of the million chickens which were there when he came, shooting winter and summer, spring and fall, he had killed no more than a thousand a year.   He failed to consider that his nearest neighbor, most distant neighbor as well, had also killed a thousand, and that just so the thousands made a million.

The birds were trapped in the barnyard, tolled under the traps by domestic chickens.   In the spring the farmer carried his gun at his work in the fields in order that no frying-size chicken might be lost.   In summer his wheat shocks needed protection and got it.   In the fall he hunted for sport, in the winter for the market.   I have heard more than a few Oklahoma "sooners" tell of knocking the birds over with a plow wrench when they became too tame and there was no gun at hand.   And so inevitably the prairie chickens were literally exterminated.

Such is the history of the great prairie grouse in every new land all the way from the Alleghenies to the Rocky Mountains. They were killed in season and out because they represented food easily procured.   The big chicken was helpless; child of the open prairies, he had nowhere to hide his head.   Though strong of wing and bold of flight, he could not leave the country to find another beyond danger, as do the waterfowl.   Like

Captain Charles Askins

Above, a point on prairie chickens in Washington near the Saskatchewan line.
Center, quail in Minnesota. *Below,* quail hunters in Virginia.

every other non-migrant, where he was born and raised, there he lived and died.

Had our bob-white quail weighed a pound instead of a short eight ounces, had he, too, been strictly a bird of the open, he surely would have "gone west" with the chicken. One salvation of the quail was that it often cost more to kill him than he was worth, whereas just about as often, a two-cent cartridge fired at a chicken meant a meal for the family.

When all is said, the passing of the prairie chicken is not to be laid to the market shooter or the sportsman, but to the farmer, the man who lived in a cabin and broke the sod.

For another thing, I believe it a fair statement to assert that four-fifths of the prairie chickens killed in this country, from the time the first bird was shot on the moors of Massachusetts until today, have been slaughtered when no more than two-thirds grown. For thirty years, wherever there have been chickens early shooting by "sooners" on the farms has gone on in spite of more and more game laws. When the young chickens reached a weight of a pound or more, able to fly a hundred yards, getting up at the shooter's feet, winging slow and straight, a dainty on the table, they have been killed. And every "sooner," man and boy, considered himself a great chicken shot, though he could hit no other game bird whatever. No, the farmer has never been a friend of the chicken, even though today he is of the quail.

In the year 1929, after many complaints had reached the Game Department of Oklahoma concerning the alleged depredations of the prairie chicken in a few counties, a three-days open season was declared on the birds. Chickens were to be shot only by residents of the state, under the usual resident license fee of one dollar and twenty-five cents. The day be-

fore the opening, it seemed as if all the small-game hunters of
the state were ready to make war on the few remaining
chickens.   The shooters came from every section, and it was
estimated that thirty thousand passed through the little city
of Enid on the way to the chicken grounds on that day.   A
garage man of Fairview counted two thousand cars passing
his station in two hours.   All the careful protection of the
Oklahoma game authorities, over a period of twenty years, was
undone in those three days.   Most of the hunters camped in
the fields, ready to start work at peep-o'-day.   Some of them
got a chicken and some did not, there being three hunters to
every grouse.   Some of the farmers charged five dollars a
day for permission to cross their places, but most of them
went down into storm cellars to keep from being shot.

That was all primarily the work of the automobile, which
is chiefly what modern game conservation has to contend with.

Today, there are more grouse in Canada, odds over, than
in the United States.   Some Americans say that Alberta can
now make the same showing of chickens that Iowa did forty
years ago.   This is decidedly optimistic, and not borne out
by the Canadian game authorities.   Furthermore, to many
of us the prairie of western Canada is a far cry, and it costs
fifty dollars for a license when we get there.   However, to
those who can afford it, the trip is well worth while, not only
for the experience of hunting prairie chickens where there
actually are more chickens than hunters, but also for the unex-
celled waterfowl shooting.

In the United States, up to the beginning of the World
War the Dakotas were the last stronghold of the prairie
grouse.   There were chickens or sharp-tailed grouse, one
or the other, pretty much all over both North and South Da-

kota. Wheat prices were high during the war, and the sod largely disappeared, together with the chicken. In the dual interest of sport and conservation, the introduced Old World pheasant, an inferior game bird, has now in a great measure displaced the chicken. Not that the native grouse cannot be bred like the pheasant, in captivity; fully as much because the pheasant is a runner and better adapted to withstand continual persecution. Some grouse remain in the rougher country west of the Missouri River. That river used to be the dividing line between the prairie chicken country and that of the sharp-tailed grouse, but now the two birds are found in the same territory—all rough country where cultivation is difficult.

In the "sandhills" of Nebraska the chicken should linger longer than elsewhere in the prairie states, for the simple reason that for years to come there should be more birds than the sparse population can eat. The Nebraska hills, under the Kincaid Law, have a settler to every square mile, theoretically. In reality many of the homestead claims have been abandoned, and houses may be several miles apart. If the farmers' lot is harder anywhere than in these hills, I don't know of it.

The elevation of this hill country is from 2000 to 4000 feet, with air sharp and bracing. The rivers, like the Loup, Niobrara, and Elkhorn, are clear, cold and swift. Over all this section are beautiful lakes, from mere ponds to lakes a mile wide and three times as long, where black bass are caught and the wildfowl remain until ice and snow drive them southward. Grouse grow fat on the sand-cherries, rosebuds and grasshoppers, while men become lean, starve out—which is as it should be, so far as I am concerned.

In the days of market hunting, Kansas was noted for its

chickens.   Incidentally, Kansas chicken shooters hitched a wire between two wagons, and with these driving across the prairie 300 yards apart, the gunners walked back of the wire, taking the grouse as they arose until the wagon was filled.

To the oldtimer no other bird can quite take the place of the prairie chicken.   Perhaps the first bird he ever killed on the wing was a chicken.   Perhaps the last bird he ever killed on the wing was a chicken, too; and then the birds were found far apart.   Country doctor, county-seat lawyer, well-to-do farmer, or retired market shooter, bearing in mind the days of his youth, August first found him migrating west after the chickens.   On the prairies of Iowa, Minnesota or beyond, he found them.   All the year he had lived frugally and saved carefully for that.   Once again the big grouse climbed from the yellow grass, cackling, defiant; and brave old days were lived over again.   And so till the gun was laid aside for the last time, when there were no more chickens and instead a long-tailed alien bird scampered before the dog.

There were supposed to be three varieties of the pinnated grouse.   The Eastern variety *(Tympanuchus cupido)* was generally known as the heath hen.   Some years ago the last survivors were perpetually protected on Marthas Vineyard. They too may all be gone by now.   The habitat of the common variety extended from Indiana across Illinois, throughout Wisconsin, thence west across lower Minnesota and the plains.   The third variety was found in the Panhandle of Texas, in western Oklahoma, and in western Kansas.   All of these birds were and where still found are much alike, the Texas variety apparently slightly smaller and perhaps more rapid in flight.

The sharp-tailed grouse, universally called "grouse" in the West, is a different bird from the true chicken. He is lighter in color, with a sharper tail, and more like the quail in his habits. He packs less, if at all, and takes less kindly to settlements. The pinnated grouse, or true prairie chicken, is very fond of cultivated fields, of wheat, kaffir, and corn, but the sharptail clings to his native hills, living today as he did when he and the buffalo had a common range in the Northwest. The sharptail lies better to a dog than the chicken, doesn't rise so wild in cold weather, and his flights are not so long. An old "grouse" is a better table bird than an old chicken, being more like a quail about this. His wingbeats are slightly more rapid than those of a chicken, and his flight steadier, though he towers higher. He is a splendid game bird, from his topknot to his feathered toes.

The chicken, or today's remaining Dakota pinnated grouse, packs in the fall, about the first of October, and thereafter tends to migrate to the southeastward. Probably this tendency to migrate is not a natural habit but one acquired. In the life of the chicken of the upper Mississippi Valley, as settlements encroached his breeding grounds would lie to the northwest, but in winter the best foraging grounds would be found to the southeast, in the great fields of standing corn, and that was where he went. In the same way the chickens of Kansas moved south and east into the Indian Territory, and Missouri, where they could find acorns and more or less protection from winter storms.*

* Sharptails do not migrate to the same extent. Nor have the sharptails of Manitoba "retreated" eastward into the vast newly opened scrub and muskeg country toward James Bay, as is erroneously reported by sportsmen. They always have been there. The northern or dark variety is found from the eastern shores of James Bay to central Alaska and south to Lake Winnipeg, but not in the United States.

Having spent many years among the chickens, I may be prejudiced. However, that I have given the pinnated grouse first place and the place of honor in this book is solely for what he was. I am confident of making no error in saying that in America one hundred years ago there were more prairie chickens than all other grouse combined. It was a prairie grouse empire, all the way from the Atlantic Coast to beyond the Rockies, from the Gulf of Mexico almost to the Arctic Circle.

In Indian Territory days of beloved memory, I have more than once sat with my back to boulder and watched a flock of fifty chickens for hours. They would be collected, cocks and hens, on a bare spot of ground on the bald prairie. Perfectly aware of my presence, yet, since I made no effort to molest them and kept still, they treated me with supreme indifference. The hens crept about coyly, pretending to scratch for food, while the cocks crowed with upstretched necks, precisely like a rooster of the barnyard, or, again, strutted like miniature turkey gobblers. Now and then all of them set up a cackle, while from far and near came the booming of bachelor cocks, which may have been shut out from this community gathering.

While watching a flock of chickens, in the early morning of a mellow spring day, I saw two cocks fight an unforgettable battle. The weaker bird didn't know enough to quit, and the stronger never meant to. At last I went to the conquering bird and "shooed" him off. At that he wouldn't fly, but ran a short distance and stood waiting for me to depart, that he might finish his job. I picked up the vanquished bird, too far gone to attempt to escape, and carried him fifty yards out into the tall grass. Shortly he showed signs of recov-

Photo, courtesy U. S. Bureau of Biological Survey.

This ingenious and time-worn photograph of dead prairie chickens brought to life by clever taxidermy has fooled more than one confiding naturalist, but few observing hunters or wild life photographers. The same is true of two photographs of mounted prairie chickens "in flight," which have been many times published as live birds. These are pinnated grouse.

Photos Edward Cave and Sumner W. Matteson.

Chicken hunting in Minnesota and North Dakota

ering, and as soon as able to walk went directly back to the mound and renewed the fight. When again too far spent to escape, I caught him a second time, carrying him nearly to the house where I lived, a mile distant. By and by he got on his feet, staggering off in the direction of the fighting ground, and while I never saw him again, I have always been sure that he went directly back and was killed.

The cock prairie chicken is a wonderfully plucky chap, and he who has once seen them fight will no longer marvel that they sometimes carry off a heavy load of shot.

That there are still some chickens left to shoot is as much due to climatic conditions as to other reasons. In the semi-arid regions of the Rocky Mountain tablelands, where it rains only at unexpected times, where wheat will not grow, nor corn, where people exist rather than live, the prairie chickens find sanctuary. Where the winds blow and the sands drift, and the ridges of hills rise broken-toothed above the deep valleys, the brown grouse boom away over the grassland, coveys in summer, great packs in winter. Draw a straight line from the northeast corner of the Panhandle of Texas to the Bad Lands of South Dakota, and it passes through the best chicken grounds that remain today, south of Canada.

Just how far the flight of a chicken might extend I do not know. When duck shooting on Trappers Lake in western Minnesota, I have seen packs of chickens cross the lake like waterfowl, a hundred feet in the air, their approach noted for a mile before they reached me, in sight for two miles after they had gone by. Doubtless these birds were on migration, bent for the corn fields of Iowa, a hundred miles distant. Perhaps no other grouse makes such extended flights, except the willow ptarmigan of the Barren Grounds.

Not all the pleasure of chicken shooting is due to the birds killed. The prairie wilderness is no less attractive than the wilderness of the woods. In association with the pinnated grouse, not to be severed, are the wide, open prairies, with wind-swept grass rolling like the sea. Roads were rarely followed in the old days; the team was headed across an unmarked prairie, hill and valley.

Blue in the distance, a cottonwood grove marks the borders of a lake. Hay flats may have been mowed, but the wild grass, undefeated, will not down, and again has reached the height of a foot. On the hillsides the sedge and redtop bend as the wagon passes over, then rise again until none but an Indian could mark the passage. It is early October, yet on the tablelands there is an icy tonic in the rarefied morning air. On the hilltops the frost opens sparkling eyes for one peep at the day, then is gone. Deep in the valleys, shaded by the ridge hills now rosebud-tinted in red, it still glares in white defiance.

The red setter and the white pointer swing and sweep across the hills and disappear into the valley. Away off on the flat, near a stack of hay, the setter stops uncertain, while two dog-like animals trot up to him. The wild dogs and the tame one spar about for a minute, but nothing comes of it, and the setter gallops off about his business of finding chickens. The coyotes, catching sight of the hunting rig, prance away with stiff-legged jumps, then strike an easy lope for the purple hills in the distance.

In the swale, where the grass is thick but not tall, where the lingering frost is turning to dew, the dogs stop. The team of broncs is sent forward at a gallop; but when a hundred

yards back the more nervous gunner insists that the team
stop and the shooters go ahead on foot.   Our old chicken
hunter is anxious about this first shot of the season, meaning
to take no unnecessary risk of the birds rising wild.   A hard
man on even bachelor chickens.

Carefully, from right and left, they stalk the standing
dogs.   No chickens break cover.   In front of the red dog
are round, well-padded spots, a dozen of them, where the
grouse have roosted.   Toward the adjacent ridge are trails
plainly written in the dewy grass, twisting, criss-crossing,
wandering apparently anywhere, yet always drifting towards
the sun-crowned hill.

"That is where they roosted," says the oldtimer.   "They
have gone to the ridge now, where the sun has started the
hoppers to moving."

Carefully and stiffly, with keen, cautious noses, and the
wisdom of much experience, the dogs follow the trail up the
hill, around the brow of the ridge and into a deep depression.
The two men might have pressed on faster had they wished,
for everywhere the wet grass betrayed the meandering footsteps of the fowl.

In the valley they have just left, skirting the foot of the
ridge, bent on seeing as much of the sport as he can, the
driver of the wagon has kept even progress with the hunters.
Suddenly he gives a loud whoop.

Dashing back to the brow of the ridge, the hunters can see
what has happened.   The wise birds, having seen the hunters
coming in pursuit, have doubled back, returning to the swale,
where the wagon has driven into the very midst of them.
Climbing, cackling, towering, curving, whipping the grass
with powerful wings, the chickens are rising on every side,

while the driver points his whip at first one bird and then
another, until fifty great grouse are up and gone.

From their vantage on the hilltop, the hunters have anyhow marked the pack accurately.   Soon they will be among
the scattered grouse.   Here we shall leave them, assured that
veteran shots will give a good account of themselves.

In northern Nebraska, in the "hay country" where in the
year 1900 very little land had ever been touched by the plow,
we were located for two weeks on Lake Creek, a tributary of
the Elkhorn River.   Lake Creek swept in a wide horseshoe
bend about the ranchhouse where we stayed.   The valley, inside the half circle, was as level as a floor, three miles across,
hedged in by towering sand-hills, bases clothed in bunch grass,
the wind cutting steadily at their bare tops.   It was all un-
fenced prairie, just as the Pawnee Indians and the buffalo
had left it years before.   The chickens would be there, we
knew, with perhaps mallards along the creek and snipe in
the overflows.   We hunted on horseback, mounted on steady
old cow-ponies.

There comes a time in the fall when the bevies of chickens
break up, the old hen and her brood separating, every bird
for itself.   Later they collect in packs, then becoming wild.
We had happened on such a time; the fowl like a great pack
that had been scattered.   It was October, nights frosty, but
the sun beating down on the yellow grass with mellow force.
We felt lazy and content, the horses were lazy, the chickens
were lazy.   Not even the mallards under the creek bank had
a worry in the world.

I had never before seen chickens in such numbers.   After
the first few hours we did not shoot many birds—nothing could

be done with them. We did not feel like eating fried chicken day after day, for dinner, breakfast and supper. Our three neighbors accepted but few, through courtesy, chicken having palled on them long since. Game has to be scarce in order to be appreciated, but we understood then how a market shooting gang a few years before might have killed five hundred chickens in a day. For honest wing-shooting we went to a snipe slash, a little distance from the house; again breaking the monotony by chasing coyotes with a pair of wolfhounds. I did try out a gun which my shooting chum owned, a little 28 gauge single-barrel, with which I killed twenty-eight chickens straight in two days' shooting. I subsequently bought a 28 double, and used it for four years with much satisfaction on chickens and quail.

And so to conclude, a further word about chicken guns, since I have promised to write of guns. In the old days any kind of gun would kill chickens, and did. Today chicken seasons are set much later, the birds are strong and wary. Shots must be taken to the utmost limits of shotgun range. The best chicken gun is simply a duck gun which will drop the birds at a good sixty yards.

Any grouse that gets up within fifty yards is to be taken. There is no need for special instruction in gun handling. It is all very much like jumping ducks, the fowl climbing, the shot sent high, the lead on a passing bird about the same as that on a mallard. With luck, in the standing corn and kaffir, a few birds may be killed. The best chance is to catch the big grouse as they come into the corn field; or post a gun or two where it is known the chickens will go out, and then have another gun and the dogs drive the field.

Chapter II

THE RUFFED GROUSE

RUFFED grouse, partridge, pheasant, and numerous un-
called-for Latin unpronounceables are the names variously tacked to the subject of our sketch. Most people would
say that this woods-grouse which flirts his tail, and flashes his
eye, and chuckles banteringly as he gaily dodges a shower of
death, is the same bird whatever he may be called. But he isn't
quite. Fact is, he is a different bird according to what he is
called. Let me explain.

For instance, *B. umbellus*, the Latin bird, I shouldn't recognize if I met him in the road, while I am on a friendly and familiar footing with the partridge. *B. umbellus* has length
of wing, spread of tail, wing-coverts, tail-coverts, markings of
rufous, cinnamon, tawny and brown; he has habits and habitat; when he is dead his stomach contains things which he must
have eaten when alive; he was discovered and named by a
naturalist, which was inevitable; the female of the species
lays eggs in the spring of the year; John James Audubon shot
'em from the back room of his kitchen when he lived in Kentucky. That is all science has taught me about *B. umbellus*.

The ruffed grouse is the bird of the Audubonites and the
United States Department of Agriculture. He lives in the
woods, and visits farms solely for the purpose of eating potato-
bugs. Having eaten the bugs he invariably returns to the
woods, being very careful not to step on the grass either com-

ing or going. The ruffed grouse knows all about bugging potatoes, and if he is carefully protected and encouraged, and not given too big doses of paris green, he will save many a faithful boy, who has been detailed to the bugs, from getting a licking. The farmer should swat the grouse-hunter, say the Department of Agriculture and the Audubonites, neglecting to say who should swat the farmer when *he* pots a grouse.

The pheasant is simply an uneducated, unsophisticated, pioneer-born, backwoods-raised partridge. He could be called a game bird, though rather a fine bit of something mighty good to eat. Without true sporting instincts, the pheasant is, nevertheless, a sly and cunning bird that is very hard to find even after you know precisely where he is through the efforts of a little dog which is barking up the wrong tree. The pheasant belongs to the age of the muzzle-loading rifle; like that weapon he is about gone, though a few of the birds and a few of the guns might still be found in the Allegheny Mountains, more likely the southern Appalachians.

The partridge is the bird I like. He alone is entitled to be known as Rex, king of the grouse, a bird of the deep woods, bold, hardy, elusive, enterprising, and unrivaled. The things that a partridge did yesterday he will not do tomorrow, and the grouse-shooter who batted a thousand per cent yesterday may strike out today every time he comes to the plate. The dog that sneaks about with cautious feet may get us a lot of shots on occasion, or it is equally possible that the partridge will do some sneaking himself, and a romping, roaring, whirlwind of a dog will be needed, in that his grouseship shall be "scared stiff" and made to hug the ground.

The partridge of today or the ruffed grouse, call him which you prefer, is a product not altogether of nature, but rather of the modern idea of sportsmanship working on the nature of a wild bird. The ruffed grouse whose forebears have never come in contact with the wise dog of a wing-shooting woods-loafer might be able to dodge as cleverly, to roar as loudly, to send flashes of sunlight and waves of sound as effectually, to shield his body, as does the sporting partridge, but he never has done so—his qualities are latent, undeveloped. But when we have educated him personally and his parents before him even unto the hundredth generation, he then becomes peculiarly our product, a creature whose instincts of self-preservation man has ably though indirectly sharpened.

The habitat of *Bonassa umbellus* is between the covers of an unread book. The pheasant is to be found in the mountains from Pennsylvania south to Georgia; also he is well known in the Ozark Mountains of Missouri and Arkansas. The ruffed grouse is widely distributed among book-learned people. The partridge occupies certain sections of the New England States, New York, Pennsylvania, Michigan, Wisconsin and Minnesota, not to mention a lot of Canada. The smallest feather of him lying in a scratched-out hole at the side of an old moss-grown log is sufficient to render an entire woodland interesting.

THE GUN

WE cannot properly shoot ruffed grouse without a shotgun; of shotguns, preferably a double gun, of light weight and small bore; of the small bores, be sure that yours is one that handles fast, and that has all the spread of pattern possible, while yet retaining the requisite power.

The partridge-shooter is one man who has to walk, and

there never is any maybe about it. The further he foots it the better his chances, assuming that he knows his partridges. His first requirement in a gun, therefore, is that it shall be one which is agreeable to walk with—a light-weight, dainty piece of baggage. If there is one feather-weight piece in a sportsman's cabinet, that should by all means be his grouse-gun—generally a weapon of six and a half pounds and under.

As to the gauge, little fault could be found with a 12-bore with 26-inch barrels, balancing the scales at the weight mentioned. However, personally I like things to be in keeping; a feather-weight gun, for me, implies a narrow gauge. If a six-pound 12 were never used with a charge heavier than 3 drams of powder and 1 ounce of shot, it would do nicely; but there will always be the temptation to try standard charges, perhaps for the simple reason that nothing else is readily obtainable. I have promised myself before now that I would never use a shell containing more than 3 drams in a light 12, but when the pinch came and I could not lay my hands on what I wanted, I did the next thing, took what I could get, often a heavy duck-load. A short, light 12-gauge is a great kicker, an arm which will eventually cause flinching except in case of that rare individual who is proof against the jar and jump of an overcharged piece.

Better than a 12 for partridge shooting is a 16 or a 20 weighing from 6 to 6½ pounds. And, let me repeat, it must handle fast. What are the features in a shotgun which tend to give it speed in covering the mark? Light weight first, but lightness will not of itself insure a fast-handling gun. A gun that has long barrels, being at the same time muzzle-heavy, is going to be slow, this notwithstanding that it may be an unusually light piece. Much of the exertion of bringing a gun to shoulder is thrown upon the left arm, and if this arm also carries the bulk of the weight, the weapon is bound to be slow.   An arm to handle fast must be a trifle muzzle-light, have barrels either short or of moderate length, and have the stock comparatively straight (and the stock should measure something under that used at the trap or in the duck-blind)—be sure the piece shoots high.

Didactic assertions carry little force unless backed by logic, so permit me to give reasons.   I think there is something optical about the fact that a short-barreled gun is faster than one with long tubes.   If we took a gun with barrels ten feet long and swung it to cover a mark, to the eye and the senses the piece would appear to be swinging like lightning, while really "coming on" very slowly.   On the other hand the muzzle of a short barrel doesn't impress us with the belief that it is moving rapidly even when it jumps to the mark in a twinkling.

The straight-stocked gun is desirable for the reason that grouse-shooting is essentially snap-shooting; not every shot will be a snap-shot, but the majority of them will be.   In a snap-shot the gun invariably comes on the mark from beneath, and the trigger-finger being quicker than the gun-movement, the shot will often be pulled just under.   It is desirable with many, and imperative with others, that a high-shooting piece make amends for a low aim.   The muzzle-light gun and the high-shooting gun work in conjunction, re-enforce one another and tend to the same results—the greatest quickness in getting the charge to the mark.

Understand, I am not an advocate of short barrels or muzzle-light arms where great accuracy of pointing is requisite, as in trap-shooting or duck-shooting, but for work on grouse in the woods, where the hammer falls as the butt strikes

Photos Charles B. Morss.

A winged ruffed grouse, and nest of the ruffed grouse

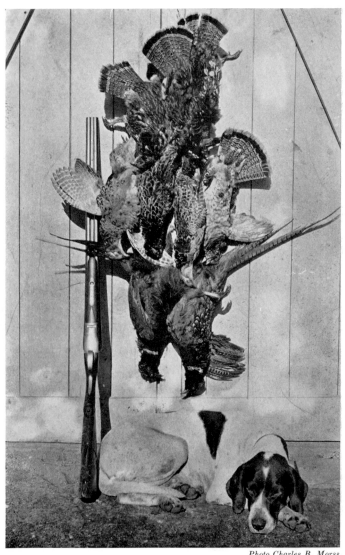

A good day with the "Biddies" and "Pirates"

the shoulder, and a half-second is all that is granted us for our entire performance of getting into position, bringing up the gun, aiming and firing, I am willing to sacrifice something of accuracy for the sake of a speed which compares with that of the bird himself.

Short stocks are best because faster, and they permit the severe contortions of the body, sometimes unavoidable, without the liability of balking the shooter that would be the case where a stock of full length was used.

For the pattern and power of our grouse-gun an extremely powerful arm is not needed. My experience has it that a ruffed grouse can be killed equally far and dropped just as dead with a quail load as the little bob-white can. Many people maintain that an old cock grouse has great vitality; which is true, but it is no less true of the quail. And as a rule shots at long range will not be secured in the woods. Three pellets of number 8 shot are as likely to kill a partridge as they are a quail, and the greater bulk of the partridge renders it probable that he will stop more of the missiles. I am, therefore, inclined to think, considering the distance at which he usually is shot and the size of the mark, that a light charge from a small-bore, the gun so choked as to give width of pattern rather than concentration, will do more effective work on the ruffed grouse than upon any other game which we consider in this book. Some people may not like it, but I have faith in a 20-bore partridge gun, the first barrel bored improved cylinder and the second quarter choke. If a man is an expert snapshot, he might do better with a quarter-choked right and a half-choked left.

While I have said that a quail load of number 8 shot will account for partridges, yet this must not be taken as implying that I advocate such small pellets for this bird. In partridge shooting there is always a possibility of being obliged to cut through leaves and twigs before reaching the quarry, and then, of course, heavier shot would be an advantage. Even number 6 shot, fired from a modified 20-bore, will usually pattern close enough. However, I prefer number 7 shot or 7½.

To satisfy somebody's curiosity, also with the possibility that the dimensions of my guns may serve as an example to some beginner, I will give the stock measurements, weight, and boring of a couple of guns which I use on ruffed grouse. The first is a 20-bore, 26-inch barrels, stock 14 inches long, drop at comb 1⅜ inches, at butt 2 inches, weight of gun 5 pounds 14 ounces. Both barrels are modified choke, to pattern 200 number 8 shot in a 30-inch circle at 40 yards. The second gun is a 16-gauge, 30-inch barrels, right improved cylinder, left half choke. The stock dimensions are 14¼, 1¼, 2½. The second gun is perfect beyond criticism in fit, hang and balance, but the muzzle-light 20 gauge is so much faster that quite often a shot is easy with it which would be difficult if not impossible with the slower-handling heavier arm.

WHY PARTRIDGE SHOOTING IS DIFFICULT

WING-SHOOTING is after all pretty much a game of anticipation. We anticipate where the bird will be at a given instant and direct our shot to that point. We cannot well anticipate what a bird is going to do, where he will be within the next tenth of a second, unless we know the bird fairly well. The flight habits of some birds are very easy to learn, as, for instance, the staid and reliable clay bird. A good trap-shot knows so perfectly what a clay bird will do when he sees it start, that he could, I dare say, then shut his eyes and make a greater percentage than the keenest partridge shot with both eyes wide open. Regarding clay-bird shooting, the fact is, between you and me, the only reason a first-class shot misses a clay bird at all is that he is so constituted that the monotony of doing one thing over and over again irks him. The difference between expert clay-bird shots is that one is more patient than another.

However, clay birds are not partridges. The one is the king of game birds, and the other is—better than nothing. A man might shut his eyes and kill a partridge, but the thing wouldn't happen often enough to become a confirmed habit. The partridge shooter hasn't any habits except the habit of trying to rival the bird in alertness and readiness to meet emergencies.

The man who can anticipate what a partridge will do under any one of a thousand different conditions can kill him, provided the charge doesn't strike a tree and he knows where to hold, and his gun pointing equals his judgment, and the line of aim and course of shot flight are one and the same.

The ruffed grouse is not an erratic bird; what he did today he will do again in the same precise way. But his repertory of tricks and flight habits is so large that he may not repeat a performance until next year or the year after. Being good judges of ground, we can fairly anticipate what a quail will do when he is sprung. We know that if jumped on the side of a hill or under a hill he probably will go over the top; we know that if he is in the open we had best not get between him and cover if we desire a straight-away shot; we know that on windy days he is liable to jump against the wind, then turn and bear away with it like a bullet. Also, we never question that certain species of ducks will tower when fired upon, that snipe will make long, curving wing-leaps when first flushed. But what will a ruffed grouse do? He may jump into a tree, perching not ten feet from the ground, and sit there scolding until you throw a club at him, whereupon he will drop out and away so fast that all you see is the blue hole in the air which he left behind him. All of which gives point to the rule of the grouse shooter, which is: "When a partridge is flushed, shoot ahead of the way he is headed, and let him do as he damn pleases about flying into the pattern."

Nevertheless, while it is no doubt true that the flight habits of waterfowl are easy to learn, and the ruffed grouse is tricky and wily beyond other birds, yet the great advantage of the veteran partridge hunter over the tyro, who simply knows how to shoot, is that the one has foresight while the other must be content with hindsight. The skilled partridge shot knows or guesses what the bird will do, and a percentage of the time he guesses right, while the novice perhaps knows what the bird did—after he is gone. It is all something like the case of John and his brother Job. Job had the gift of foresight. Said John in regard to his brother: "My brother Job is jist one day smarter'n I be. He can tell what's goin' to happen the day before, and I can allus tell the day after." Telling what is going to happen the minute before or a second before often makes all the difference in grouse shooting.

There are certain things which we may with some confidence expect a flushed grouse to do in a recognized situation. For example, a bird springing from thick underbrush must top it in an abrupt rise, but he will rarely go higher than he needs to in clearing the growth, and will then bear away on his course in sharp, descending flight. There is a chance to catch him as he appears for an instant above the bushes—be ready for your opportunity; it lasts but a fraction of a second. On the other hand, a partridge sprung in the open woods, where the trees are free of limbs to the height of twenty or thirty feet, may dodge behind trees and fly off low to the ground, but there is an equally good chance that he will go straight up for the leafy cover. He may jump the space from ground to limbs in half a second, but if you have to dislocate an ankle, twist your spine, and shoot without a thought of aim, fire at him anyhow—failing to do so marks you as not a partridge shot. Make it a rule to shoot at every bird that gets up within range, no matter if there is so much brush in the way that a solid ball couldn't get through—being a partridge shot, you are not supposed to have waited long enough to know that brush was there; next time it may not be, and if you wait for a sure shot on partridges you are hopeless.

When your dog makes a stand, pause long enough to note the problems before you ere going in. If the find is made in the edge of the timber, it is reasonable to expect that the birds will fly farther in when they rise. If the bevy is in a clump of cover, get on the forest side of it, and if luck is with you, the birds will break out all around you—that is a grouse hunter's snap, so snap true and win.

Many grouse shooters are fond of a solitary ramble, and there is much to be said in favor of it, since a man does an amount of clean thinking and sweet feeling when all alone that he misses in discourse with the most sympathetic. But if the business is strictly bagging grouse, two gunners in company will do proportionately better than one by himself. Too often when the dog has finally pinned his bird in thicket or clump of trees it is evident at a glance that the wise grouse will inevitably go out on the side where the gun isn't. It doesn't matter from which direction the gun attempts to approach, the partridge will go out on the other side, in all probability escaping unseen. Two sportsmen, working together, can circumvent him, one or the other sending his missiles home.

The hunting companions should, as a rule, walk a short distance apart, but near enough for each to be perfectly aware of the other's whereabouts. It will then often happen that a bird flushing wild before one gun will fly directly toward the other. That means another snap in ruffed grouse shooting, for once the partridge has mapped his course, over the hill and into the brier thicket on the farther side, he will whiz directly past a man without batting an eye.

In grouse shooting two shots are easy, one where his grouse-ship has been caught in the open fields, where nothing remains for him but a straight and hazardous dash for life. The second providential opportunity is the driven bird, the bird flushed by another, which then comes sailing past us through the open woods. Under circumstances of this nature ruffed grouse wing-shooting is no more difficult than stopping any other bird, as a quail, chicken or duck. I might add that while such lucky occurrences as catching our grouse in the open are rare, yet half the contents of our game bag is due to them.

There is a saying that of all misses the worst is made by the man who fails to shoot. This axiom applies with peculiar force to the grouse hunter. He must shoot, and, moreover, he must take his bird before it gets hard or impossible. Further, he must have the hair-trigger liveliness of Finnegan himself. There are some game birds which the man of methodical swing is deadly upon. But do not count the ruffed grouse among these. Snap him, man! snap where he ought to be—and about one time in three he will be there.

Chapter III

THE SNIPE

IT is the unwritten law that as fish shall not live without water, neither shall snipe live without marshlands. The written law, even that granting the most drastic protection, is not worth the paper it is written on for snipe food. And snipe live on food.

The greatest snipe land ever known on this continent was the bottom lands of the Mississippi and tributary streams. Bottoms now drained and turned into the greatest corn land that marshland ever has attained. And just so our onetime wealth in snipe has turned to corn. The snipe were not killed off by the market shooter or the sportsman—they were starved out by the drainage dredge, the disk plow and the corn cultivator.

Again, inasmuch as where there is snipe ground there will snipe be found, we still have some of the saucy longbills with us today. Say about one for every former hundred, or perhaps every five hundred—who knows? Jack is a nomad, coming in the night, going when no man sees. But let the water overflow wild grasslands, let his needed marsh worms grow abundant in oozy black loam, and he is sure to come again.

Whatever food value the snipe has to humanity—and no daintier tidbit ever was eaten—he is worth ten times as

much to the gun. He is a dull hunter who can finish a day
on snipe without wishing at the end of it that he could bring
his bag all back to life, and turn them loose in the full strength
of wing to hazard life and death over again in their gallant,
dashing way.

The World War had an ill effect on most small game.
Agricultural products were in demand and high-priced. In
the years of America's neutrality particularly, more ground
was brought into cultivation. Irrigation had a boom,
marshes were drained. Wild lands were cleared and waste-
land cultivated. Now the cry of overproduction has gone
forth. For one reason and another some of the marshes are
being reflooded; which is all as it should be. Even Congress
is trying to bring back the vanishing wild life. It is well if
it can last.

The golden time of the snipe shooter in this country was
from about 1870 to 1890. The birds were found in untold
numbers, and breech-loading guns had been developed.
About 1885, in the open, grassy glades lying between the
cypress swamps in southeast Missouri, I saw the snipe roll
up before the gun like grasshoppers in front of a Kansas
mowing machine. Step into the grass where the water was
half over your shoes, and the first rank of snipe got up,
scaped, crisscrossed and settled down. And advance, and
the second rank arose, thicker than ever, a hundred birds to
where you could count one, rolling over the first rank and
settling down. How many birds a man might kill was only
a question of ammunition.

Forty years ago big bags were the rule, and the majority
of the birds were killed in the spring. This was not so much
because snipe could not be killed in the fall as for the reason

Photo Nat'l Assn. of Audubon Societies.

Nesting Wilson's snipe or jacksnipe

"Whatever food value the snipe has to humanity . . . he is worth ten times
as much to the gun."

Photos Charles B. Morss.

Snipe shooting

that in the closing months of the year gunners were busy with the quail, chickens and ducks, while in the spring no game was so convenient or so attractive as the snipe. Bags are now limited by law, and the Federal Government prohibits all spring shooting, which is right beyond cavil or criticism. Now the best snipe shooting is to be had in other countries. Snipe are said to be immensely plentiful in India, also in the Philippine Islands. The Argentine pampas, we are told, hold waterfowl and waders in their oldtime abundance. Northern Europe, strangely enough, has the same tremendous flight of waterfowl that America once knew. I have reports from Finland, Lapland and Scandinavia indicating that ducks and geese breed there in numbers beyond computation. The American sportsman of means can still find his shooting, in some other country if not in ours.

SNIPE SHOOTING

MY own best snipe shooting has been accomplished in the strictly gun-pointing, instinctive style of aiming—no aiming at all in the rifleman's acceptance of the term. I simply threw the gun butt to the shoulder, face some distance from the comb, covered the mark by means of a trained or acquired knack of aligning without direct control of the sighting eye, and pulled trigger when I *felt* I was right. I killed a good many snipe; did it as positively as in any other style, and with greater ease. However, a man's shooting style is a law unto himself rather than a law for the other fellow. Every man should shoot in the manner he finds the most killing, regardless of how somebody else goes about it. Naturally, if he finds the snipe a difficult bird for him, then it would be well to inquire if there is something wrong with the "system" adopted.

Long observation of the work of many brilliant snipe shots leads me to conclude that the correct style on snipe is the "delayed snap." The tubes are brought up under the bird, along the course of flight, and when opportunity comes they are raised to cover the mark with lightning quickness. *Never swing after a snipe along the line of flight*, except an overhead or passing bird.

There is a wide difference of opinion among gunners as to the difficulties of snipe shooting. One man finds the longbill a simple proposition, while another swears that no living target is so hard to connect with. I have seen very fair duck and quail shots who could do nothing with snipe, and expert snipe shots who performed very indifferently on the webfeet. The trouble seems to lie in adopting the wrong style for the bird. Very few men can regularly snap wild ducks in full flight, and fewer can account for jacks by swinging after them.

The jacksnipe has no such even flight as the quail, prairie chicken or the duck. He has long, curved wings, wings apparently too strong for his small body. This causes him to wabble, glide and lurch like a kite with too short a tail—when he jumps he himself doesn't know precisely what he will do. He may be in gentle humor, slow and lazy in his movements, but still his flight will always be more or less erratic.

If the gunner attempts to follow the jack's flight with his piece, the mark will now be above the muzzle and now beneath, and about the time he makes his allowance for lead, the snipe will tack, causing a wide miss. Deliberate swinging will not do for the snipe, and rapid swinging is not much better.

The object of the swing in shotgun shooting is to reduce lead on fast birds, and its success depends on the mark's keeping a straight course at uniform speed. The snipe doesn't keep a straight course, and he is not speedy enough to make reducing the lead a great object. If a snipe were as fast as a blue-winged teal, being at the same time as erratic as he is now —well, you could search me for the right kind of style for shooting that snipe.

In snipe shooting a good deal depends on the weather. In cold, windy weather, when the birds will be wild, when they mean to go out of the country, the first time flushed they are likely to attempt sprinting. A sprinting snipe and high wind provide the most confusing combination. The bird's wings whip rapidly, at the rate of once every half-dozen feet, he rolls from side to side, bears up and down, corkscrews—all movements too rapid for the best judgment to anticipate. When the snipe does all these things and at the same times rises wild, he becomes unhittable except through luck. However, a man has no business after snipe when they will not lie to dog and gun.

In real snipe weather, warm, sunny days, favorable cover and good feeding grounds, the longbills rarely rise with the intent of deserting the country for good. They are then lazy, saucy, fearless, content to get out of the way temporarily. They get up scaping, protesting, rise to a height of a few feet, tack gently over the marsh, and drop back to their knitting. Now and then a bird may make a bluff at vanishing for good, rising high and winging so far away that he blends with the sky, but stand still and presently he returns, makes a half circle and drops like a plummet within twenty yards of where he started. If you have any conceit about your shooting, try to stop one of these fellows as he drops from where the clouds ought to be.

When snipe are at home, when they have become attached to some snipey corner and do not mean to leave it except they're carried out in the game-sack, when they arise with a gentle spring which carries them no more than twenty feet at a rate of forty feet a second, when every long tack seems to be the last ere they settle back into cover, then snipe are easy to kill. They can be snapped with the same certainty as if hanging "dead" in the air. Give them a chance by withholding fire until they have reached a distance of thirty yards.

The old theory that after flying a certain distance a snipe settles down to rhythmic action and steady wing, that no shot should be fired at him until all his gymnastics are exhausted, is a pure absurdity. I have had an old gunner tell me that before he learned the secret of snipe shooting, he fired at birds all day and never touched a feather. Then he brought his good gray matter to bear. He saw that the bird jiggered and jagged and jostled until he had reached precisely forty yards, after which he took a beeline. Presto! He had it! Merely wait until the snipe flew forty yards, and you couldn't miss him. The next day, according to the story, the old snipe-liar killed twenty-six straight, and had missed but a mighty few since. I suppose that many of us have heard such stories, but the thing to do with the snipe, as with any other game bird, is to take him before he gets too hard to stop; in short, while he is well within range and has not yet reached top velocity.

To go further and achieve expert work on the longbills requires perfect and rapid co-ordination between vision, mind, nerves, and muscles. Good judgment, instant decision, and coolness also have a bearing. With the snipe, thought must be translated into action with greater rapidity, perhaps, than is needed in shooting any other game bird. If for the interval of a quarter of a second the bird makes a straight, level dart, the gun must be equally prompt. Failure to meet an opportunity, be its duration ever so short, means a balked aim, a subsequent endeavor to follow the intricacies of the bird's flight, an uncertainty as to when the trigger should be pulled, and a probable miss. The crack snipe shot is the man with quick nerve response, who is, besides, faithfully trained to alertness and precision of movements. The man who is constitutionally slow, vacillating, deliberate in aiming, will always have his troubles with this bird.

I have spoken of the full snap or rough snap, and of the half snap or delayed snap. I might illustrate the difference in this way: The rough snap shooter is like the boxer who sees his opponent within reach and makes a long "round house" swing at him. If the other fellow stands still, the blow lands all right; but the man being socked has plenty of chance to dodge. The half snap, so far as snipe shooting is concerned anyhow, is like the blow of a fighter who leads with his hand already extended to within a few inches of his opponent. Seeing an opportunity, he snaps the blow over, and rarely fails to land.

In wind shooting everything depends on the marksman's being able to foresee the line of flight, for the brief space necessary to cover and fire. Then the difficulty of connecting with any particular bird simply depends on its speed of flight and line of flight. For example: A baseball is thrown straight to a baseman; he can see what the ball is to do, barring wind, from the time it starts, and can deliberately set himself to make the catch. About that order of skill is demanded in clay-bird shooting. The outfielder in baseball must have such judgment that he can tell the instant the ball leaves the bat where it will drop 300 feet away. This skill is to be compared with the duck shot in making his lead. The snipe shot is the infielder of wing shooting. On the ball field the infielder takes a hot, sizzling, short-bounding grass-cutter, and on the snipe marsh the gunner takes a dodging, swerving, corkscrewing atom of game-bird life. It follows that the gunner must have his gun in position or he misses the snap.

It is a generally accepted opinion that snipe invariably rise against the wind, and that the gunner should consistently hunt down wind, with the bird beating back toward him in its spring. There is some truth in this, though snipe do nothing invariably and can rise with the wind any time. Still, the probabilities are that snipe will jump into the wind, just as most ground birds do. If the birds are tame and lazy it is not necessary to hunt down wind, for they can be hit readily enough anyhow. But when the jacks are wild, rising at long range for the gun, it is well to take every possible advantage. Beyond a doubt they will remain within reach longer when headed toward the gun, while the "driver" is the one that gets away from us most of the time. Try to so work the ground that Mr. Longbill will cross the gun, if that can possibly be done.

Snipe have somehow or other obtained the reputation of being hard to hit. Very few oldtime snipe shooters will agree that this is true. Mostly this reputation of our bird comes from the tendency of one writer to follow another, with implicit confidence that what has been written so many times must be true. Great, too, are the stories concerning the

erratic flight of a snipe. Walter Rich tells of a snipe which
sprang before him, turning complete somersaults, sidewise
and edgewise! An Englishman goes him one better by telling
of a snipe which circled the field breast up, like the stunt in
aviation of flying upside down. I never like to see an
Englishman beat a Yankee like that. Edwyn Sandys tells of
a snipe match between a couple of friends in which one man
killed twenty-three in twenty-five and the other twenty-five
straight, which is more like snipe shooting as I once knew it.

I think it was Frank Forester who popularized the scheme
of withholding fire until the bird had covered a fixed distance.
Frank also popularized not cocking a muzzle-loader until
a quail was on the wing. Thereupon he reached over and
cocked the left barrel, shifted and cocked the right, then had
so completely recovered his coolness that the bird could
not be missed. Ever since I learned to read I have been
learning of the chap who could "wait out a snipe," who could
kill passing ducks without a lead, who could shoot quail from
the hip; but I have never yet seen a man who could do these
tricks with any certainty. Taking snipe guns as they come
and snipe loads as they are, not half the birds would be
killed at forty-five yards if they were nailed to a post.

Whether snipe shooting is going to be easy or not, on any
particular day, depends on the snipe. Understand, I perfectly agree with Sandys when he says that he doesn't believe
any snipe ever voluntarily ducks, dodges or corkscrews, with
deliberate intent of evading the gun. The snipe's flight
habits are governed by the wind, the weather, the cut of his
wings and the state of his crop. Perhaps he learned how to
fly a million years before guns were invented, and he flies that
way yet. Birds follow instinct, when scared; we cannot

change them—we have to follow the birds.   A mallard towers, a greenwing flares, a dove swerves, and a snipe tries to make his long wings beat faster than he has the power to move them, and just what those wings will do to him he himself doesn't know.

The weather makes a difference with all game.   Take a cold, blustery day and the ducks will come in; take a warm, still day in the fall and the chickens, which would not let you get within 200 yards of them the day before, will lie to the dog.   It is the same with a snipe.   The very first snipe that gets up may give us a good line on how all the snipe are to behave that day.   If he gets up wild and goes far, take your snipe as you can, for you won't get many.   On the other hand, if he gets up at your feet and goes away tacking and "scaping," that is your snipe day.   Hit 'em all, why not?

From what I have observed, bad weather, mostly cold, besides having an effect on the flight of the snipe, makes him dislike to crouch.   Snipe can sometimes be seen on the ground, like other waders.   You may be sure a snipe has seen you before you see him.   If he raises his head high and stands alert, you will have a dickens of a time getting close enough to that snipe to shoot him on the wing.   Van Dyke tells of shooting snipe under this condition with a small-bore rifle, which might be done.

A wild snipe, one killed in blustery weather, is nearly certain to have an empty crop.   There you have another reason for long rises and slim bags.   Why is his crop empty? The worms also do not like the weather, and they are temporarily hibernating, like a bear in midwinter, not coming to the surface and not making noise enough for a snipe to hear. Your snipe, consequently, is soured on your whole blamed country, or at least doesn't mean to take a chance on getting killed for the sake of dining where there is nothing to eat.

Most game birds have been set apart and classed for two or three qualities which they possess. The first is their size and edible quality, the second their tendency to crouch and so remain until the gun is close, and the third their steadiness of flight. The snipe is highly edible and he crouches and lies to the gun. He is small and, though a strong flier, finds difficulty in combining momentum and balance. When he tries to go fast from the start, as he will when in a bad humor, he gets up a sort of rolling motion, with first one wing and then the other starting from a higher position, and much as an airplane when one wing is elevated, he drifts to the other side. Here we go then: right wing higher, he drifts to the left; left wing up, he drifts to the right. Whip, whip, whip, too fast to count, the bird bearing to right or left with every beat of his wings, and we call that a corkscrew flight.

Snipe, however, are not always wild. Indeed there are not many wild days during the season, for snipe time is a season of sunny noons and little frost in the morning. Moreover, he is a gourmand, if not a glutton. After stuffing himself to the utmost capacity of his crop, he sits blinking in the sunshine. Sighting danger, he crouches, hoping it may pass him by. Forced to rise by dog or hunter, he gets up protesting, "*Scape, scape.*"

STORIES OF SNIPE SHOOTING

FORTY years ago, I used to pay seventy-five cents for a round-trip ticket from St. Louis to the best near-by snipe grounds, on the Missouri River bottoms. I loaded my own shells and they cost me a cent apiece, one hundred being my allowance for the day.   My bag might consist of fifty snipe, a dozen blue-wing teal, and perhaps a curlew or two.   The total cost of the trip, including a German lunch at a roadhouse, did not exceed two dollars.   The ground was as level as a floor and perfectly easy to walk over: just a great wet meadow, extending for miles, with snipe all over it—a thousand might have been counted in a day.   I fancy that a day's snipe hunting may now cost the St. Louis gunner somewhere from a dollar a bird up, if he is fortunate enough to have a place to hunt for little Jack.

There are times when the duck shot is right at home in snipe shooting, even though he knows little of shooting snipe. I once long ago was out with a friend near Malden, Missouri. It was March and the snipe had lately come in and were wild. We followed them about over a wide, half-submerged glade, a mile long, lying between heavy timber on one side and a cypress swamp on the other.   We were hunting with dogs, trained dogs, but they did more harm than good.   I killed a few snipe, but my companion, a fine duck shot, couldn't hit them.   I noticed that when a bird tried to pass us, Jim got him, but he missed those going away.

At last we drove the snipe, several hundred of them, into a patch of elbow brush at the end of the swale.   Posting Jim where the birds would come out, I went to the other end and drove slowly toward him, now and then shooting a bird myself.   Presently his gun began to crack: one shot, two shots, a rattle of shots from the pump.   The birds were passing over his head, to right and left, in singles, pairs and flocks.   I had never before heard such a continuous banging at snipe, nor have I since.   Better still, he was hitting them, for they

Above, nest of Wilson's snipe or jacksnipe.   *Below left*, woodcock, jacksnipe and green-wing teal.   *Below right*, yellowlegs and jacksnipe.

It might be . . . well, what do *you* suppose a dog would find out here? Snipe,
woodcock, quail, or an old red grouse?

flew like miniature webfeet, except not so fast. Just how many he killed I had best not say, for it makes people feel badly to learn of the great bags that used to be made. The point is that Jim wasn't a snipe shot at that and never did become a snipe shot.

Along an old, little used irrigation ditch in Wyoming, I once found a snipe colony—a lot of enterprising pioneers that had trekked far into a new country. They had preempted the ditch and staked every claim—not a plover, kildeer or sandpiper on it, nothing but jacks.

It was not a snipe country; no lake, slash, or marsh anywhere. The ditch led from a swift mountain creek to the North Platte River; no snipe along the river or creek. Neither was it snipe weather, nor was there a single condition that would lead to a thought of snipe. It was fall of the year and frosting every night, otherwise dry as tinder with a drought on. The vegetation had first turned yellow, then brown, was now fading to the color of the neutral-tinted earth. Snipe had no business to be there.

Along a two-mile stretch of the ditch, I shot morning after morning. At the ranch-house where I boarded, the hired man was from Iowa—he had learned to eat snipe. Patsy Carrigan, who lived at the head of the ditch, was from Ireland —had been an Irish market shooter; he would eat snipe. The widow Beasely, whose son, Tom, accompanied me to retrieve the game, received a daily allowance of ten birds—they had learned to eat anything that wasn't "pizen." The remaining folks in the neighborhood took due pride in being able to afford three square meals a day. Some of them admitted that, the beef failing, they would eat potatoes, and potatoes failing they would eat cabbage, but under no circumstances could they imagine a time when they could be brought to eat snipe.   Thus my bag was limited, not by law or the supply of birds, nor by my inclination to shoot and conscientiously distribute my bag, but solely by the neighborhood's appetite for snipe.

The snipe were there and they stayed there, despite our best endeavors to eat them.   On the first day along the ditch I flushed what I estimated at 200 birds, killing a self-fixed limit of twenty-five.   On every subsequent day, when returning from sharptail grouse shooting among the cañons beyond the valley, I took to the ditch and killed the twenty-five snipe.

When I would start in at the lower end of the canal the snipe would begin to rise, some on my side, some on the other, flying upstream a short distance and alighting.   I condensed them as we went.   However, they got onto me.   It dawned on those snipe that so long as they kept beating upstream ahead of me, I would continue to follow and pester them, but if they could get in behind me, that settled the disturbance for the day.   Persistently they doubled back on me.   And that suited me, for in topping the high bank to circle they gave me a sky background, hung in the air sharply defined, and I took a deal of satisfaction in dropping them fairly upon the bare ground of the embankment, much to the liking of my retriever, Tom.

Perhaps the only really odd thing about my experience on the Wyoming irrigation ditch was that I began shooting with a stock of 200 birds, killed 300 and there still remained full 200.   It seemed I had tapped a migratory stream of snipe, and for every miner's inch of birds that I took out as many flowed in.   Doubtless the ditch would hold just so many jacks, and if it had not been for me the newcomers would have kicked out those that came before them and sent them on their way, such being the habit of the world.

On one occasion in northern Nebraska, I had a bit of sport with the snipe, both odd and unexpected. I was chicken-shooting in the sandhills, thirty miles from O'Neill, thirty miles from the nearest town, for the matter of that. It was late October and the first snow of the season had fallen the night before, a good six inches of what might be termed a warm snow.

It looked like anything but a chicken day, and I didn't mean to go out. However, a pack of 300 chickens came along, alighting in a patch of standing corn a short quarter mile from the house. I knew the cold snap would make the birds wild as hawks, as they were wild enough anyhow; but I thought I might slip up and catch one or two napping. Taking a cautious dog which would heel at the wave of a hand and stay there, I tried a stalk.

The scouts began to rise when I was still a hundred yards away, and the rank and file followed to the last of them. I sprinted, hoping to catch the laggards, but there were no laggards. The pack flew about a mile, dropping in the tall grass in plain sight.

I followed hot-foot, and hot-headed too, judgment giving way to temptation. They were wilder than before, the last bird clearing the snowy sedge when I was still two gunshots distant. They flew farther, too, maybe two miles, passing beyond a high ridge. Nevertheless, stubbornly I took the course, with dog ranging, searching the deep grass of the valleys or a hillside covered with wild rose bushes. The chickens allowed me to get close enough to reach them with a Government rifle, and then went off north—to Alaska for all

I cared. I quit them cold; literally cold, for it was winter weather, though October season.

On the way home, hidden in a deep, narrow valley, I came across a deserted claim-shack. The eight by ten cabin was built of cottonwood logs, a trifling amount of lumber and innumerable tin cans, flattened out to make weather boarding. The man who built that house and went away may have left hope and ambition behind, but little of those commodities remained in the shack, not having been put there in the first place. The barn was no better than the house—a few poles covered with now decayed prairie grass. Neither structure was much more prominent than a respectable muskrat house.

Idly curious, I went to the house, finding a baby cab, minus a wheel, an old buckboard without tongue or seat, a rusted-out mowing machine, and a hayrake with part of the teeth gone. The man who owned all this wealth had come from somewhere and gone into elsewhere long since. The story, plainly told, was an old one in the sandhills.

One permanent thing the starved-out homesteader had left behind—a three-inch flowing well. Pouring a stream which I came to find was ice-cold in summer, smoking-hot in winter, it was always "on the job." That day the water made a break in the even expanse of snow-covered ground, spreading over an acre or two, a black oasis, covered with smartweed and, farther on, patches of grass still green. I drank from the end of the rusted pipe, and my dog waded out into the shallow pond. A jacksnipe got up and scaped off, as big and natural as life!

That jack was an alarmist, one of the sort that begin a panic. That was what he did, started a snipe panic. Wherever he flew a snipe arose, and where one snipe went down another got up, until they were whizzing and scaping all over the little spot of water-logged ground. However, I noticed that not one of the birds left.

My waterproof boots were already beginning to leak, and I had no intention of provoking them further. I circled the bit of snipe haven, taking such birds as got up within reach, and the dog retrieved every one. Circling the pond as regularly as a runner on a cinder track, by the time I had made three laps, having beaten a path to walk in by this time, I had fifty birds—and no more shells. Neither could I see but that the snipe were just as plentiful as when I began.

It was a white day and a stormy day, for the old dog went home with the ice tinkling in his coat, but for me it was a red day, a red-letter day, the like of which I shall never see again.

The following morning I returned. The sun was shining, a gentle wind blew blithely from the south, the snow had melted from southern exposures, and I had plenty of shells in my pockets. Not a snipe remained—not a single snipe. But there were teal, and mallards and sprigs in the smartweed, and when I had hidden in the old "barn" they kept coming back despite all I could do.

Blessings on the man who sinks a flowing well in the arid sandhills.

Chapter IV

THE WOODCOCK

THE American woodcock has a near relative in the wood-cock of Europe. The latter is a trifle larger than our bird, a trifle more dun-colored, a trifle more simple-minded, and a trifle fonder of winter weather. Both species are migratory, but ours continues his travels until he has outfooted the ice and snow, while his foreign cousin seems as fond of the English winter climate as is any other Briton.

The woodcock never has been found in any numbers west of the Missouri River. This is all explained in a word. He is a bird of the woodlands, of swamps, of moist country, of the rain belt, and, like snakes in Ireland, if carried to the arid countries of the West would get out of there just as quickly as he knew how.

Formerly our cock had two great migratory lanes of flight in America. One was down the Atlantic Coast, along its swamps and tide-water rivers, from Labrador to Florida. The other and heavier flight was down the Mississippi, where the rich, moist land, the lakes, swamps, and heavy timber were much to his liking. Never a hazel thicket, a bramble-covered hillside, a patch of buckbush, a cypress slash but at one time had its woodcock. In the Mississippi Valley, the home of market gunning, thirty to fifty years ago woodcock were in season in July. The Migratory Bird Law came too late to

44

save the woodcock of the West, but there are still enough for sport in the East.

Perhaps the woodcock is the daintiest tidbit in bird flesh in the whole realm of nature. Moreover, he is a game bird, lying well to a dog, springing close to the gun, taking a sporting chance, and presenting an elusive mark. His only near relative in this country is the jacksnipe. The kinship is shown in the appearance of the birds, their methods of making love, and their feeding habits. The woodcock is the finer bird, higher colored, more exclusive, more difficult to find and harder to hit.

In the breeding season he struts like a veritable peacock, wings dragging, tail outspread. Then in the twilight he springs into the air with wings humming like taut wires, towering in widening circles until lost in the gloom of the upper air, whence he comes pitching down to his mate, headlong, with the sound of a spent bullet.

To me it has always seemed that the woodcock belongs to another age of the world rather than to the one we are in now. I can imagine him the last survivor of a great family of woodsbirds, all like him in appearance, some as large as a pheasant, some plain, but the majority far more brilliant than our cock of the woods. They lived then in a congenial clime, a time of great, moist woods, of rank undergrowth, of a thousand plants unknown to us, where the sun filtered through only to break the density of everlasting twilight. It was under those conditions, I imagine, that our woodcock, as all the other many species of woodcock of his day, developed his nocturnal habits, his big black eyes that blink half blinded in the strong light of the sun, and all his woods traits which remain, notwithstanding, from his appearance and habits, he should be a marsh bird like the snipe. With all his brilliant and larger kindred buried in the unknown history of an unknown world, let us cherish him. No more pleasing bit of coloring, no more charming inhabitant of the silent woods, is to be found in America today.

Not caring to follow custom when with propriety I can avoid it, I will not give a naturalist's description of the woodcock. Authorities differ, and some day I might purchase a Latin dictionary and more satisfactorily name him myself. Anyway, I am English, ten times removed, and English is good enough for me. Besides, he is a cocky little rascal, and woodcock suits him to a dot. A Louisiana plantation hand calls him a blind-snipe, a Mississippi colored brother a briah-snipe, an old Kentucky uncle, recalling the days of his youth, remembers when there were wood-snipe. Of course all these names came from the whites, who have taught the blacks all they know.

Naturalists know everything about the woodcock that is immaterial to the gunner. I have read everything about the little red hide-and-go-seek, light-of-the-woods, and still don't know much. Having shot woodcock for a quarter century, all I have learned is how to shoot him according to law, and according to the shooting form I happen to be in.

The woodcock is a bird of mystery to the automobilist and the rural resident. People who were raised right next door to his modest little nest never have seen him except when they visited the city and paid five dollars to see him without his feathers. The United States Government pronounces him a migratory bird, of which I had a suspicion before it made the announcement.

In regard to the migratory and other habits of the woodcock, I shall not tell you anything that I know or have read, but only what I have surmised. My theory is that the woodcock goes south when it gets cold in the North, and north when it gets hot in the South. Certain tribes can stand more cold and others more heat. For example, the bird that breeds in northern Mississippi may winter in South America, while the one hatched in Nova Scotia is likely to think that South Carolina is about right for a winter "resort."

The woodcock is not so particular about the weather as is his cousin the snipe, being better able to adapt himself to climate, and having a wider range of food. The snipe has to bore holes in the ground for his dinner, and the cock can bore, too; but if the worm develops legs and gets to crawling around on the surface of the earth, it is all the same to him. He has a bill that can probe, likewise feet that can scratch. If the early worm fails to be early enough, he goes down into the mold on the sunny side of a rotting log and gets him. He catches the worm when he comes out with the groundhog in the spring, and the frost-bitten grasshopper in the fall. Consequently we have the woodcock with us from dandelion time even until the fox grape is ripe.

Woodcock are not so gregarious as buffalo, but they follow their leader just the same—in migratory time. I never have seen a flock of woodcock, nor anyone who ever told of seeing a flock, but I have heard them passing in the night. Hearing them, what do you suppose I wished to do? To get up and go along! Precisely the way the woodcock doubtless feel; hearing the passing of their mates, they get up and follow,— every one which is in the woods, or the briar thickets hard by, or in the swale below. By and by, across all the length and breadth of woodcock land, the straggling army is in motion.

Presently, seeing cane along the river or laurel in the
mountains, some of them drop out. Others keep dropping
out from twelve o'clock until, at daybreak, the last bold cock
folds his wings in the rice fields of South Carolina. A few
more days and the right wing of the Atlantic army has come
in contact with the left wing of the Mississippi Valley army,
and all across the Gulf Coast from Texas to Florida the woodcock are feeding, I surmise.

With the exception of some few birds killed in North
Carolina, my personal observation of the woodcock has been
confined to the states lying along the Mississippi River, from
Wisconsin to Louisiana. Louisiana is perhaps the best state
in the Union for shooting woodcock in winter, though there
are numbers of the birds in Mississippi and Arkansas. Even
there "the old gray mare is not what she used to be."

The woodcock nests on rather high ground, anywhere in
the woods, in brush and briar patches, incubating very early
in the spring. I have found the birds on their nests in
southern Illinois when the ground was like iron, found them
on their nests with snow powdering their backs. Nothing less
than a tenpenny nail driven by a hammer would have gone
into the ground then, yet the birds were doing nicely. I have
never seen the track of a cock in the snow, however, and I
wouldn't advise anyone to go woodcock shooting in zero
weather.

In summer our bird retires to heavy cover, where there are
swamps and "oozy" spots; or even to the mountains, they say,
to moult. In the fall he scatters all over woodcock territory,
being about as apt to be found in standing corn as anywhere.
His winter haunts are about confined to the northern limits
of cane—wherever cane grows rank you are apt to find wood-

Above, photo Nat'l Assn. of Audubon Societies; below, by Charles B. Morss.

Above, "The woodcock nests on rather high ground, anywhere in the woods, in brush and brier patches." *Below,* "No more pleasing bit of coloring, no more charming inhabitant of the silent woods, is to be found in America today."

A mixed bag in woodcock cover

cock all winter. Also in such country there will be open water, and the kinds of bugs which do not hibernate in winter. But do not search for your Christmas cocks where cane never grows.

WOODCOCK SHOOTING—DOG AND GUN

Henry Sharp, an English authority and a good one, says that in proportion to birds bagged, more shells are wasted on woodcock than on any other bird. I can almost agree with him, and would be quite ready to do so except for some of my experiences on ruffed grouse. However, I have missed plenty of woodcock myself, and have seen others do the same. In fact, I have never yet seen a first-rate performer on woodcock outside of half a dozen market gunners who happened to fall under my observation. I have not seen the great woodcock shots of the New England states.

There is a good deal of luck about woodcock shooting. The bird is not so very fast, and, caught in the open, he is one of the easiest of our game birds to bag. At times one open shot after another will be afforded until the shooter begins to believe he is "it." Again we must fire at dodging, twisting, twittering glimpes of reddish light, in heavy cover, missing so regularly as to take the heart out of Old Optimism himself.

The best woodcock shot is the man who has instinct and intuition in place of time and system. If the marksman can foretell with any certainty where the bird will break cover, whether his next whip will be up or down, to one side or the other, being able at the same time to point his gun accurately without knowing how, to pull trigger without remembering that he has a trigger, he can kill woodcock quite regardless of his shooting ability. Ordinary shooting depends on style, system, shooting form and study of the bird's habits, but, the woodcock being unsystematic, irrational, contrary, nothing remains but to outguess him.

"What made you shoot to the right of that bird's line of flight and high?" I asked a shooter after he had made a successful shot which looked impossible. "By all reason that bird should have dropped away after he topped that dwarf oak, in place of continuing to rise and quarter away."

"I dunno," he replied. "Just had a hunch that he had started for a long flight and would keep on climbing."

That is all there is to woodcock shooting—just have the right hunch and send a wide-spreading shower of shot about where he will be when they get there.

The dog is all important in woodcock shooting. Some birds can of course be killed without his services, but the sport is wearisome and worrisome. The cock is a cunning rascal, despite the innocent look in his big twilight eyes. You may mark him down to a dot, but there is no certainty that he will stay put, and less that you can flush him again if he does, tramp as you may. When in good cover, for every bird that rises wild two will refuse to get up at all. A cock is wise enough to know when he is well off, and he generally considers himself well off when under the leaves in heavy cover. Let a dog pin him, however, and the wily chap knows that his wings should serve him best.

The English use spaniels for cock shooting, cocker and field spaniels, but I have never seen one of them trained well enough to beat a good setter. The small dogs are too wild, too busy, and too noisy for our American woodcock and woodcock covers. I can understand the value of spaniels where the birds are driven to the gun, as sometimes happens in British shooting.

The woodcock dog requires brains rather than legs, and a delicate nose takes the place of fast searching. He is the bloodhound of bird dogs, and must detect the faintest scent, stopping, to work it out right under the gun muzzle. Above everything he must have his mind on woodcock, know that he is hunting cock and nothing else, and have a love for the bird which exceeds his liking for any other game. Having such a dog you will get woodcock, if there are any, and lacking him, turn the gun on some other game.

The woodcock gun should be light, for it must be carried in readiness and handled with extreme quickness. It should be open-bored, because usually there is but time for a rapid snap; yet the pattern should have some density if it is to cut through twigs. Density demands a quantity of shot, pattern being open, therefore I have gone to the 16-bore, using $1\frac{1}{8}$ ounces of shot. A weight of $6\frac{1}{2}$ to $6\frac{3}{4}$ pounds is about right. I prefer the second barrel as open as the first, because it frequently happens that this second barrel must be fired when the bird has already gone out of sight, his whereabouts guessed at. Spread is needed then.

The 20-bore will certainly kill woodcock, but the gun should be choked a bit more than the 16 is, and of course has to be held closer. If you have the requisite skill, with confidence in yourself and the arm, then the 20-gauge is a good woodcock gun.

ODD BITS OF SPORT

I REMEMBER seeing a picture in "Lewis' American Sportsman," of a man shooting woodcock by torchlight. The scene

was located in the Louisiana swamps.   A handsomely dressed
gunner stood in the foreground, a very long-barrelled fowling-
piece in his hands.   With him was a negro carrying blazing
pine-knots.   To either side great walls of cane arose thirty
feet, while the party walked down an open glade, free of
vegetation and highly illuminated by the torches.   In the
outer rim of the firelight the woodcock stood here and there,
staring at the unaccustomed light.   The stage was all set.
Soon the birds would jump, followed by the cracking right
and left, ere the cock topped the cane.   Being a boy, I found
the picture appealed; I meant to shoot woodcocks at night,
by lamplight, the first opportunity.

In the Lower Egypt section of southern Illinois is Crab
Orchard Creek, a tributary of the Big Muddy River.   One
summer, thirty-five years ago, I went from St. Louis to see a
boy friend who lived down there, he having written of
quantities of game—quail, wild turkeys, squirrels, snipe,
ducks, and lastly woodcock.   I went down in July because in
those days that was supposed to be the best time to shoot woodcock.   Terry declared that he knew where the birds "used" at
night.   Another night shoot was to be staged, patterned after
the enticing Lewis.

Crab Orchard Bottoms were heavily timbered then, while
along the fringes, between the woods and the cultivated fields,
were rank patches of blackberry bushes, wild grape-vines,
sumac, papaw, and similar growths.   The creek itself was
walled in by switch cane and rushes.   At one point our creek
had made a cut-off, plowing through for a short cut, leaving
a half mile of meandering slough in the old creek bed.   This
slough was from thirty to sixty feet wide, its bottom soft,
black muck, which had washed in and was unable to wash out.

Here deep or again shallow, the water never dried up, and all along the shores that July day when we investigated the moist soil was bored full of woodcock holes.

Terry informed me that the cock fed on the slough at night only, spending the day in the briar thickets and dense brush, now in full leaf, where we couldn't do a thing with them. Since I was bent upon shooting at night, that made no difference to me. Jacky Morton, an English lad, gone to length and legs, agreed to be torch-bearer, for the privilege of going along.

About ten o'clock we arrived at the lower end of the slough and started to patrol it, Jacky in advance with two good lanterns held above his head on a T pole. Somehow those lanterns were less effective than the Louisiana torches appeared to be. There was no evenly illumined circle of light, but the lantern rays flashed and danced, now extending far up the slough, and again leaving it black dark in our immediate vicinity.

The woodcock were there, no mistake about that, dozens of them, maybe hundreds; but they didn't behave according to Hoyle. They didn't sit staring at us with big, wondering eyes until we kicked them up, and then bat along a few yards until killed; not those Crab Orchard woodcock. They flew much more promptly than they would have done in the daytime, usually being heard but not seen. When they did spring in sight, there was one flash of wings and they were gone.

Notwithstanding the inexplicable behavior of the woodcock, we plodded on hopefully. Other things were there. Water-turkeys and shypokes got up at our feet, which we might have killed awing, by torchlight, had that been worth

while. Two or three times we shined the eyes of coons or
possums, and a young fox barked at us. A flock of wild
turkeys flew from a giant water-oak above our heads and
were gone before we could think of shooting. The sum of
our experience was zero as to game bagged, with a com-
pensating disillusionment as to the hunting lore of Lewis.
Later we had a lot of good shooting among those woodcock,
but not after dark.

I spent one shooting season down in Mississippi, on the
plantation of Colonel Al. Jones, which gave me my best
memories of sport with the "briah-snipe" of the Deep South.
My Southern colonel was not the typical tall, aristocratic,
gray-mustached Confederate veteran—as fine a gentleman as
ever lived. That wasn't Colonel Al. Jones. He got his title
from being a country auctioneer, his reputation from being
a jackleg lawyer, a small politician, a trouble-maker and
trouble-finder, a nuisance to his neighbors, a long-winded
argumentative bore to his acquaintances. He owned the
Encyclopædia Britannica and sprung it on me continually by
way of backing up his assertions. The Colonel never lost
an argument, except it took place before a judge and jury;
which being absent, I went to bed early. He made me
grouchy, save when I thought of the neglected shooting I was
enjoying on his weedy plantation.

Game was there in quantities, and I was almost surfeited
with shooting quail, snipe and turkeys. When riding home
from town one evening I saw a glint of something, whipping
over a second-growth pine, which looked to me like a woodcock. Old Sam, one of the black tenants, was with me, and
I asked him if there were any woodcock in the country.

He thought I meant Southern giant woodpeckers! * There were plenty in the Hatchie bottoms, but Colonel Jones, he had quit shooting them, finding them "bad smellin' an' wuss eatin'."

I wasn't exactly surprised at the Colonel, take it any way at all. To Sam I said, "No, briar-snipe, Sam."

"Sholy, sholy, suh. Ah mistrusted you-all wouldn't eat dem wood-knockin' buhds. Briah-snipe Ah seed many a time, but dey is wustest buhds to hide Ah ever rec'lect. Dah's sho to be some right now ober in Squiah Roguhs' pasture, by de cattail spring."

Squire Rogers and I being very good friends, I asked Sam to ride over with me and show me the woodcock.

In an old, disused field, full of blackberry briars, saw-briars, dewberry, and greenbriars, among young pine, we found the cock. Taking a cowpath, which led down a neglected road, I saw four flush, and Sam declared he had seen a couple more dodge into cover.

Below the field was a swale three hundred yards long and a third as much across, where the spring broke out under the hill, spreading among willows and buckbush. I had little doubt that the birds were in there in numbers, that they visited the swale nightly, though remaining in the heavier cover throughout the day. Back of the field was a forest of pine and oak interspersed, with dense patches of undergrowth— I thought the woodcock might be found in the woods, too. The chances for sport looked excellent.

Colonel Jones and I had gone quail shooting together a few times, and, since I was in perfect practice and he was rusty,

---

* Most likely the ivory-billed, a bird over 20 inches long. However, the pileated woodpecker, next in size, is often called "logcock."

results were rather with me.   He attributed my superiority, such as it was, entirely to my gun, a fine little 28-bore, full-choked.   Constantly he bemoaned the lack of a similar weapon.   For my part I even more earnestly longed to change mounts with the Colonel.   He rode a handsome mare which could both foxtrot and singlefoot, and there was no getting her away from him.   Worse luck, the best I could get was a clumsy plow-nag, liable to stumble any time she was pushed beyond a walk.

I had found to my sorrow that the Colonel liked to make a good safe bet—fortified, I might say.   Just give him a chance to corner you in his encyclopedia!

"Colonel," I remarked casually after supper, "I beat you shooting the other day, didn't I?"

"You did, suh, but it's all the fault of my gun, and you know it.   That little gun o' youahs holds the shot togethuh and kills a thud futheh."

So at last a little bet was fixed up which promised me a return on my investment in the Colonel's good nature.   I was to shoot more woodcock next day then he might shoot of quail, strictly wing shooting.   If I lost, my little gun was his for the remainder of the winter.   If he lost, his saddle mare was mine for the same length of time.   We would exchange guns for the match.   Sam and his boy Tobe were to go with me to see that I shot no woodcock except it was flying.   I was to take one dog.

The Colonel was willing to allow me all the dogs on the place.   He wanted to make a side bet of some kind about the use of a dog in hunting woodcock, but I was afraid he would get out his encyclopedia.   To get his mind off the question, I stipulated that for the hunt we were also to exchange horses.

I shall not describe my afternoon's woodcock shooting.
The birds were more plentiful than I had ever seen them elsewhere. My old stub-tailed pointer, Grover, did his work
perfectly, and Tobe's keen young eyes were of great assistance
in marking. I killed some birds but missed so many more
that I should have lost the match simply by poor shooting.
Still, despite the Colonel's gun I had fifteen cock, my largest
bag on these birds. It was dark when I got home, to find
the Colonel in rather testy humor. He had red Mississippi
clay ground into the back of his hunting coat.

"If I had to ride that cussed critter again, I'd have the
niggers take her out and shoot her," he announced savagely.
"The dogs pointed and I started for them on a trot, jist a
trot, suh, and she fell down. It was only luck that youah
pea-shootuh wasn't broken. I reckon I'd have done about
as well if it had been, for it ain't my fit at all. I shot into
a covey as thick as bees leavin' a hive and only killed two.
Blew one apaht, at that."

The Colonel brightened as he looked me over for woodcock. He slapped the back of my coat, which was empty.

"Aha, son! Didn't make a killin' eithuh, did you? I
got ten birds, I did. Guess that's about ten moah than you
did."

"Come here, Tobe, with those woodcock!"

Tobe came up with the birds strung together by their
necks. The Colonel gave one glance and snorted:

"Why, you chump! Them ain't no woodcocks—nothin'
but ole briah-snipe! Of all the Yankees you are the greenest
that has come down heah since the Wah."

"Look it up, Colonel," I suggested.

He went with foreboding haste to his encyclopedia. And

he learned beyond the possibility of a doubt or an argument that it had been the worst day's quail shooting of his lifetime.

We rode up the lane together a couple of days later, he for his office, while, carrying the little 28-bore gun loaded for woodcock I started out to see what I could do with it instead of with the Colonel's misfit 12. He prodded his plow-horse viciously, trying to make her keep pace with my smooth-going mount.

"Colonel," I said, "it is a good thing you didn't win this gun. I'd hate to think of having the stock broken sometime when that brute falls down with you."

"You go to hell, suh," replied the Colonel. "You and your damned woodcock!"

Chapter V

THE WILD TURKEY

SOMEBODY says that our wild turkey is more of a pheasant than he is a grouse. While there may be some truth in this classification, yet it seems to me that in appearance he is a grouse rather than a pheasant. Like a grouse, he has a compact body, short, broad wings, habit of strutting and a roaring rush of flight. On the other hand, he resembles a pheasant in his disposition to run rather than fly, and in manner of flight, since he wings much higher as a rule than do grouse or quail. I have seen turkeys flying across open fields between woodlands reach an altitude of a hundred and fifty feet. Driven pheasants do the same thing, they tell me, but you never can send a grouse or a quail up into the sky like that. Neither will our great bird lie to a dog any better than does the pheasant. Perhaps the truth is that he is the "daddy of 'em all," the grouse having descended from him on one line and the pheasants on the other.

I should consider our wild turkey more or less disgraced by being forced into close kinship with the pheasants. An English cock pheasant is nothing but a brown leghorn rooster which has been shot at and otherwise licked until he has dropped his tail. I dare assert that the pheasant is not a whit handsomer than the barnyard fowl, either, nor a much better game bird. Put a lot of brown leghorns on a deserted farm and leave them half a dozen years to take care of themselves, and they will fly as fast and as far as a pheasant. Furthermore, except to the eye of a barbarian, who must have a riot of color, the ruffed grouse is a far more beautiful bird than any pheasant.

When America was discovered, the wild turkey was plentiful up and down the Atlantic Coast from Massachusetts to Florida. Northward he was found in the woods of Ontario, and his westward range extended across the plains and into the mountains of Colorado, New Mexico, and Arizona. His southward limits are perhaps not yet perfectly defined; certainly his habitat extends over nearly all of Mexico, Central America, and very likely a portion of South America. The Mexican bird is not precisely our bronze species, but he is similar in all essentials.

The wild turkey is not migratory; he is a sticker and a stayer, clinging desperately to the home where he was reared. If wild turkeys were in a certain bit of forest last year and none are to be found there this year, be sure that they are all dead, every one. They were scarce in the territory adjacent to St. Louis after about the year 1850; yet, despite the fine-toothed-comb raking of the mighty hunters, they stuck and stayed, a bird being killed now and then within thirty miles of the city up to 1890; possibly a few might yet be found along the breaks of the Merrimac River. I am told that turkeys can still be shot within ten or fifteen miles of Richmond, Virginia.

Wild turkeys are still fairly common in the wilder regions of the Allegheny Mountains, with a few in Pennsylvania, more in West Virginia. They are more plentiful in the hill country of North Carolina, Virginia and east Tennessee. Other mountain sections where sport with these birds is pretty well

Turkey yelping, where yelping still brings them

Photos Nat'l Assn. of Audubon Societies.

"From the time of John Smith right down to now, wild turkeys have never
had any real protection in America."

assured include the Ozarks of Missouri and Arkansas; also the pine forests of New Mexico and Arizona. To find the birds, however, in anything like the numbers once seen, it is necessary to go down into the mountains of Mexico, in Yaqui Indian country and farther south. The Florida swamp lands have long been noted for these fowl, and as much might be said for the tidewater sections of Virginia and the Carolinas. The heavy forests along the Mississippi from Cairo down always have contained turkeys and always will, perhaps— that is, unless the Government manages to prevent overflows, thus rendering the bottoms fit for human habitation. For good and sufficient reason, turkeys and people do not thrive in the same neighborhood.

There never was any question of perpetuating wild turkeys. Turn any breed of domestic turkeys loose in the woods to shift for themselves, and in a few years you will have turkey shooting. Maybe the birds will be white, maybe black or the typical bronze; but they will be wild as heart could wish and perfectly able to take care of themselves. The wild turkey never starves, never freezes, never is drowned out, and never dies from lack of water. The enemies nature has provided have few terrors for him, but the American backwoodsman has pursued him with a devilish ferocity that no Indian ever matched.

From the time of John Smith right down to now, wild turkeys have never had any real protection in America. The big fowls have been baited, trapped, snared, shot on the roost, chased down on horseback, deceived by the love-call in breeding season; mother birds have been killed on their nests and gobblers decoyed by challenging them to battle. In Oklahoma I have known the prairies and creek bottoms to be fired in order to drive the turkeys out.   Surely man has exercised his ingenuity in getting rid of the wild turkey.   Had he been a beast whose destruction was required that humans might exist, no more radical means could have been found for his extinction.   It seems that the rarer turkeys become in any vicinity, the greater the effort put forth to kill the last one.   Where there are turkeys, young America's chief ambition seems to be to shoot these birds.   In the same woods, deer will be let alone in closed season, but not the turkey.

Some years ago, among the breaks and bluffs of St. Clair County, Illinois, a wild turkey gobbler began to be seen occasionally and talked about oftener.   Man and boy, from September until January, half the male population of the neighborhood made an effort to bag that turkey, and he was still alive.   Then a tracking snow fell, and to the number of twenty-five the hunters collected.   They struck the gobbler's track, put him to flight, and, alternately tracking him and searching for him, kept him going all day.   At last, near nightfall, the tired old fellow ran into a brush pile, where a cur dog found and killed him.   No more wild turkeys were ever heard of in that vicinity, so far as I know.

Down in the same state's "Lower Egypt," in Williamson County, there was a fine flock of turkeys one fall.   Gradually they were killed off through the winter and spring, until but one hen remained.   While I was out crow-shooting in late May, with a native—who, however, had no gun—this hen sprang into the path in front of us and ran slowly away. Knowing she had just left her nest, or maybe having that much decency anyhow, I refused to shoot, and was soundly berated by my companion for pure foolishness.   He declared that somebody was "shore to git her, anyways," and it might as well be us. He was right about that, for she never lived to hatch; and I never had any doubt as to who the "somebody" was in this case.

The fate of that lone hen and of the lone gobbler has been the fate of a thousand other last turkeys in as many rural communities in the United States. Let turkeys become scarce, and everybody hunts them; let them be killed to a single bird, and the desire to kill it becomes a craze. Then they sit around and talk of the "sights o' turkeys that used to be aroun' hyar."

Regarded as they are at present, as fair game for any man who owns a gun, at any season of the year, wild turkeys cannot possibly exist in any settled American community. Therefore, to find them in such numbers as to make hunting them worth while, we must go to places where the country is rough, mountainous, swampy, unhealthful, or for some other reason not a fit abiding place for man. Where I now live, thirty-five years ago five hundred turkeys could be seen in a day. Not a single wild turkey is left within a hundred miles of here. People talk regretfully of other days, but if the turkeys were back it wouldn't take a Philadelphia lawyer to tell what would happen to them. The deer that tried to return to the jack-oaks fifteen years ago would give the turkeys a pointer.

The wild turkey has never had a high place in the regard of wing shooters. He is not a bird that can be taken with dog and gun, like grouse or quail. The turkey is too big a mark for the wing shot and too helpless once the gun gets near him. I have seen times and places where turkeys would hide like a ruffed grouse and break cover like a prairie chicken, but then it was turkey killing rather than wing shooting.

However, ordinarily the shotgun never gets within killing range of this tremendous game bird of the woods.   The only proper weapon to be used against him is the small-bore rifle.

Perhaps not one of my readers in a thousand will ever kill a wild turkey, but every one, without exception, has eaten turkeys, tame or wild.   This has been the fate of our great grouse—not shot for sport, but killed for the table.   Neither the city sportsman nor any other sportsman is responsible. Our giant bird has not been killed off in a sportsmanlike manner; no ethics govern his pursuit; he has just been "hogged" out of his life any old way to get him.   Read any book or any article on turkey hunting by way of confirming this assertion. See if instructions are not given for calling the turkey in mating season, for sounding the rallying note of the flock, for building blinds, for putting out bait, for finding him at night on the roost, for treeing him with a barking dog, for running him down on horseback; and, as you go along, note how rarely the writers advise still-hunting the turkey.

Acting on a conviction which I had been very slow in reaching, I some years ago said that no game bird or beast should be decoyed and shot through imitating its love-note or its rallying call.   It is just as reprehensible to call a turkey as it is to call a moose—all much of a piece with the old back-woods custom of drawing the doe up to the rifle by imitating the distressed bleat of her fawn.   It is not many years since books on field sports gravely advised us, when a bevy of quail had been scattered, to hide, wait a sufficient length of time, and then whistle the little beggars up to the gun.   How many sportsmen do that now?   Yet is it any worse than calling a scattered flock of turkeys up and then raking them with a three-foot spread of shot?

I have shot turkeys after all the accustomed and advised methods, I think. Not a good caller myself, I have had experts accompany me in the Missouri Ozarks, southern Illinois, the North Carolina hills, Mississippi canebrakes, Arkansas swamps, and in the mountains of eastern Oklahoma. Calling turkeys is a fascinating game, aside from the shooting, and if the fowl were plentiful enough I should have little against it; but I believe that today it should be outlawed. With a skilled man handling the call, the chances are ten to one against the game. Since the whole thing is so absolutely dependent on the ability of the caller, any kind of gun or any sort of marksman being able to do the killing, once the bird has been enticed within easy range, it is not sport for the man who takes pride in pitting his skill as a shot against the natural ability of his quarry to escape.

Almost everyone is so familiar with the manner of calling turkeys that I am not going to dwell upon this, the commonest method of turkey hunting. Perhaps, however, short descriptions of other and more novel methods of turkey hunting would prove interesting, though in these tales I must necessarily become reminiscent.

In southern Illinois I hunted a season or two with a man who had a trained hound which would slow-track turkeys in preference to trailing any other game. He followed them at a trot, sometimes a walk, baying as constantly as though chasing deer. The hound never crowded the birds, so they rarely took wing, but would run before him a half day at a time. We followed the hound on horseback, and, knowing the runways, could cut in ahead of him with an almost absolute assurance of getting a shot.

A particular flock were generally found in a patch of timber through which a cyclone had gone, felling the timber, which lay in impenetrable masses.   One of us would put the hound into this tangled thicket, while the other rode on ahead to a big hickory tree, standing by itself in a field a mile from where the turkeys were to be started.   Almost with absolute certainty the fowl would leave the fallen timber at the northwest corner, thence running down an old disused woods road to the open fields, and across these within easy range of the hickory.   Standing under this tree, I have killed birds enough to make a respectable flock.   Occasionally, though, the turkeys concluded to fly across my field, and then it took sharp shooting with the rifle which I generally carried.

Having crossed the open field, the fowl were now in a solid body of jack- and post-oak woods, including three or four sections.   Through this forest the hound would drive, with the turkeys circling west and then south.   An hour or so later the big fowl were confidently expected to cross a certain gap in the stake-and-rider fence of a woods pasture.   There we made it a point to be ahead of them.   Some of the birds would run through the gap and others, flying on top of the fence, stopped an instant to look back and listen to the coming hound.   Many a bird we knocked from the top rail of that fence.

It didn't take us long to learn that turkeys had regular runways—runways which they followed with the same persistence that deer would.   Unless interrupted and scattered somewhere en route, this flock of turkeys in question invariably went northwest into the big woods, circled through this, eventually coming out to the south, where they followed a wooded branch to a creek, which they kept eastward until opposite the "cyclone woods," into which they went again, having made a complete circle of perhaps ten miles. We rarely failed to get birds in front of this hound unless other hunters got ahead of us and scattered the flock.

Another shooting mate of mine, a quarter-blood Cherokee living on Grand River, Indian Territory, had a mongrel bird dog which was a most killing brute on turkeys. He would wind, trail, and point them the same as quail; and then at the word—or without the word, if he were alone—would dash into the flock and tree them. Having his turkey in a tree, he sat down under it and barked as long as the turkey remained, or until someone came to him. It was nothing uncommon for this dog to go out alone, tree his turkeys, and then bay till his master heard, caught up a horse, grabbed his old lever-action 10-gauge, and galloped down for his turkey. This dog had a mastiff-like bark which could be heard two miles, yet it never seemed to frighten the turkey out of his tree; merely made the bird sit the tighter. We killed an average of three birds a week over that dog from November to February, the majority of which he had treed when hunting by himself.

A long-whiskered Mississippi friend of mine was a confirmed night hunter, forever poking about the woods listening for turkeys to go to roost. Having located them at dusk, when they "flew up," along in the night he would creep under them and get his turkey. By way of making a bigger killing, I was frequently invited to accompany him after the fowl had been "roosted."

Having been pestered too much, the turkeys became very wild—so suspicious of the slightest noise in the dry leaves that it was impossible to approach on the darkest night without sending them pounding off in every direction. Dave's resourcefulness was equal to the occasion. Cattle and hogs ran at large at the time, some of the cattle usually wearing bells.   Of course the turkeys associated the sound of a bell with the presence of cattle, of which they had no fear whatever.   Dave got a cowbell, and, as he approached without more caution than cattle would show, allowed the bell to tinkle noisily.   Not a turkey ever so much as fetched a "cut" until the guns were fired directly beneath him.   Again, I have known this clever woodsman to crawl about here and there as he approached, imitating hogs rooting in the leaves, grunting for all the world like a satisfied porker among the acorns.   He never would let me crawl straight, but I had to root around here and there too, being sure of making plenty of noise. Rooting and grunting like hogs worked just as well as ringing a bell, and we always got turkeys.

One season, about the year '87, I helped to kill a lot of baited turkeys.   The Missouri swamper with whom I stayed that fall made a business of trapping and turkey hunting, claiming to have killed a hundred and fifty of the big birds in one year.   His method was to bait islands in the swamp during time of high water, when the turkeys had some difficulty in obtaining food.   He got into his blinds by means of a dugout, pushing it through lanes cut into cane, getting into the blind so quietly that the birds rarely were alarmed.   He usually kept half a dozen blinds baited at a time, passing from one to another, often securing fowl from several in a morning. He and I rarely agreed in our turkey-killing tactics, for I wished to practise on them with a rifle, and he desired to get as many heads in line as he could before turning two loads of BB's loose on them.

An army officer, whose acquaintance I made in St. Louis, invited me out to his post in the Osage Indian country.   He declared that he shot the fowl over a bird dog, precisely as he would quail, first having scattered them along the tall grass of the creeks.   His stories had a Munchausen-like ring to me at first, for he affirmed that he had shot a wagon load of the birds in a day.   Afterwards I believed all he said.

It was in the fall of '85 when I visited the captain.   The first flock of turkeys we saw was on Hominy Creek, in what is now Osage County, Oklahoma.   This "gang" contained what we estimated at 250 birds.   The flock was flushed among the post-oak ridges, but flew about a mile into the heavy timber of Hominy Bottom, where they scattered in the rank grass and lay like quail or grouse.

As soon as we got into cover our dogs began to point, and when we saw a dog standing we never knew whether we were to tramp up a turkey, a chicken, or a bevy of quail, not to mention the possibility of a deer springing from the rank grass.   I remember my first turkey now as well as I did that night in camp.   I was expecting quail, and even when the great bird broke cover I thought it was the bunch of small birds all rushing out in a body.   The turkey rose at ten feet, quartering away, rising at an angle of forty-five degrees, and I drove the whole 10-bore load through him at thirty feet!   Thereafter we shot turkeys, quail, chickens and ducks indifferently, just as luck brought us one bird or the other.   Nearly all the turkeys lay like quail and flushed like quail, except that rarely more than one or two got up at a time.   I have forgotten the number of birds in our mixed bag of that afternoon, and maybe I wouldn't tell if I could.   There was no bag limit in those days, and we had the fair excuse of shooting game to supply the army post.

I have written at some length of my own experience in

turkey killing, but it has not been done with the intention
of instructing my readers to follow the same methods, which
I have learned to be ashamed of.   I believe that a wild turkey
should be regarded as *big* game, the same ethics to govern
his pursuit that govern deer hunting, and the same weapon
used, a rifle.   The greatest pleasure of turkey hunting comes,
not from the shooting, but from fairly hunting the wildest and
wariest bird that lives in woods so wild that he there can still
find refuge.   There still are, let it be said with due respect,
a few real turkey hunters, who by choice pursue the big bird
only as we would have it done as we sit in judgment.   They
are men who love stillhunting for its own sake, who love the
rifle as the stillhunter's natural weapon, and who appreciate
the wild turkey's superb ability to avoid his enemies.   To
these hunters the turkey's passing spells catastrophe.

Notwithstanding his hawklike vision and extreme wariness,
the turkey has certain habits that give the stalker an advantage.   Unlike the deer, he sleeps in the night and feeds by
day.   Searching for food implies movement, and besides the
bird can be seen more readily than the deer.   The mind of
the fowl is at least partly occupied with his foraging, while
the deer has nothing to do but guard against danger.
Furthermore, the bird is noisier than the animal; I have heard
turkeys scratching in the leaves 200 yards away.   Additionally, a flock of turkeys leave plenty of sign—tracks along the
watercourses, wallowing places, upturned leaves, lost feathers
are sure to betray the presence of birds.   Lastly, and perhaps
of most importance, the flock has a limited ranging or "using"
ground.   Just as each bevy of quail has its own corner of ragweed and cover, every flock of turkeys has its own limited bit
of woods.   Find where a gang is using and you may be sure

that right then they are somewhere within a mile—this unless they have been greatly disturbed and persecuted, when they may quite desert their home.

Having found fresh sign, and knowing that the birds are probably within sound of his gun, the hunter can still further restrict the grounds over which he must search by his knowledge of where turkey food can be had and where it cannot. Early in the season the fowl are certain to visit the little meadows in pursuit of grasshoppers; later, their diet may be acorns and they will be found in the water-oak slashes or on the post-oak ridges; in winter they will often forage in pea fields, corn fields, and cane patches.

Rest assured that the fowl will feed from daylight until about ten o'clock, and then go to water, after which, as do nearly all game birds, they lay up and rest several hours. It is not often that the gunner can walk * up within range of turkeys, especially if he doesn't know precisely where they are; but if he has learned where they feed, where they water, where they rest, and by what routes they travel, he can almost certainly get in ahead of them and wait for their approach. The great secret of success in turkey stalking is to let the turkey do the stalking while in some spot selected with good judgment the hunter awaits them.

The greatest weakness of the turkey's line of defense is his extreme regularity of habits. If feeding in a certain field, he invariably enters it from one direction at a fixed spot, and invariably he passes out of the field today where he left it yesterday. Traveling from point to point, he doesn't straggle, but foots it by a fixed route, which he will take to-

---

* If you must do the stalking, there is real advantage in a windy day—more luck if the fowl are using in a clutch of little knolls.

day, tomorrow, and next year. Familiar with the ground and knowing his flock of turkeys, when the birds fly the hunter can tell just about where they will alight, or where they will go to should they run, when they will collect, and what they will do subsequently. It is knowledge of this kind which makes the "native" unrivaled as a turkey shooter.

The surest way to bag your turkey is to get right on the ground where he fed undisturbed the day before. Get there at daybreak and find a comfortable seat with your back to a tree. Keep quiet and smoke a pipe if you want to. Let the squirrels run across your feet and jump on your back if they like—they can't see you, neither can the turkeys. By and by the turkeys will come. Keep absolutely still and they won't be any more afraid of you than were the squirrels. Question is, how well you can hold yourself in and not move. Pick out a fat young gobbler and, be mighty quick and accurate to break his neck with a rifle ball.

Chapter VI

THE BOB–WHITE QUAIL

THE bob-white quail is the true American game bird of romance. All that is tenderest, sweetest, most appealing in American sporting literature has been written of the quail. Looking back over the hundred and fifty years or more of American wing-shooting, we can see all the great characters of our hunting history tramping the fields for bonny Bob, writing of his habits, dwelling upon the witchery and charm of his pursuit.

Traversing the wilder lands of earlier days go our first noted bird hunters and naturalists, Wilson and Audubon. Later come Forester and Lewis, followed by Colonel James B. Gordon, Gloan, Mohawk, Val. Young, Edwyn Sandys, Van Dyke—poet-hunters every one. Even today we have our Rutledge, Buckingham, Stedman, McGaffey and others, paying loving tribute to the bob-white quail. The man who can shoot quail with no more sentiment than he would feel in shooting clay targets is a barbarian, a pure heathen.

Forester has written of York and Jersey as they were in the old days, setting strong-limbed lads and stout old veterans to tramp with us forever across New York's rolling fields and Jersey's pine and sandy barrens. Wade Hampton, soldier and statesman, despite defeat in battle and disappointment in life, felt that the world was still good to him, that it always

would be good to him, so long as he had his horse, his double
gun, his merry setters, and the quail calling to him on his
broad plantation, in his beloved Carolina. "Pious Jeems"
takes us across the snowy cotton-fields and yellow, sedge-
grown hills of sunny Mississippi, and Ernest McGaffey
touches, wizard-like, the hedgerows, ragweed fields, and
thickets of hazel, brier and sumac in the black corn-lands of
Illinois. To all such quail hunters and their kind, past and
present, the man to whom the world has become a bit stale,
who has seen love and war and success and failure, who has
read the things that man has written and seen the things that
man has done, has still a delectable new world before him this
side of heaven. It is the quail-hunter's world just waking
from a sound twelve hours of October sleep, the flush of a
maiden on his face, the pride of eternal youth in his "coat of
many colors," the contagious vitality communicated to all
who come in contact with him when his day is young.

In the past great arguments have taken place as to whether
our bob-white was a quail or a partridge. Northern shooters
held tenaciously that he was a quail and Southerners that he
was a partridge. He was named a quail in the North because
he was about the size of an English or European quail, and
in the South because in habits and appearance he was more
of a partridge than anything else. It was elementary human
nature for the early settlers in America to name the birds
after some similar bird in their home country. Hence we
have quail for bob-white, partridge or pheasant for the ruffed
grouse. As a matter of fact our little bird undoubtedly belongs to the partridge family, though he is far from being a
European partridge. By way of settling differences in no-
menclature, which hardly seemed likely to be settled in any

"The best shooting is to be had in the South."   Quail in North Carolina.

"As for seats of the mighty, please give me a log,
and let me sit there with a gun and a dog."

other way, we have called our bird the bob-white, after his mating call. I do not like "bob-white" particularly, as a name, but think it merely a nickname which will eventually die out. Ninety men in a hundred who go shooting in this country speak of the sport as quail shooting, even the South becoming accustomed to the name, and so, I suspect, eventually the bird will be known as the American quail.

Colinus virginianus is, as said above, a far different bird from the European quail. The quail of Europe is migratory, traveling from his northern breeding grounds into Italy and Spain, or across the Mediterranean Sea and into Africa. Many of these birds are trapped during both their northern and southern migrations. Trapped and netted for the market in Italy, Spain, Greece, and other countries bordering on the Mediterranean. Whatever may be said of game protection in this country, Europe has nothing on us, except that trespass laws are far more strict, and the landowner is apathetic in seeing that his rights are enforced. The quail of Europe is now of minor importance as a game bird compared with the position he occupied a hundred years ago.

The American quail is the widest in distribution and has the most friends of any game bird that ever existed. Even the farmer has long since turned friendly to the quail and dislikes to see them shot. Formerly they were abundant in the East, from central New York south to Florida. Some quail remain in New Jersey, on Long Island, and in Delaware and Maryland, but the quail shooter of the Atlantic seaboard has to go south of the Potomac for really dependable bob-white shooting. Southern Ontario still has some quail, but it has been fifty years since any visitor might sensibly go to Canada for quail shooting. For the visiting sportsman, quail shooting is now to be had south of the Potomac, south of the Ohio, and south of the Missouri, Kansas, Colorado line.   Virginia has plenty of birds, though it is becoming increasingly difficult to obtain permission to shoot them.   The best shooting is to be had in South Carolina, Georgia, Florida, and Mississippi.   West of the Mississippi, fine shooting is to be had in Arkansas, Louisiana, and Texas.   Arkansas will always hold birds because much of the state cannot be cultivated or thickly settled.   The same might be said of Louisiana, while Texas has quail over the entire state, though in the west end the Mexican blue quail displaces Bob White to some extent. Quail seasons do not open as early as they once did, most of the birds being killed, perhaps, in December; south of the Tennessee line, and south of the Red River of Texas is America's winter playground, and thither the non-resident quail shooter must find his way.   Not a bad way to travel, despite any preference for northern birds.

Quail are supposed to be easily winter-killed, and hard winters are given as a reason why few birds are to be shot north of the Ohio River.   However, winters have not changed except to become milder, and we must admit other reasons for the scarcity of small game in such states as Ohio, Indiana, and Michigan.   There are far too many people who have gone in for intensive agriculture; there remains too little cover; and there are too many automobiles, too many shooters.   Ohio classes the quail with song birds, not to be shot any more, yet they tell me that these birds increase very slowly if at all in that state.   The trouble is partly due to a lack of cover, and more particularly, I suppose, to just this sort of thing: A few years ago Oklahoma threatened to close the season on quail for a number of years and such a bill was up before the legislature. Living in Oklahoma, I felt like protesting. But a friend of mine said, "Never mind, Askins, we will still shoot all the quail we want, and it will keep them damned city hunters out of here." That may be what has happened in Ohio. The quail hunters have ceased to shoot quail, but how about the "rabbit-hunters"?

It is generally considered true that all animals and birds on our earth had reached a balance many thousands of years ago. So far as birds were concerned, the favoring factors were climate, food, cover protecting them from enemies, and protected nesting sites. On the other side were certain enemies that maintained the balance. Remove the natural enemies of a given animal species, bird or mammal, and it is apt to increase with tremendous rapidity. We all know the history of the Australian rabbit. He had lived in England for hundreds of years, about holding his own, maybe decreasing slowly. Taken to Australia he overran the country. Because Australia lacked our North American mink, weasel, wildcat, fox, coyote, owls and hawks to hold him in check. In the same way our Virginia white-tailed deer is said to have become so numerous in New Zealand as to be a menace to agriculture. Of this I am skeptical, since it doesn't take much to excite a farmer where his crop is being a bit injured. Man's hand is appearing there against the deer, you see.

In reversal of things, an American farmer went to British East Africa. Wheat was a good price, and he attempted to raise wheat, which the country produced readily. The buffalo came in and broke down his fences, likewise came thousands of other game animals. In one year he killed eighty buffalo to keep them out of his wheat, and he neglected to count how many antelope. Game was a greater asset to the colony than wheat, however, and the Game Department interfered with the slaughter. In Oklahoma, along the Cimarron River, where a fringe of jack-oaks exists on sandy soil which will not bear cultivation, a few deer managed to survive the opening of the Cherokee Strip. The state gave those deer all-year-round protection; the law was fairly observed, and the natural enemies of the deer kind were nearly all extinct. The deer increased until they overflowed into the cultivated fields, and then a great cry went up from the farmers that the deer were ruining them. During the winter of 1929–1930 two thirds of those deer were killed, and a politically governed game department was entirely unable to control the situation.

We are thus enabled to see that man, though invariably not the sportsman, is the great disturbing factor in that balance which nature would otherwise maintain. In some small measure, unintentionally, man's influence has been favorable to the production and increase of game birds. Food has been mentioned as one of the factors that lead to an abundance of game. Farmers produced wheat and corn and oats and in every new settlement quail multiplied. Prairie chickens grew more plentiful in the early wheatfields of the Dakotas and Minnesota than they ever had been on the bald prairies. That was only a temporary improvement, however, for while the food was there the cover was gone, and the game began to follow it. Then there were improved guns, active all the time.

Forty years ago Oklahoma was a good example of what nature could do for small game when unmolested. Near my present home a market hunter, who was otherwise honest, told me that in one clean-up he took 112 dozen quail from one single quarter section of land. That was about 1900. He got ten cents apiece for the birds. There are farms now in that immediate neighborhood where not a quail could be found. Recently an oil man who had turned farmer attempted to buy quail for restocking. The game breeder told him that while he could furnish no birds at that particular time, he might later, and the price would be from $5.00 to $7.50 a pair.

Some forty years ago a party of us from St. Louis went down into the Osage country. We drove in with a camp outfit from Caney, Kansas. After we got into camp, it seemed that the dogs could find a bevy of quail every hundred yards. After sundown, in a widened section of the creek, flock after flock of wood-ducks came in to roost, nothing coming except wood-ducks. No such game preserve will ever be seen again in America, and no man had a hand in protecting or preserving that game. The turkeys, deer and chickens which were there in abundance were eating acorns, the quail living on wild sunflower seed.

The shooting man has gone through his inheritance. To-day he must build up rather than tear down and destroy. Game protective legislation has some effect. Bags can be limited, and seasons. Neither the Federal Government nor any state has money to give game any real police protection. There is, I believe, about one Federal warden to each state, who might, if he gave all his time to it, protect one township out of one county in all the counties and townships of his state. State game rangers are not much more effective. It takes money to protect game, and, besides, it will have to be produced before it is protected. I am told that in England, where a remarkable amount of game still falls to the gun, it requires $3.50 to produce one pheasant.   We are fast coming to that in this country.   Whether we like the idea or not, what we need now is not so much game protection and game laws, which are good enough, but English *game keeping.*

A man or a club, on suitable land, can produce all the quail that it is reasonable to shoot.   Take ten sections of land, with climate and cover right, put a good man on it, a man who understands game breeding, together with the destruction of vermin, and game laws, other than the law of trespass, will become a matter of minor importance.   In some localities a hundred bevies of quail can be raised and will thrive on every section of land.

Fortunately the sentiment among farmers is favorable to quail.   The little brown birds are regarded as friends of agriculture, keeping down insects, and not injuring any crop whatever.   There is no such favorable sentiment toward any other game bird, not even the prairie chicken nor the pheasant.   Nevertheless, in course of time, in this country, as in England, the game found upon a man's farm will come to be regarded as a tangible asset of no mean importance.   Once a farmer comes to realize that the game found upon his place is worth just so much money per bevy, and the more cover he allows to remain in odd corners, seeded with little patches of field peas and cane, the greater his income from his farm, then quail preservation will be fixed on a permanent and solid basis.   Tell a farmer that he is to have one hundred dollars for twenty bevies of quail, ready to the gun at the opening of the season, and the man who shoots a bird illegally had as well rob the village bank.

Naturally, the place for game farms and game preserves is in the South, where hard winters are not a problem and winter shooting is permitted, both by law and by human comfort.   Many American sportsmen are now going to England and Scotland to lease game preserves.   That is a simple means of taking the course of least resistance, but the whole thing can be done better and more cheaply at home.   The young man of America will be just as keen to enter the game-keeping profession, once he knows the meaning of it, as he is to become a forester or a member of the Border Patrol.   There is not a doubt in my mind that we can develop just as good game keepers in this country as they have in England.   We perhaps will do better, for the American enters a thing whole-heartedly when he undertakes it.   I think we can produce quail, ready for the gun, at fifty cents a bird, and that is more cheaply than it can be done in any other country.   It is true that is far from "free shooting," but when a man has squandered the estate left him by his father he must buckle down or be poverty-stricken all his life.

We once depended on finding odd corners of America where ideal shooting grounds yet remained.   The writer, a shooting man, has moved from state to state in quest of ideal grounds.   When he has found such a corner, an isolated corner, apparently, the automobile has come along and shot him out.   The automobile has pretty well killed free shooting, and is to finish the job.   There is no remedy except the shooting estate and the shooting preserve, where the sound of a strange gun will bring an active game keeper in a car of his own.

Chapter VII

THE DOVE

IN writing of the mourning dove as a game bird, we have no quarrel with the sentimentalist nor conflict with the naturalist. We admit that Noah picked out a true little bird when he sent forth the dove to find land, but we surmise that Noah's dove was really some other kind of pigeon; for do not some Europeans call all pigeons doves?

In Nature's scheme of things, man's scheme, too, nothing is permitted to exist that is not of some use. When tame pigeons were shot from the traps, they lived a merry life if a short one. They live a haphazard life now and few are bred; there is no purpose in breeding them; they have no value to anybody; no law protects them, and no penalty is attached to shooting them at any time. The dove that is protected by sentiment, because of his cooing, is shot from his perch in a dead tree, all through the year; the sporting dove is rigidly protected, except for the open season, and then runs his hazard on fleet wings.

The dove breeds everywhere in the United States, but as a game bird exists only in the prairie states and in the South. His chosen summer home is in the wheat-belt, in the semi-arid lands west of the Missouri River. In a strip of territory extending from the Dakotas southward into the Panhandle of Texas, he is the most common summer bird. On a horseback

ride in August I have counted more doves than all other
birds combined. In the winter he migrates to the Gulf Coast
and southward.

We have seen ten thousand doves pass a given point in half
a day. No great numbers are killed by the sportsman, but
a heavy toll is taken by pot-hunters. They drive about in
automobiles, shooting the birds along the roads, much
furthered in this by the habit the dove has of perching on
dead trees and telegraph wires. From the shooting man's
point of view the dove is merely a miniature waterfowl. He
has the same speed of wing; he is no less difficult to hit, and
can swerve and duck and dodge in a way that no mallard can
imitate. The sporting method of pursuing him is the same
as with the wild duck.

He may be jumped from the stubble, like prairie chickens,
but more often a blind will be built among the weeds and
sedge, perhaps in a fence corner, where a "line of flight" extends between pond-hole and foraging ground. As the birds
pass, now high, now low, now close in, now a long gunshot
away, such toll is taken as a man's skill may permit. Here the
duck shot is at home, and the quail shot at sea.

More rarely and in less sporting fashion some oldtimer
may hide in a dark recess in the bank of a pond where the
evening shadows cover him. He has opened his one box of
shells, for the bag limit is but fifteen birds, and, lighting his
pipe, is smoking in comfort. The sun drops lower back of
him, and he sees the birds coming from the east, in a line a
quarter mile wide; flocks like passenger pigeons, singles, pairs,
small bunches, their shadows floating on the short, parched,
yellow grass. The doves have finished feeding for the day
and are coming to water.

Now the front ranks are overhead and the gun is ringing. The ejector works in the fraction of a second, and deft fingers send the live shells home.   In one minute ten shells are fired, and, keeping mental tab, the hunter remembers that seven birds were struck.   He finds six.   In less than half an hour the shell box is about empty, and he has his fifteen doves, besides has dropped two crows and a hawk.   The old hunter relights his pipe, and as darkness creeps up from the east, settles down to watch the birds coming in against the pale canopy of the western sky.   They "fall in" now and surround the pond, side and side, close packed, a 200-yard ring of packed birds, all drinking.   The dove shooter climbs to his feet, and the birds rise with a prolonged roar of swift wings, show an instant against the sky, and are gone.

The dove is peculiarly able to adapt himself to conditions. In Illinois, in my time there he nested mostly in the orchards, building a simple nest on the low limbs of the apple trees.   He most likely still does, and the same in Iowa.   In the prairie country, where trees are scarce, he has learned to build his nest on the ground and to roost on the ground.   In either instance, pigeonlike, he raises more than one brood in the course of a season.   Nest-making begins in May and ends in September, sometimes later.   In the latitude of Oklahoma young birds are sometimes not strong enough for the annual migration, being left in the North for the winter.

Our dove is a grain and seed eater, though of course he picks up such insects as come in his way.   No farmer has an unfriendly feeling for the turtle dove, because he destroys nothing, eats what would otherwise be wasted, and is actually beneficial in getting rid of weed seeds.   Doves are never seen foraging among the fruit trees, as the robins are, but take to the open fields and the grain that has been scattered by the harvest. They nest all over the plains country, from Canada well down into Texas, and westward high up in the Rocky Mountains.

The big farm tractors, which nowadays enable the farmer to turn his stubble in early July, have worked a serious injury to the doves, and the last five years have shown a steady decrease in the numbers of these birds. They begin their migrations earlier now than they once did, and by September first the majority of our doves have left the wheat country and gone south into kaffir corn and rice belts. This saves a good many doves, because the season opens after the bulk of the birds are gone.

An insect-eating bird can get along without much water, but the grain-eater needs moisture to soften up his dinner. Therefore our little game bird finds his problem in discovering his waterhole within reach of his dining room. Severe droughts occur in the wheat belt in July and August, but ponds remain here and there. With no ponds there will be no doves. He is a strong flier, though, and minds little if he has to make a flight of a dozen miles between a certain fallow stubble field and a "tank" which brings his kind in the late evening from all directions. A lot is said about how straight the crow flies, but the crow wavers and swings this way and that. To and from water, the dove keeps to a compass line. A certain point by which he passed yesterday and the day before will be right on his line tomorrow, so long as feeding grounds remain unchanged.

I recall a certain little field of standing corn, on a direct and heavy dove flight. About three o'clock the birds began to come from the southeast, from a distance beyond the range of vision, going to a prairie pond which I knew very well. Presently the "line" was filled with birds going and coming, always passing over the field of corn, but never stopping. They came mostly in flocks, possibly a hundred in a wide line, or again in small bunches, one after another, some almost sweeping the ground, others a hundred to two hundred feet in the air.   The low-flying birds swerved when they saw me, but the "tall" birds held their course.   Any and every kind of shot was afforded that could be had at passing waterfowl.

For two weeks the flight continued, and every day, sometimes taking no more than an hour, I bagged my limit of doves.   In mid-September a cold wind came up from the north one night, and the next day the birds were gone.   A bag could still be made at the pond hole, but the fall rains started, and dove shooting was over.

The dove is supposed to have a speed of from sixty to seventy feet a second.   He may pass within forty feet of the gun, which makes the shot hard, because the swing is so rapid, or he may drive by at a distance of sixty yards, which again makes the shot hard, because of the calculation for lead. Theoretically a passing dove at sixty yards would demand a lead of a dozen feet, if shot are to connect, and an allowance of ten feet is not uncommon in dove shooting.   Complicating the lead, if the gunner is seen and the doves have been shot at before, the wise little chaps may tower, may drop abruptly, or may swerve and rise at the same time.   Often I have observed doves coming which suddenly caught a glimmer of gun barrels.   Instantly the forward motion was checked and the bird attempted to wheel; now it was impossible to tell whether to make the lead in front in the direction a bird had been going, or in front of his head which was turned the other way. Actually, our sporting bird was drifting, side to, in the direction he had originally been flying, but in a jiffy he'd make the turn and be going the other way. Some of those birds can be hit by aiming directly at them, and others can't be hit at all.

The easiest shooting is in the stubble, where the birds are jumped and drive away like pigeons from a trap. They then fly close to the ground, and hitting them is a matter of prompt use of the gun, before the birds are out of range. A dove jumping from the stubble at thirty yards can be caught the same as a clay bird from a trap, but it is to be remembered that the marksman is walking, and he has to get his legs under him and balance before aiming. All that time the bird is whipping away from there for life, and the gun that catches him within 45 yards is in luck. Of course only a percentage of the birds drive straight away; the others quarter or swing about the gun. The drivers are the hardest, just as they are the hardest from the traps.

The easiest of dove shooting comes at the pondholes. This is really very much the same as English driven-bird shooting, except that the doves drive themselves. It is necessary that the shooter be well hidden, for the dove has too much sense to fly right over a gun in the open. Sometimes a blind can be made under the bank, sometimes it is necessary to dig a pit. From habit, the doves wing right over the water, then make a turn to come back and alight. Shots can be taken overhead, as the flocks wheel to come back, or side shots, either coming in or returning. A man may have his choice of shots, in accordance with his skill, or he can vary his shots, now all incomers, now allowing them to pass overhead, and holding low as they go away. The surest shots will be those passing, at from twenty to thirty yards, and if the game is very plentiful, as sometimes happens, the cautious shot can bag almost every bird.   In fact the writer did once bag twenty-five birds straight, one shot to the bird; but he never did try that more than once, since it took all the fun out of the shooting, which from sport became hard work.

I have mentioned the pondhole shooting as less a sporting proposition than pass shooting.   This is so for several reasons.   The birds are thirsty, less wary than usual, and if driven away from water may desert the country.   Also, they slacken speed as they circle the pond to alight, and are thus more easily hit.   The recompense is that a bag is almost certain, even when the doves are comparatively scarce, and a greater variety of shots may be had than is possible with almost any other game bird.   Some of those doves will tower, again drop away.   We may have to hold two feet above some towering and outgoing bird, or again so low to catch a bird dropping in that it goes against the grain of us, seemingly a certain miss.   Again our dove can whip like a snipe, becoming past hitting.   Just the passing "duck shots" are fine, for a lead of four feet will miss and a lead of six feet may drop the racer like a stone.

Two or three factors a game bird must have.   He is to be steady enough in flight so that he can be hit; he must have speed sufficient to make hitting him a problem, and he must be worth something when he is killed—that is, good to eat.   The dove has all these qualities.   Just fry or broil him, as we would a quail, and he is not so bad.   Make a pot pie of him, and the epicure will be satisfied.   In the South they have a way of cooking him that is different.   The dove is cleaned and stuffed with a piece of bacon.   Now he is wrapped in clean, damp paper, and in with him is a chunk of butter about the size of a walnut. Further wrappings of paper are made, and the whole placed in the ashes and live coals of a wood fire, in an open fireplace. A bit of steam comes from the cooking birds, but that is from the damp paper. The inner paper is heated hot, but not scorched. In an hour or so the dove is done, cooked in his own steam, all the juices preserved, meat so well done that the bird is ready to fall from the bones. Now we have a tidbit that is only to be compared with a rice bird, cooked by a Philadelphia chef. Really our dove, properly wrapped and cooked in this way, is better eating than any other game bird whatever.

The dove is especially attractive as a game bird because he is ready for the gun at a time when other game is not in season. No ducks are to be shot in September, no snipe, and no other upland game bird except the dove. Guns have been resting in their cases, and shooters have been getting a bit rusty too. Now the dove comes in, affording enticing sport of himself, besides tuning us up for the duck shooting that is to come presently. A half case of shells may be expended on the doves, and Western shooters look forward to the dove shooting as anxiously as they long for the return of the mallards.

Down in Georgia the winter dove shooting is made an event. From various sources, principally black, comes the news that a heap-sight of doves is using in Squire Bascom's big pea-field. Possibly that field contains a hundred acres, a cotton patch on one side, cotton pickers at work, the other side bordered by pines, with the river below. The darkeys have been slow in harvesting the peas, too busy with the cotton, and the doves have discovered a made-to-order foraging ground. They are there by hundreds and hundreds. The reason that the shooting is an event is, a party of guns, maybe eight or ten, are needed in order to properly work the field and get sporting shots.   Guns are lined up at the corners and between.   Two or three men go down the middle, maybe some unarmed blacks besides.   The doves are driven in all directions, and come by the guns in hurtling flight.   Very possibly sides have been chosen, and the losers will have to pay for a dinner, and maybe for some very fine bootleg whiskey that is made around there some place.   Some of the guns can account for nearly every dove that comes within reach, and some of them can't—most of them cannot.   Misses and hits, it is all happening too fast to count.   A colored boy gathers birds for each gun.   The birds are loath to leave, and wing up and down the field, perhaps alight again.   The driving guns wade through from end to end and back again.   So many hours are fixed for the shooting, perhaps the entire afternoon.

In the old days there was no limit as to the number of doves which could be legally killed.   And in the old days the planters came from neighboring plantations, within a radius of half a dozen miles, on horseback, each hunter accompanied by his own colored attendant.   That night they gathered at the Squire's, and if any man got away before supper, the Squire would be offended.   Eggnog and hot toddies loosened tongues, and all the notable shots were remembered by the shooter, and all the notable misses by someone else.   Nowhere was life so well worth living as in the South, just a little while ago.

Chapter VIII

THE UPLAND PLOVER. THE CURLEWS

THE upland plover is a true bird of the prairies. Though he will follow the plow in foraging, he refuses to nest except in the unbroken grassland. This gone, he disappears. His breeding grounds once included all of North America, from middle Texas to Alaska. Always he was in the greatest abundance on the Western plains.

Plovers nest early, as soon as the frost is out of the ground and the ice off the ponds. As they eat grasshoppers and other insects, they are on short rations in the spring until the bugs get active, but pairing starts very shortly after they reach their summer home. The winter migration starts with equal promptness, the young being mature by mid-July. Then the "uplands" drift southward. It is not a set migration with long flights. The birds come to a given locality, linger and go on all through the summer. August finds the vanguard in the Panhandle of Texas, and by the middle of that month the last plover is gone from the place of his birth. Though an attenuated flight in these days, the southern migration covers an immense territory, some of the birds still remaining in the Nebraska sandhills when the "scouts" are in old Mexico. Eventually some birds reach the pampas of Argentina.

91

A restless, free citizen is this prairie dweller, seeing the world, abiding no place for long, tolerating never a touch of wintry weather. He is a sprightly and graceful bird, upright and alert, with musical though plaintive cry, fast and steady on the wing, wild and difficult of approach when much molested. His nesting duties over, he devotes himself to the grasshopper family, growing fat, even to the point where his skin bursts when he falls. Now as a table delicacy he is second to none, not even the woodcock, the ruffed grouse or the quail.

In the old days the number of the upland plover which bred in such a state as Minnesota was past computation. Forty years ago in Minnesota and the Dakotas I have seen more plovers in one day than I have all told in the last twenty years. Drive as far as we might, two kinds of birds were always with us, rising on every hand, far and near, the song of one and the cry of the other never silenced—the bobolink and the upland plover. Pairs and small flocks of the plover could be seen running through the short grass, forever running away from the team, forever rising with plaintive calls, forever gracefully circling to wing back to the spot they called home.

This was too fine a bird, too delicate, too edible, too tame, to exist among pioneer people as the country became settled. In the early days he was shot without compunction in the spring and summer. Most of the homesteaders, sodhouse and shanty, had lean times for a year or two, and, bacon failing, there was the prairie plover. Though he might nest in the yard and forage in the garden, providing company for the settler's lonely isolation, he was sacrificed just as were the wild turkey, the prairie chicken and the deer. Among the possessions of the canny Swede or other immigrant was usually a shotgun, and he made good use of it on birds that refused to be driven from his door.   Hunting seasons he did not know, open or closed.

The upland plover was never a great game bird from the marksman's standpoint.   Gunners used him as a practice mark, before chickens were ready or ducks on the wing.   His flight was steady, and he winged without fear, in easy reach of the gun.   He is a different game bird now, rising beyond the reach of a long-range duck gun, and flying far.   Given his old numbers he would be a splendid game bird, but the Bureau of Biological Survey has rightly taken him from the list of birds which may be shot.   This act, together with the extreme wariness our bird has developed, present the only hope that the beautiful prairie plover will not ultimately go the way of the passenger pigeon.   I am placing him here among American game birds because, whatever the ruling of the Biological Survey, and whatever the necessity for that ruling, he is the finest plover that ever existed in this or any other country.

In the book of authority to which I refer at the moment, the scientific name of the upland plover is *Bartramia longicauda*.   Which reminds me of my pet dislike against Latin names.   Every new naturalist that bobs up strives for or finds reason to change the name that some forerunner gave to every bird and beast.   The upland is here described as from eleven to thirteen inches long, with a wing extent of from twenty-two to twenty-four inches.   The following description is from Walter H. Rich's "Feathered Game of the Northeast":

"Above the upland is mostly of dusky hue, with a greenish, satiny sheen to the feathers, mottled with tawny and whitish yellow, the light colors mostly on the edges and tips of the feathers; the top of the head and back darkest, and the yellow tones predominant on neck, breast and wings. The rump dull blackish, this color carried down over the central feathers of the tail, with these barred as are the other feathers, but the outer ones are much lighter, shading from the central feathers through ever lightening tones of orange-brown to creamy white on the outer pair, all showing subterminal bars and white tips. Scapulars and inner secondaries are regularly barred with black on a dusky ground. Chin white, shading into the yellowish brown of the forebreast and neck, and these parts streaked with fine dusky lines on the sides, growing larger and heavier on the throat, and taking the shape of arrowheads on the breast. Axillars and linings of the wings pure white, very evenly barred with black; for the rest of the under parts yellowish white. Primaries brownish black, the first white-shafted and brokenly barred with white on the inner webs. Barrings often show on other primaries, though generally obscured. Bill yellow, black tipped. Feet dull yellow; iris dark brown."

That doubtless is a good description of the upland plover, but I question if many readers actually learn from it a whoop about what the bird really looks like.

THE CURLEWS

I am placing these birds with the upland plover because, while they belong to a different family they have pretty much the same habits, and often are found in the same territory. The curlews are described as waders, but are really more

birds of the fields and upland pastures. Gunners know the
three birds that are classed as curlews simply as long-billed
and short-billed curlews. They formerly bred in large numbers in Minnesota, Iowa, the Dakotas, and thence well north
into Canada. In the day when chicken shooting began on
August first, a curlew or two generally was found in the bag.

In the writer's day curlews never have been very plentiful
on migration. Occasionally the spring duck shooter would
kill a few curlews in May, along with the snipe and the teal.
A bag of them was always noteworthy. In the spring the
curlew went north in large flocks. They drifted south in the
fall very much as the upland plover did, and like the latter
were found in high and dry country, not in the marshes.
Anybody would know a curlew by his call, which is merely a
repetition of his own name, curlew: *"Curlew-e-e,"* a very far-
reaching cry. His bill also is a distinguishing mark, and
there is no mistaking it.

The curlew is a fairly white-meated bird, as tender and
toothsome as a tame chicken. He can be fried or broiled or
baked—good eating any way you take him. This is sur-
prising, in view of the fact that in flight he looks something
like a bittern. Whatever nature has done for the curlew to
make him good eating, he has done a good deal for himself,
by refusing a fishy diet and living instead on the same sort of
food as the upland plover—insects, fruits and seeds. I have
never seen a curlew feeding in even shallow water, though
doubtless they do so on the seacoast.

The curlews have pretty much disappeared, and are no
longer legal game. These birds, at least the sickle-bills, are
so large, so even in flight, that hitting them never was much
of a problem when they came within reach. On the prairies,

when yet in families, if one curlew was shot the remainder would continue to wing about the gun, calling, until all were killed. Their size and habits were such that they had no protection from the gun; which finally made an all-year-round closed season imperative. The man who would kill curlews as they were shot in the old days will have to go to some other country.

The only remaining curlew country known to me is that adjacent to the eastern foothills of the Rocky Mountains. On the plains of western Texas, on the high, dry shortgrass lands, curlews can be found throughout most of the year. As no insect-eating bird can exist when ice forms, the winter range of our bird extends south into Mexico, and beyond.

THE LONG-BILLED CURLEW, OR SICKLEBILL

(Numenius longirostris)

THIS is the largest and the longest-billed of the curlews. His length is from 24 to 28 inches, with a wing extent of from 36 to 40 inches. In flight he looks as large as a small goose, though of course he weighs much less. The bill is the distinguishing mark of the curlews, that of the longbill being eight inches, appearing of yet greater length. The eggs, four in number, are as large as those of a domestic hen. The young leave the nest at an early age, and families remain together until migration starts. I have seen a thousand curlews in one day's drive, along the Red River in western Minnesota. The sicklebill was another fine game bird that could not withstand encroaching settlements, with the shotguns, reapers and plows.

THE HUDSONIAN CURLEW, OR JACK CURLEW

(Numenius hudsonicus)

THE Hudsonian is a smaller bird than the longbill, being from fifteen to seventeen inches long, with a wing expanse of around thirty-three inches. He is more buff-colored than his large relative, and has a much shorter bill, about four inches long. A distinguishing mark is that the linings of wings are a pale red. The eggs are more greenish than those of the larger curlew, somewhat the color of duck eggs. He breeds farther north than the longbill, and in the United States is apt to be seen in migratory flocks, which may still be started on the marshes or on snipe grounds. The Jack curlew is, I believe, a stronger flier than his large relative, and is said to go farther south in winter, even to Argentina. Our Jack curlew was the bird most likely to fall to the gun of the snipe shooter in the spring. The last large flock of Hudson's curlew that I saw was in western Oklahoma, about fifteen years ago. Some thirty of them winged past me no more than fifty feet high. Having been shooting teal, I gave the birds too much lead and missed with both barrels, much to my regret, at the time. I have seen a good many curlew since, in eastern New Mexico, but in pairs and singles. While this bird may nest mostly in the Arctic regions, I think it also breeds on our plains. Any time within my memory, half a dozen Jack curlew was a big bag.

THE ESKIMO CURLEW, OR DOE-BIRD

(Numenius borealis)

THE "doe-bird" is the smallest of the curlews, having a length of from twelve to fourteen inches and a wing extent of twenty-seven to thirty inches.   His bill is from two and a half to three inches, but considerably down-curved, not straight like a snipe's.   In color he is the reddest of the curlews.

The Eskimo curlew is more a bird of the seacoast than its relatives, and formerly was shot in large numbers by shore-bird gunners.   It travels in large flocks and at times will decoy to a stool set out for yellowlegs or other shore birds.

This bird is said to be merely migratory in the United States, breeding in the far north, even about the shores of Hudson Bay.   Its winter migration carries it into a similar plains country to ours, well down into South America.   Those that I have shot have been travelers, passing over the marshes in snipe time.

Chapter IX

THE GROUSE OF REMOTE PLACES

The Canada Spruce Grouse

The Sage Grouse

The Willow Ptarmigan; Willow Grouse

The Dusky Grouse

COMPETENT authorities tell me that I have not yet reached the end of the grouse. Nor am I likely to, for this book makes no pretense of including game birds not commonly shot. To avoid discussing too many birds in one chapter, I have selected the grouse of so far secondary importance that I consider of most interest to the sportsman.

THE CANADA GROUSE, OR SPRUCE PARTRIDGE

THIS bird belongs to the order of *Gallinae*, family *Tetraonidae*, subfamily, *Tetraoninae* (grouse), genus *Canachites*, species *canadensis*. That sentence contains an entire lesson in the scientific study of birds. If you fully understand it you "know all about" this grouse, whether or not you ever have actually seen a wild grouse of any kind. This bird is variously called spruce grouse, spruce partridge, Canada grouse, swamp partridge and black grouse. By any other name he would taste like spruce buds at certain seasons of the year. Perhaps his most common and correct title is the name I have used in the chapter heading, Canada spruce grouse.

The spruce grouse is a true Canadian bird, although a few are found in northern Maine and in Montana. A near cousin, the Franklin grouse, replaces him in the Northwestern mountain states and British Columbia. The present habitat of this bird extends from Maine away up to the northern limits of spruce timber, well within the Arctic Circle.

Possibly even more than the ruffed grouse, the Canadian is entitled to be called a "woods" bird; for while the former sometimes comes out into the open farms to feed, the spruce grouse never leaves the depths of the forest. Not only does he love the deep woods, but he prefers the most impenetrable parts of it, having his home in swamp and bog and densest evergreens. Furthermore, he is more markedly a tree bird than is any other grouse. When flushed, he almost invariably takes refuge in a tree, and in winter may remain there, eating and sleeping, snug and warm, days and nights at a time.

His tree-dwelling habits are little to the liking of the shotgun man, but it is inferred that time, education in the ways of the white man, and experience with the deadly nature of the gun may show him the error of depending on the branch of a tree for safety, whereupon he will take to his wings and become a first-rate game bird. Mr. Walter Rich thinks that the future history of the spruce grouse will be very similar to the past history of his ruffed cousin. In the beginning the ruffed grouse was no less tame than the Canadian is now, but he learned, and so will the spruce partridge.

Above, the Canada grouse. *Below,* the sooty grouse.

Nor is it all of hunting to hunt, as
the interlude snapshot reminds us.

At present the spruce grouse is little hunted by wing shots, since his habitat is in the big-game regions, where the men who may visit his home grounds do so for the sake of game larger than birds. However, when the ruffed grouse are pretty well gone and the last of the prairie chickens have been shot, we may confidently expect the Canadian spruce grouse to afford fine sport for many succeeding generations. It is confidently predicted that within a hundred years this bird will be among our most highly appreciated American game birds.

Like the ruffed grouse, the spruce partridge is non-migratory. Wherever he finds a summer home, where he first treads lightly over marsh and bog, there he remains when the shallow water has turned to ice. In this he differs from the Franklin grouse, which migrates up and down the mountains with the mountain ptarmigan, having like habits. In summer our Canadian feeds on berries, insects and fruits, his flesh then becoming equally palatable with that of the ruffed grouse or a quail. In the winter, forced to a diet of spruce buds, he naturally acquires considerable spruce flavor.

In appearance the Canadian grouse resembles the partridge more than he does any other grouse. He appears to be a sort of missing link between the partridge and the grouse. In size he is about the same as the English partridge, being shorter, square and blocky, with movements in running and flying similar to those of a bob-white quail. He is the most handsomely marked of all the grouse, or of any partridge, unless it is the Massena.

His general color scheme is a dusky bluish gray, with barrings and mottlings of black. His breast is black, he is black beneath the throat, and has a black tail with orange tips. Between the black of the throat and that of the breast is a white bar extending from eye to eye. The foregoing applies to the cock, the hen being marked very like a ruffed grouse hen. Should the gunner after moose or caribou bag such a grouse with a bit of naked vermilion skin above the eye, white standing collar, legs feathered to the toes, he can safely decide it to be a Canada spruce grouse.

Unlike the prairie chicken, the sharptail, the English red grouse, or the ptarmigans, the spruce grouse neither migrates nor packs in winter, but, like the quail, remains in a bevy where hatched. Whether he could be handled by dogs or not, as is the ruffed grouse, is uncertain. Time alone can prove this. Possibly if his beloved timber were thinned, he could be driven to the guns, as is the black cock of Scotland, also a woods bird in his native habitat.

There are two other varieties of the spruce grouse, and there is the Franklin grouse, often mistaken for the Canadian.

THE SAGE GROUSE

CONSIDERING the wild turkey as belonging to the pheasants, the sage grouse is odds the finest bird in appearance of all American members of that family. He is larger than any other grouse found in America, and is only to be compared in this respect with the black cock of Europe, with the bustard and certain other very large grouse of Europe and Asia. Our sage grouse was formerly known as the cock of the plains, being found within the Rocky Mountains and the adjacent tablelands. Indeed he was formerly very abundant on the plains, east of the Rockies, wherever sage grew, and sage grew everywhere about the Rockies, above an elevation of 4000 feet. Hence our cock of the plains was a most familiar bird to all the hunters and explorers of the mountain regions. He is a proud and stately bird, strutting like a turkey, dancing like a dervish, unafraid of cold or heat or drought, and independent of a food supply that would be requisite with other grouse. He is now a lordly fellow in his mountain fastness, a proud, high-stepping highlander, a trophy for the veteran wingshot.

The birds when young lie well to the dog and afford the very finest wing shooting. Neither is a two-thirds grown sage chicken bad eating, being much the same as a young prairie chicken. It is only after he has been forced to a diet of sage leaves one winter that he is not such good eating any more—unless a man has acquired a taste for old-fashioned country sausage, well seasoned with sage.

The sage grouse is perfectly independent of civilization, caring nothing for wheat or grain or cultivated fields. His proper home is where the elk bugles and the grizzly gathers berries, on a mountainside. I fear we shall never be able to wean him from his diet of sage leaves, since they say he has no gizzard like other grouse, so cannot grind grain readily. Instead he has a stomach, well adapted to digesting buds, leaves, and fruit, with of course his share of insects in summer.

He is a strong flier, winging high and far, going readily over high mountain passes. Furthermore, he is a traveler, and the place you found him today may not have him to-morrow. Again, like other grouse, he becomes wild and wary with age and when the weather is sharp.

The best sage grouse shooting is now to be had in Utah, Wyoming, Nevada, and Idaho. There the man with the smoothbore still finds good use for it on sage hens. Formerly the cock of the plains was found as far eastward as middle Nebraska. He has been forced to retreat to the mountains, where nature protects him if man will not. At that, sage hen shooting is a common sport among the mountaineers, and mountain ranchmen. However, this grouse has been holding his own this past twenty years because much of his range can never be cultivated, nor thickly populated.

Just as the wild turkey, the ruffed grouse, and the blue grouse are typical birds of the forest, the sage grouse belongs where we find him, wherever sage brush grows: deep in the mountain valleys, high on the mesas, and on the sides of the peaks, even up to timber line. Nobody will ever tame the cock of the plains, nobody will ever domesticate him, but he will long remain the finest feathered ornament that nature has given to the gray and rugged old Rockies.

THE WILLOW PTARMIGAN, OR WILLOW GROUSE

As shown by his scientific name, *Lagopus lagopus*, the willow grouse belongs to the tribe of ptarmigans, the only member I shall have occasion to mention. He has the ptarmigan characteristic of a coat changing from dark to light in winter and is feathered right down to his toenails. In mid-winter his coat is pure white, except the tail, which is black bordered by white, and black wing primaries. The summer coat is grouse-like, a mixture of white, red, and brown, but since these birds moult three times a year, they have a mottled appearance at times, no two in precisely the same coat.

The willow grouse is said to have the widest range of any of the grouse family, occupying all northern Canada, thence extending into Asia and the north of Europe. He belongs to the prairie division of the grouse clan, preferring the open barrens and almost treeless regions of the Arctic to the heavy forests farther south, though in winter he retreats to the borders of the timber. Preferring the highlands in summer, in winter he migrates to the willows along the streams, where he feeds on the buds of the swamp willow and other dwarf vegetation, whence comes his name.

The ptarmigan, of one species or another, is the most truly Arctic game bird in existence. In Europe he is found in Finland and Lapland, thence across northern Russia and Siberia. Where the summers are brief and the winter nights long is his chosen home. In the United States he is found only on the higher mountains, where our ptarmigan was once quite plentiful from New Mexico north to the Canadian border. Ptarmigan have not been shot largely, but have been killed out by sheep which have trampled their nests to pieces and destroyed the eggs, this being true also of the dusky grouse. Range sheep are responsible for the destruction of much American game, both birds and animals.

A characteristic of the willow grouse is that, living so much of his time in the Arctic night, he has acquired more or less nocturnal habits, feeding very early in the morning, very late at night, and sometimes all night. In the middle of a summer's day he takes his ease, getting into the shade of a rock, with a great partiality for a snowbank, if he can find one. Winter visitors to the far North can have the rare experience of shooting a good game bird in the middle of the night—wing-shooting.

I am paying particular attention to the willow grouse here because I believe that sometime in the future he is to become a standard American game bird. Really this grouse has all

the essentials of a prairie chicken. He lies well to dog and
gun, has strong scent, remains in the open, is powerful in flight,
though less noisy than other grouse, and his numbers com-
pare well with the chickens of an earlier day. In all respects,
except accessibility, he appears to equal our prairie grouse
as a game bird. Moreover, owing to his migratory habits,
his breeding grounds far to the north of any arable land, his
numbers, his habit of packing, he should remain with us long
after the chicken and the partridge are gone.

The bird squats on the approach of danger, even lying
more closely than the chicken or the ruffed grouse, being in
this respect much like a bob-white quail. This trick makes
the bird dog highly useful, and in fact without one it often is
difficult to flush a ptarmigan after marking him down.
Though migratory, with probably the ability to cover longer
distances than any other grouse, his bursts of flight when
flushed are shorter than those of the chicken, more like those
of an English partridge. He is, by the way, not much larger
than an English partridge.

It is seldom that we read an account of ptarmigan shooting.
The late Edwyn Sandys wrote of the bird, telling of ptarmigan shooting, when after caribou, well up in the Barren
Grounds of Canada. Occasionally some American big-game
hunter carries a shotgun into Alaska and has a bit of sport
with this bird. Ordinarily the big-game hunter of Alaska
or Yukon sees plenty of willow grouse, but wing shooting is
not included in his plans. Like the spruce partridge, this
grouse is generally killed with a .22 pistol or rifle.

In that good time coming when every species of game in
this country will be under the jurisdiction of Uncle Sam, and
all Canadian game will be protected by the Dominion Govern-

ment, with reciprocity between the two countries and no license to pay except a Government license, I am anticipating that thousands of American sportsmen, Canadian no less, will make annual trips to the Barren Grounds of the North, just as Englishmen get their finest shooting in Scotland. They will not be big-game hunters either, but bird hunters, in search of spruce partridges and ptarmigans, or willow grouse.

THE DUSKY GROUSE, OR BLUE GROUSE

THE dusky grouse is a fine big fellow, somewhat the color of a dark dominick hen. He is strictly a bird of the forests and of the mountains. No forests, no blue grouse; but he is at home anywhere in the Rockies and contiguous mountain chains. Formerly plentiful from Mexico to Canada, his numbers are much reduced now, and probably Montana has more dusky grouse than any other state.

The weakness of the self-defense of this bird is that he must breed on the ground. Sheep are driven into the mountains in early spring, just in time to trample the nest of every grouse that comes in the way of the flocks. Cattle of course do some damage also, but a flock of sheep covers the ground so closely that nothing can escape.

Owing to his habitat, and to the people who inhabit the country with him, the blue grouse has never been a great sporting bird. They have always been shot by the Mexican sheep-herders, from the time the sheep are driven to the mountains in April until they come out in November. Cowpunchers have always killed some, and they furnish part of the diet of prospectors, who also have no regard for seasons. Big-game hunters carry a pistol or a small rifle to shoot this grouse, and fishermen often do the same thing. Like most woods grouse he will take to a tree and sit there until killed. When in full flight he should be a fine mark for a shotgun, but few are killed on the wing. His only friend as yet is the forest ranger, and these men are too few to afford him much protection. The best hope for the dusky grouse would be national game reservations, where no shooting was allowed whatever, and no sheep could be pastured.

Chapter X

QUAIL OF THE SOUTHWEST

THE MEXICAN BLUE QUAIL

THE MASSENA PARTRIDGE

THE CALIFORNIA QUAIL

THE Mexican blue quail is the common name of a quail which is found from Oklahoma westward, throughout southwest Texas, across New Mexico and into Arizona. Whatever ornithologists would call this bird, nobody in Texas would know what you meant if you inquired for anything except the blue quail or the Mexican blue quail. He is a bird of the mesquite thickets as well as of the brush-covered valleys of the great Southwest plains.

The blue quail was formerly plentiful in western Oklahoma, but doesn't take as kindly to civilization as does Bob White, and has gradually disappeared, to be replaced by the latter. The blue fellow is a wilder bird than Bob, more an inhabitant of the desert, yet paradoxically is capable of being half domesticated.

An acquaintance of mine who lived in east Colorado had a bevy of blue quail which lived close about the farm house. That bevy had been there when the house was built, and, curiously enough, while the birds scattered and bred like other quail, he never did have more than the one bevy. Those birds knew where the chickens were fed, where the pigs were fed, when the steers came and munched their feed corn, and were at home anywhere from under the barn to the back porch. As a man will when wild things trust him, our farmer became very fond of his one flock of blue quail. They were company for him at a time when homesteads were a long distance apart. He expected them to meet him at the garden gate in the morning; they were a part of his daily life. He wouldn't have killed one of them for a gray horse. One day, coming from town, he heard shooting, and saw a car parked in front of his home. The car drove off as he approached, but that was the last he ever saw of his quail.

A bevy of bob-white quail never would have been all killed off like that. They would have scattered widely, and not every bird could have been shot. This in a way accounts for the blue quail disappearing when the wild lands are settled. He is more of a runner than a flier, and that is much to the liking of a pot-hunter. The little chaps can run like a wild turkey, and have much the appearance of a turkey, a very miniature turkey of course, as they race down a corn-row or through openings in the chaparral. The blue quail had as well been called the chaparral quail, because there is where you find him in southern Texas. He is well able to take care of himself where only natural enemies are concerned, but is easily killed off by shooting, especially if shot on the ground.

I was out shooting with a good Texas quail hunter one day, down on the Nueces River in south Texas. I was shocked to see him fire into a bevy of blue quail as they raced down a field of kaffir corn. Taken to task, he said "Shucks, it is harder to hit a blue quail running than it is flying."

That is one way of looking at it, but between shooting on the ground and shooting in the air, very shortly the blue quail are not what they used to be; not in a section that is heavily shot.

I used to get a lot of fun out of the blue quail. Hunted with a dog, found in the cultivated fields, when the dog pointed I knew very well that he wouldn't be holding the birds. Now the dog would start in trailing down the corn-rows, a very much disgusted dog, maybe, and I'd follow along contentedly, knowing what those birds would do. Possibly that field was half a mile long, and those birds would never stop running until they got to the thickets at the farther end. It might be that this first bevy would encounter another or more on the way and all would join in the running procession. Now and then I might get in sight of those birds, running in single file, every one in the same row, footing it swiftly with top-knots erect. I might have had a running shot now and then, but I hadn't come a thousand miles to shoot quail on the ground, and I knew that eventually I'd get enough to eat.

Reaching the thorn-brush at the end of the field, those quail should have been as safe as a bug in a rug. However, they were not, for no sooner were they in the brush than they took a notion to fly right back to where they had started from. They came by me in singles, pairs, a half dozen in a bunch, all going straight back past me. I bagged a mess of quail, if shooting true, for not a bird would remain in cover, once they took a notion to go back, and they didn't all start at once. I had time to reload, while the old lemon-spotted pointer just watched the shooting, with brow awrinkle and ears acock, marking where the dead birds fell. "Boss," he seemed to say, "this kind of thing is not to be forgotten."

Again, I have trailed the birds along dusty cow-paths or the winding chaparral roads, always dusty so that the trailing was as easy as in the snow. I might follow those three-toed tracks a mile, for these little chaps travel widely as compared with bob-whites. By and by I'd see them, in some straight stretch of road, possibly a quarter of a mile ahead. I didn't hurry them, because if I did they would jump the road and take to the brush, where not a thing could be done with them. On the other hand, I knew those birds were making for an open field ahead. Once in that field I meant to crowd them so fast that they couldn't keep running, whereupon one after another they would rise fifteen or twenty feet into the air and curve back around me—making for the brush this time. I'd get them as they rose like green-wing teal off a pond.

Shooting blue quail in Texas in the old days was worth while, and it is now. In places bobwhites and blue quail may be found in the same field, but as Bob goes west with the white man, the blues go west in front of him.

In New Mexico and Colorado the blue quail is sometimes called the mountain quail, because he goes very high up on the hills. I have seen them on the mesas 7000 feet above sea level. But the blue prefers the foothills as a rule. Flushed in the mountains, he probably will go straight up the highest hill, and it is here one learns it takes strong legs and good wind to follow him. Not many birds can be bagged in the mountains, and the best dog would probably be some kind of spaniel that would rush into them and make them fly. Once badly scattered they would permit the gun to come in reach, or they would lie to a dog the same as other quail. I have never hunted them so.

The blue quail is good eating, just as tasty as a bob-white, though it rarely gets so fat. The Mexican bird is just about the size of Bob, though longer and looking larger. As to appearance "on the hoof," he has a topknot, something like a bluejay's, but shorter, composed of some white and some mottled feathers. His general color is lighter than Bob White's, and his handsome coat scintillates when he takes the air. His flight speed is just about the same as that of our Eastern quail, but he doesn't rise with the same roar as Bob White does. I think that when flushed in the open he is easier to hit than a bobwhite, but no Texan would ever agree to that.

THE MASSENA PARTRIDGE

(*Cyrtonyx montezuma*)

OF the different species of American quail, really partridges, by far the greater number are found in old Mexico, with diminished abundance on this side in near proximity to the Rio Grande.

Despite our game laws, steadily becoming more strict, game must decrease in this country. Forests will be cleaned up if not cleaned out; fence-rows, briar patches, and quail cover generally must disappear as farms become restricted in area, together with general adoption of a more intensive system of agriculture. At present there are few states north of the Ohio River where worth-while quail shooting can be obtained, and in these only very restricted districts. I believe that it can be safely asserted that in the entire country we have less than half the quail now that we had in 1900, and double the number of hunters. The solution of the small-game shooter's problem, no less the large-game hunter's, is to turn to Canada and Mexico—Canada for the big-game hunter, Mexico for the bird shooter. In the day to come when the Mexican revolutionist must eventually starve himself and be educated into a reasonable frame of mind, then being willing to welcome American sportsmen and to earn an honest dollar by acting as guide or host, we can confidently expect northern Mexico to become a great shooting ground.

Of the numerous species of quail found in Mexico, and to some extent in New Mexico, Texas and Arizona, one of the very finest is the Massena partridge. While naturalists have placed this bird in the genus *Cyrtonyx*, giving Bob White the generic name *Colinus*, yet in every essential the Massena partridge is simply an enlarged edition of our bob-white quail.

Like the Virginia partridge he prefers to live in cultivated fields, in the vicinity of homes and houses. He doesn't pack as does the California quail, but remains in bevies as hatched. He crouches and hides even more closely than Bob does, scattered birds refusing to take wing until pointed and tramped up, and his scent is said to be even stronger than that of our quail, dogs winding bevies at fifty yards or more and singles at half that distance. When pointed and flushed the bevies break out as one bird, directly in front of the gun, rise to six or ten feet and boom off with a tremendous burst of speed. Once scattered in the grass, singles will not run, neither can they be flushed by the sound of a gun or the flight of other birds, as often happens with bob-whites, but every individual bird hugs the ground until pointed and walked up. The flight is rather shorter than Bob's, being from 100 to 150 yards, and they much prefer to alight in the open even when cover is adjacent. Mr. H. T. Payne, a good authority, says that for work with a dog he much prefers them to any bird he has ever shot, and that in Sonora, old Mexico, from twelve to fifteen bevies can be raised to the mile.

The breast of the Massena partridge is as spotted as that of a guinea hen, while the back is much the color of the back of Bob White. This quail has a "semi-erectile" crest, something like Bob's, but running farther back on the head, in fact drooping back over the head. The head of the cock is about equally barred with black and white, the black dabbed on without regard to design. The short tail of the bird gives him a square, blocky appearance, and he is always plump. His flesh is just as palatable as our quail's, and not excelled by any member of the family, unless it is the mountain quail, of California and Oregon.

THE CALIFORNIA QUAIL; VALLEY QUAIL

Of these quail there are two kinds, differing in minor features only: *californicus*, and *californicus valicola*. Both are typical blue quail, so much alike that the ordinary observer would consider them one and the same bird. Should the gunner, anywhere in the Southwest from New Mexico to the coast, shoot a bird of a general slaty blue color, with a topknot composed of six feathers which stand up and roach forward, the cock having a black head with white markings—a bird which runs in the half erect attitude of a turkey, runs nearly as fast as a wild turkey, too—he can safely conclude it is a "blue" quail, or at least a member of *Lophortyx*. The only bird that is liable to be mistaken for either the California quail or the valley quail is the mountain quail, a larger bird, with his topknot extending backward instead of forward.

As to the general characteristics of this quail, including both, he can exist in an arid country, unsuited to Bob White, he chooses to run in seeking safety rather than to fly—though again like the wild turkey, he will squat and hide when he strikes suitable cover, and when he does hug the ground he stays there until tramped up.   He is strong of wing, affording splendid shooting, once the bevies are broken up and scattered.   Lastly, he has the habit of collecting in packs in the winter, like prairie chickens, not remaining in bevies like Bob White.   Great stories have been told as to the number of birds in one of these packs, up to 5000 in one great convention.   Such flocks might have been seen at one time in the history of California shooting, but I think we might safely divide the number by about fifty now.

A difference of opinion exists as to the "gunning" qualities of the blue quail.   The Eastern sportsman, accustomed to shooting bob-whites, reviles the blue runner bitterly because of his tendency to run and to keep running, thus tormenting a good dog; but your true Californian swears by the game blue fellows, nor will he have it that a finer game bird ever existed.   Talk to a Coast man of the "valley" quail and you will instantly get a line on whether he is a real native son. Incidentally, both the California quail and the valley quail are valley quail to him.

When everything is said for and against these birds, there are undoubtedly times, places and opportunities when the finest possible sport is to be had from a well-scattered flock of blue quail—it matters nothing whether they are actually California quail, valley quail or a little of both.

Ornithologists explain that the greater difference in the two birds is not in appearance but in habits and habitat.

The valley quail prefers the good cover of the Coast Range valleys, from San Francisco northward, while the California * quail is partial to the high, rolling, thinly clad foothills of the mountains of southern California.

Possibly the way to tell the difference between a California valley quail and a valley quail is that one will run up the hill and over a mountain, where there are mountains, while the other will not, in the absence of the mountain.

* Commonly given the other bird's name, valley quail, to distinguish it from the mountain quail, *Oreortyx,* above mentioned; of which, by the way, there are three varieties.

Chapter XI

IMPORTED UPLAND GAME BIRDS

THE HUNGARIAN PARTRIDGE; GRAY PARTRIDGE

THE European red-breasted partridge is known as the gray partridge in England, and as the Hungarian in this country. It is the common partridge of Europe, distributed pretty much all over the temperate sections, and extending much farther north than the bob-white quail does in this country. The Latin name of this gray bird, which may be given to distinguish it from other partridges, is *Perdix cinerea*, while the type bird, a more northerly species, is termed *Perdix perdix*. The other partridge, common in England, is the French or red-legged, carrying the title of *Caccabis rufa*. Our early importations came from the plains of Hungary, hence the name. Either he is indigenous to the British Isles or the Romans brought him over, concerning which history is uncertain.

He is known as the gray partridge in England to distinguish him from his red-legged cousin, a trifle larger bird and more of a runner, which is well liked for "driving" but does not lie well to dogs. The gray partridge is intimately connected with English sporting literature, from Colonel Peter Hawker to Stonehenge, to Sir Ralph Payne-Gallowey and Earl Grey. Charles Dickens, in "Pickwick Papers," has his quasi-heroes attempting to shoot partridges, and in all the world, in prose and poem, no bird has had so much written of him as has the English gray partridge.

In the days of the flintlock he taught the English sportsman how to shoot awing, by the simple means of affording him an easy and enticing target.   Even the bell-muzzled snaphance was used in partridge shooting, on bevies at rest.   Earlier still, partridge hunters used snares and nets.   English writers of the period gave instructions for netting.   At night a steady pointer was taken out, wearing a bell.   When the bell became silent as the dog stood his birds, a net was drawn over both dog and partridges.   Presently the gun became fashionable, and netting a sure indication of poaching, a severe offense.   Many an Australian family's history traces back to some ancestor who found his way to the big island because he was too fond of partridge hunting with a net.

The English or Hungarian partridge fits in well with American needs.   He is accustomed to civilization, to living in cultivated fields, to gleaning in sight of the reaper and the plow.   He is a half domesticated bird, multiplying where his natural enemies are decimated by the gun, while some of our own game birds retreat steadily as the sod is broken or the forest felled.   Where man can live in comfort, producing his food from the soil, there the partridge thrives.   Yet he is a sporting thoroughbred, flying strong and straight, lying to a pointing dog, getting up within reach of the gun, flushing in the open with a roar of wings, scattering in the open to take his chance with the gun.   Furthermore, he is just the size that a game bird ought to be, when a day's bag has to be carried in a back coat-tail pocket.   Often when shooting a mixed bag of quail and chickens in the Nebraska sandhills, I have wished for a bird just midway between a chicken and a quail. We have him in the gray partridge—though I doubt if he yet is established in my old sandhills hunting territory.

The partridge weighs from 14 to 16 ounces, just double the size of the American quail. He is stronger of wing than a quail, not faster but of more prolonged flight. It is nothing unusual to see a bevy of partridges fly a half mile. On the wing, the bird has a greater resemblance to a prairie chicken than to a quail. He also resembles the prairie grouse in alighting in the open, whereas the quail will go to cover, if there is any. Of the two birds the partridge is the more difficult to find and the easier to bag when he is found.

I am reminded of the first flock of Hungarian partridges that I ever saw. This was on the game preserve of the late Paul Rainey, in northern Mississippi, about twenty-five years ago. We were standing in the yard of the bungalow when a bevy of some kind of large birds winged by, looking not unlike a whole flock of blue pigeon hawks. I watched them till they passed beyond the range of vision in the distance. Two darkeys, one of whom worked for Mr. Rainey, also witnessed the flight. "Whut's 'em bu'ds?" queried Sam.

"Paterges," replied Mose.

"Shucks, nigger, ain't no paterges git 'at big!"

" 'At's all you know 'bout it. 'At come from feeden 'em up. Mars Rainey done plant cow tuhnips foh 'em."

However, although a frequenter of the turnip fields of England the gray partridge unfortunately is not so easily fed up. It has been hoped that he can be introduced into every section of the United States, but I doubt if he takes kindly to all the severe variations in climate that we have in much of this country. His native climate is temperate and moist. Snow

Photos Nat'l Assn. of Audubon Societies.

Ring-neck pheasants, male and female

Above, native bob-white quail captives for breeding and stocking. *Below*, Hungarian partridges for the same purpose.

he doesn't mind, nor cold, but I doubt if he ever thrives in the semi-arid sections of our Southwest, or survives the long, hot summers of the Gulf states.   However, all through the East, thence across Ohio, and over all the prairie states, where the American quail has practically died out, the gray partridge should take his place.   In the Pacific Northwest he has found a homelike region.

In the days of Colonel Peter Hawker and General Hutchinson, partridges were shot over dogs precisely as our quail are now.   Times changed in England and the partridge began to be driven over the guns, as were grouse and pheasants. The aristocratic sporting Briton took kindly to that sort of thing: it enabled him to shoot a lot and to have company at it —and he could hire the walking done.   Shooting became a social affair.   The day before the English partridge season opened, far more shooters gathered at the manor house or the castle of the estate, whichever it happened to be.   Formal dress for dinner was the rule and, if in those bygone days the women did not participate in the shooting they nevertheless were on hand for the rest of the good time.   All had their brandy and soda before dinner, wine with the dinner, and a good, stiff English night-cap before going to bed.   Nobody can ever accuse the sporting English, men or women, of being darned chumps when it comes to enjoying life.

To detail a day's shooting, we must begin with the beaters, bright and early.   Assembled in charge of the head-keeper and under-keepers, they carry sticks and tin pans, or anything else that will make plenty of noise.   They are instructed to drive a certain section of the estate.   The gun-bearers trudge away for the shooting butts, maybe a half dozen miles, each carrying two guns which belong to his master for the day.

Ponies are brought out in charge of grooms, and the sportsmen ride away for their stands. These stands are built, perhaps, of turf, like miniature sod houses, down in some valley, preferably back of a hedge, which the birds must top and so rise higher to the gun. The sod butt is designed to hide in. Grooms take away the horses, the shooters take comfortable chairs in the stands. Gun in hand, the "loader" kneels back of the marksman, a case of shells beside him. A pair of guns are in every stand, and the loader must recharge one as the other is fired. Loading the spare gun is a profession of itself, because the guns must be handled just so, the loaded gun being passed to the shooter's right hand while the empty piece is taken from his left. No Englishman could be induced to shoot a repeating shotgun, because that has never been done. If the object is to see how many birds can be killed as they pass, I'd bet on an American with a couple of pump guns and a man to load them.

Presently the long line of beaters is heard coming in the distance. They are converging and concentrating the partridges in front of them. Shortly comes the warning call, "Mark." The birds are seen coming. Every gunner carefully selects his own birds, and as carefully refrains from shooting at those of another. The guns kill according to their skill, the birds being dropped not too far in front and not too far behind.

In time the rounded-up partridges have all gone over, such as have escaped. The dead are gathered by serving men and dogs. If the bag averages fifty birds to the gun, that is a successful drive; some marksman may have killed a hundred. Birds are counted in pairs, never singles—that is not done either. Mrs. H. B. Duryea, an American woman, told me that she had killed fifty pairs of Scotch grouse in one hour and thirty minutes, on the preserve of the late W. B. Whitney. The last thing is to pack the birds in hampers, ready for the London market.   Lunch is coming.

With it come the mesdames and the honorable misses— on horseback and in carts in the old days, maybe sometimes in cars now.   An English woman looks well in tailor-made clothes, and she wears them on the opening day.   An English cook has it all over ours when it comes to putting up a cold lunch.   If there is anything good to eat cold in the whole of England, it is in that lunch—or anything good to drink, for that matter.   One can well believe in the elegance of that lunch.

There surely must be a lot of solid sporting glamour about such an outing, on a perfect English autumn day, say what you like.   The parklike wooded hills and cultivated valleys, the orderly army of servants in gala dress, the many sleek horses, the correctly dressed and decorous sportsmen and sportswomen, the rows and rows of shot partridges, all form a picture of our British cousins at play in a way which, if not yet our way, we must admit is impressive.   It is a great day, the first day of the open season on partridges.   Appetites are sharp, for breakfast came very early.   The old fellows stick to their Scotch and soda, the youngsters to their claret, the women to their champagne.   The men talk as shooters will, the women chatter as women will, and the laughter of the beaters comes from a neighboring grove.   They are fed this day from milord's table, have ale, beer, and a great demijohn of brandy all their own.

We will let them linger over that lunch, ere they are off for a second drive, when nobody will shoot so well and not so many birds will be killed.   The gun-bearers, the grooms, the keepers and the beaters at evening will gather in the great hall for the tenants' dance, given in honor of a great occasion, the opening of the partridge season.   The gentry will have a party of their own.

We of this country know all about driving game as a co-operative proposition.   We practise it by the thousands in our deer hunting, our jackrabbit and coyote drives.   Already we know the driving of pheasants and hand-reared ducks to the gun, on private hunting preserves.   Maybe, in a hundred years or less we too shall know the partridge drive as a social function, when shooting has become an expensive luxury, when nine guns in ten have dropped out because of the expense, and the tenth may bag birds without limit.

Chapter XI (Concluded)

IMPORTED UPLAND GAME BIRDS

THE RING-NECKED PHEASANT

The owl sang "Oo-ooo-ooe" in the sycamore tree,
And his mate answered loudly, "Who-ah-me!"
But Carl and his wife never heard him.

The billygoat butted the gate unlatched,
The bull calf bawled in the cabbage patch,
But Carl and his wife never heard him.

The coyote wailed his plaintive cry,
And the old red hound bayed fierce reply,
But Carl and his wife never heard him.

The hired man crept o'er the kitchen floor,
Till he stubbed his toe on the cellar door,
But Carl and his wife never heard him.

Came "Curt, curt, curt" from the turkey flock,
For the old red pheasant was thrashing the cock,
And Carl and his wife sure heard him.

THE Chinese ring-necked pheasant is an inhabitant of Asia by nativity, a migrant long since to Europe along with the white race, and is a resident of North America from importation and personal preference.

America is much to the liking of our ringneck. Nature, they used to say, abhors a vacuum. That was the old explanation of why water rises in a tube from which the air has been exhausted. And that is perhaps why weeds grow on land where no grain is produced and why the pheasant is spreading over North America.

The ringneck found a vacuum in the United States, a place where nothing existed, a place for a good, live, enterprising game bird, educated to the wiles of civilization and the gun. He found the quail gone, the ruffed grouse gone, the prairie chicken gone, the wild duck going, and there was all the room the red bird from Asia always had needed and always had lacked.

Just why the pheasant found himself peculiarly adapted to America's game shooting needs is a matter of pheasant character and education. He is a bandit, and bandits thrive where honest men cannot find a job that resembles a snap. A bandit cannot be exterminated and can't be hung, because you have to catch him first. Same way with the pheasant. He knew more about men and guns and stealing a living before America was discovered than American game birds ever learned afterwards. If we didn't like him we couldn't get rid of him any more than we can get rid of the English sparrow; but he pays his way and we like him.

As to character, he is as wise as an old black crow which never mistook a crooked stick for a gun. He is as wise as a country politician who never said anything, never thought anything, never did anything, who carefully kept out of people's way, so was elected vice-president or something. The ringneck will come into the barnyard to lick a tame rooster, provided the owner stands by and laughs; but if the farmer dodges back into the house for a gun, the bird is gone where the soldier went who lived to fight another day. He has had a thousand years' experience with men, and not only knows what they do but how they do it.   He knows that legs sometimes serve better than wings, better than courage, better than taking any chance whatever, so he runs.

If our ringneck arose in bevies, like prairie chickens and quail, winging to an open field to lie like a stone to gun and dog, we could exterminate him as fast as we could import him, all the same as a partridge.   But mark down a bunch of pheasants, see exactly where they alighted, go there for the shooting, and the pheasant will be a quarter of a mile off, streaking for the tall timber.   Beat the timber with a good dog, and while the pointer is slowly drawing about on foot-scent, the pheasant will slip out of one corner and silently fly away.   A cock pheasant, unless a young bird, is not killed by any system of searching for him.   He is accidentally caught napping, or maybe, like a white-tailed deer, he is taking a chance that if he keeps still you will pass him by; only to find, when too late, that "the best laid plans o' mice and man gang aft agley."   In that way, by accident, where the birds are thick, one of our very limited bag limits can be made in a day.

A ringneck, flushed in field or cover, may not consider himself safe until a mile away, half the distance being covered on foot after he alights.   Therefore all the pheasants on the place are not going to be killed—perhaps not any of them, unless enough guns are present to "drive."   The systematic style of pheasant driving adopted in England gets results, if you want shooting and game in the bag.   Flushed by twoscore beaters going through the coverts with stick and hullabaloo, these birds can be driven in swarms over a line of guns and slaughtered.

They tell me that in England pheasants cost an average

of about $3.00 a bird to produce, shoot, and market.   An
English gun may possibly account for a hundred pheasants
in a day.   The cost to that gun or to the host who provides
the shooting will be $300 a day.   We expect to get our free
American shooting for $1.25 a year, and so long as we do,
our bag limit will be from nothing at all to perhaps three
birds for a good day.

What is accomplished in Europe through private owner-
ship we are endeavoring to bring about through state owner-
ship.   The states haven't yet worked up much momentum,
but they have spent a pile of money on pheasants.   If the
6,000,000 shooters we are supposed to have in this country
could pay $25 a gun, that would mean $15,000,000 dollars a
year for game.   Game keeping would become a profession,
and the farmer could pay his taxes from the game his farm
produced.   On the other hand, the shooting may slowly drift
into the hands of clubs and individuals who are willing to
pay from $100 to $10,000 a year for something to shoot at.

The pheasant is a farm bird.   He has some of the habits
of a wild turkey, since he will take to his heels at the first alarm;
but, unlike the turkey, he has no intention of retiring to heavy
forests and never coming out.   In England he is spoken of
as a bird of the coverts, supposed to be found in small bodies
of timber or brush, but in this country he is doing well in all
kinds of cover, from the weedy "old fields" of abandoned New
England farms to what used to be the open plains of the old
West.   Not very long ago Major Frazier asked me concerning prairie chicken grounds.   I sent him to South Dakota,
where twenty years before I found all kinds of chickens and
sharp-tail grouse.   The Major did not find chickens or
grouse, but he had splendid pheasant shooting, he wrote me.

That is a country of severe winters, with fierce blizzards, which force even the native chickens to the willow-bordered streams for protection, but the pheasant doesn't seem to mind. A pheasant can roost in a tree or on the ground, on top of a haystack or on the lee side of it. Which is reason for observing, incidentally, that unlike our native grouse he hasn't a one-track mind.

Though of course in season eating his share of insects and all kinds of creeping things that he can swallow, the pheasant is a grain eater. Almost anything the farmer raises, the ringneck finds good. He has been bred on farms and among farmers for a thousand generations. He eats wheat, oats, corn, beans, peas, millet, green vegetables, and the farmers say he will scratch up a hill of potatoes and eat them. His size is some protection against winged vermin, and ground vermin find him safe in a tree. When the wheat is cut he takes refuge in the standing corn, and the corn gathered, there are acorns in the woods.

All the ringneck asks is to be able to nest in security, and in nesting time, like the turkey, he takes to the tall timber. If any game bird can exist and increase in this country, notwithstanding the gun or any other persecution, it is the pheasant. As indicated in our rhyme, he has the habit of coming into the barnyard at feeding time; then the tame rooster runs, the old gander keeps out of his way, and the turkey gobbler gets a prompt licking. People admire him for his courage, just as they do any other bold outlaw, who takes by force what he could not otherwise secure. He will drink at the horse-trough when the pond goes dry, and if the field is plowed, leaving the garden full of weeds, into the garden he comes.

An odd thing about the pheasant that makes him particularly adapted to game farms and hand rearing is that he can be hatched under a domestic hen or brooded by a leghorn, yet on being freed he promptly goes wild. Turn a hatching of young pheasants loose, after they get old enough to take care of themselves, and at once they disappear, to return only if starved into so doing. They will be somewhere, doing nicely, thank you.

For another odd thing, they won't stay put. When winter comes, the birds you turn out may be in the next township. Raise a bevy of bob-white quail under the same conditions, and you have a bevy of pet birds that won't stray two hundred yards from the house. You can domesticate quail or even prairie chickens, but you cannot domesticate pheasants, if allowed their freedom. Attempts have been made to make game birds out of guineas, but the guinea is too tame. He will wander far over the farm, but will come home to roost at night, and if disturbed will fly to the shelter of the buildings he considers home. Not so the pheasant; he roosts wherever night overtakes him, to continue his travels the next day.

When selecting a game bird adapted to America, necessarily he had to be from a climate similar to ours. The Chinese ringneck is a member of a large family. Pheasants of one kind or another occupy pretty much all of temperate and tropical Asia. Some species live with the peafowl in India, others with the blackcock in southern Siberia; a certain species may live in the mountains, and another prefer the level plains. Our bird comes from a country of heat and cold, of open fields and heavy cover—in which he is equally at home. Transferred to this country, the change has not affected him, except to make him more prolific. Like the original American pioneer, he is pushing west, also east, north and south.

First introduced in the Northwestern states, Washington and Oregon, he traveled south into California, and east into Idaho, Montana and Utah.   Stocked first in the Dakotas, he has pretty well covered Minnesota, Iowa and Wisconsin now. Colorado has probably more pheasants than any other game bird.   New York and Ohio have pheasant shooting where no upland game bird, except woodcock in New York, could be shot otherwise.   And the fine red cocks are pretty much all over Illinois, Indiana and Michigan.

With necessary protection, supported by vigorous propagation, our bonny red ringneck will follow in the footsteps of the sparrow and the English starling, making his own way, taking care of himself, spreading from farm to farm, from county to county and state to state.   I expect to see the pheasant acclimated everywhere in course of time, north of the Ohio River and north of the Red River of Texas.   He can hardly exist in the South among the darkeys, with their insatiate taste for fried chicken, and Texas will have to become a "wet" state before the ringneck will tolerate the thickets of chaparral.

Part II

WATERFOWL   SHOOTING

Chapter XII

DUCK SHOOTING BANKRUPTCY

A HUNDRED years ago wild ducks bred all up and down the Ohio River, the Mississippi, the Missouri, the Arkansas, the Platte, and all the thousand lakes and ponds lying between. Fifteen years ago, in a magazine article I remarked that the ducks going north were not flying high and far beyond their old homes for the love of wing-practice, but because of spring shooting. At that time, treaties recently made with Canada had finally given the United States Government authority to protect migratory birds, to prevent spring shooting and to end market gunning. We thought the problem of conserving waterfowl was solved in favor of the birds. Now, in the year 1930, after fifteen years of protection under the Migratory Bird Act, and after various vast Gulf Coast wild life refuges have been closed to shooting for nearly or all that time, as a guess I would say that there remain only about one half the waterfowl that we had fifteen years ago.

What is the reason? A while ago the best reason was the Great War. The next good reason was that Congress never made any real, practical effort to protect migratory game, but relied upon the prestige of a Federal law to enforce itself. If Congress had made any such effort to enforce the Migratory Bird Act as that great body has to enforce prohibition, we'd have had such numbers of ducks and geese that farmers would have been howling about the destruction of crops. Instead, enough money was appropriated annually to hire twenty-five Federal wardens to police forty-eight states! In the entire fifteen years I, for one, have never seen a Federal warden, except those at headquarters in Washington. The law fell more or less into contempt. State game authorities had the right to enforce the Federal law, but, between you and me, they thought it was "George's job"! Tell a state game warden that ducks are being shot out of season, and he may or may not pay any attention, but tell him that a deer has been illegally killed, or quail, and he will be concerned at once. It is only of late years that a determined effort has been exerted to promote the welfare of waterfowl. I have in mind reading the other day that $300,000 has been appropriated to purchase and set aside the Cheyenne Valley in Kansas as a Federal waterfowl reservation. Previously a great scope of country had been set aside on the upper Mississippi. That is precisely what the waterfowl need, water—water and some place to breed and to rest in security. We are all still hopeful that the Bureau of Biological Survey, Department of Agriculture, is going to come through.

Now for the first reason and the great reason why the webfeet have decreased one half. During the war agricultural products brought high prices; word went forth from Washington to produce more wheat and corn and everything else that the farmer could raise. Wild lands were brought into cultivation, lakes, ponds, sloughs and marshes were drained and water was used for irrigation, under instructions from the Department of Agriculture. The Canadian farmers were doing the same thing as ours. And along with this

Photos Nat'l Assn. of Audubon Societies.

Above, redhead mother duck and young, and a camera shot of a duck changing its mind. *Below,* friendly lesser scaups (bluebill or broadbill) on a protected lake; Canada geese, adult pair and young.

Above, a goose and duck stand on Currituck Sound.   *Below,* mallards in one of the
Louisiana refuges.

came the automobile, to be followed by concrete roads and droughts.

Money was pretty plentiful after the war and wages were high. Every man could afford to own an automobile and a gun, and most men did. Men became shooters who never had shot before. The automobile took thousands of men around every countryside where but one had gone before. Ducks found neither water nor food, but a hundred guns awaiting their flight. Bag limits and other restrictive laws were unavailing, because the birds were legally killed, and ten legal guns carried in automobiles could kill more birds than one market gunner possibly could in the years that were passed. If no ducks came near us and we heard of a spot 100 or 200 miles away, we could get there before breakfast, and we did. If there was any place in America where water-fowl resorted, with no road to get to them, a road was built. The ducks were compelled to fly high between Canada and Mexico, and to nest in the far North.

Now, then, what is to be done about it? My own theory is that duck shooting should be made more difficult in place of easier. I have not been able to promulgate that theory in the current sporting magazine, because the more duck shooters there are the more readers those magazines have. Arms and ammunition companies are interested because their sales are dependent on the game supply, but they are not interested to such an extent as to be willing to curtail their output. The magazines would hold, whether they said so or not, "No shooters, no readers"; the arms companies know that "no shooters, no guns sold." So everybody is encouraged to shoot.

The Bureau of Biological Survey has recently issued a regulation cutting down the bag limit to fifteen birds a day.

That is a step in the right direction. The logical next step would be, or should be, a Federal license of $10 a gun, instead of the usual resident license of $1.25 a gun. That would give the Government money to work with and game authorities would no longer have to depend on special appropriations. Ten dollars a year is no great sum to expend for the privilege of duck shooting, or shooting any other game. Shooting is a luxury, and these days has to be paid for the same as any other luxury. The average man who makes a duck-shooting trip spends not less than $10 a day for his sport, and he would be glad to pay $10 before he started for the assurance that he would find something to shoot at when he reached his destination. Plenty of men now spend $50 a day for their duck shooting. Nevertheless there are numbers of others unwilling to pay more than the usual license fee of $1.25. That is just what I am driving at. The man who thinks more of a bottle of bootleg whiskey than he does of the privilege of shooting ducks, ought to have the whiskey and go without the ducks. In other words, let every man have the luxury that he appreciates most. However, it is no doubt true that a great many shooters would refuse to pay a license fee of $10, and that again is what I am driving at. So long as we have 6,000,000 licensed shooters we shall never have any ducks. Whatever the Government does or conservationists do, we shall never have any ducks, so long as it costs only $1.25 a year to shoot them.

The only other way out of it is to have the United States conserve water and the states conserve ducks by producing them wholesale. I have noticed that when Oklahoma has a very wet spring, ducks breed in numbers within the state. It is a matter of water and to be free of molestation. If the

Government ever gets to a point where the rivers are dammed in order to prevent overflows in the Mississippi, waterfowl will breed in the lakes so formed. The more ducks that are bred in a state, the more ducks that state will have in shooting season, and the more ducks America will have in shooting season. Moreover, local ducks remain about home a long time, while migrations from the far North come and go sometimes within a few days.

Waterfowl are readily bred in state hatcheries, far more easily raised than pheasants or other upland birds. I suspect that the reason this means of restoration is not promoted is that state game authorities look upon the returns as uncertain, for their particular state. A friend of mine, by keeping wing-tipped mallards, raised a flock that were as tame as domestic birds, and it was the same way with a pair of Canada geese. In the spring his fowl got to flying about the neighborhood, and then disappeared, both geese and ducks, and never came back. That is, I suspect, what the state game authorities think would happen if they raised a hundred thousand mallards. The birds would go off to the Gulf Coast or to Canada, and never come back. Therefore if the states are ever to go into the production of game it will have to be by general agreement. Oklahoma won't raise ducks for Texas to shoot, or Kansas for Oklahoma to shoot. On the other hand, if pheasants or Hungarian partridges, or bobwhite quail are ever turned loose in proper cover, there they are.

The only remaining obstacle to the production of waterfowl is that involving means for remunerating the farmers for feeding the birds. Take a small lake which may carry a thousand mallards, and the surrounding corn and kaffir fields will suffer.　Farmers will become insistent that the birds be killed or driven away.　However, pay a farmer $1 apiece for every bird shot on his land, and he will forget all about the grain that was eaten.　A dollar each is a lot of money to pay for every duck killed, we might admit, but that is just what we are coming to, and will have to come to.　On some big English estate a thousand pheasants may be killed in a single day, but we are told that every one of those pheasants costs $3 to produce.　We are coming to that, and in due course of time every duck that is killed will cost the man who shoots it not less than $1.　When that happens we shall have less than 6,000,000 duck shooters, and those who do shoot will take it as a matter of course if the license fee is $25 instead of $1.25.　Give a farmer $1 a bird for every duck killed on his place and he will construct ponds and lakes of his own.

Chapter XIII

THE MALLARD. THE BLACK DUCK

IN contrast with what I have to say in this volume of the lives, history, occupations and diversions of our waterfowl, it should be borne in mind that an encyclopedia could be filled with the subject. Attempting the subject in part of one book is comparable to whittling at a giant redwood log with a pocketknife.

For a beginning, we select the mallard, because he has afforded more sport to more people than any other waterfowl that ever lived. A cosmopolitan gentleman, a well-dressed and highly respected citizen of the entire world, he is equally well known to the Tartars of Siberia, the Lapps of northern Europe, and the Aleuts of North America. England welcomes him during migration, also Mediterranean countries, and far-away Brazil and Argentina. He goeth wherever he listeth, and a little thing like another ocean to cross gives him no concern. The naturalists call him *Anas boschas* and to many gunners he is the greenhead.

Many consider the mallard the handsomest of all ducks, not excepting the wood duck. He is the recognized leader and commander of the webfoot tribe, specializing in knowledge of the ways of his arch enemy, man. When the mallard says, "Go," all other ducks are gone, and when he says, "It is safe here," his word is taken. As witness, every species

141

of duck comes to mallard decoys.   The raucous quack of an
old hen mallard will arouse all the webfeet within a quarter
of a mile, and few will hesitate to obey her command.

The late Joseph A. Graham used to remind me, when I
faltered over a decision, that the mark of a brilliant mind was
instant decision.   If so, the mallard measures up to the mark,
for his decisions are made like the lightning's flash.   The
glint of the rising sun on a gun-barrel, the gleam of a keen
eye peering from beneath the brim of an old slouch hat, the
sight of an empty red shell on the naked sand, and our mallard literally "goes into high."   He is like the Indian's turkey.   Asked which was the more difficult to hunt, turkey or
deer, the Indian replied: "Deer see Injun, stamp his foot,
say, 'Maybe Injun, maybe not.'   By'm by Injun get close,
deer say, 'Looks like Injun, maybe not.'   By'm by Injun
shoot deer.   Turkey see Injun, say, 'Injun, *Injun! Injun!
Run!*'   Injun never see turkey no more."

The mallard is the embodiment of duck wisdom.   You
may catch him napping, but, unlike people, you can't fool
him twice in the same way.   His glossy head is armored on
the inside—by brains.   He is the finest waterfowl that ever
lived or ever will live, a gay and gallant sporting character,
a warrior of parts, who carries his legion safely past many a
well hidden ambuscade.   Nevertheless, he is always willing
to declare a truce with man, willing to become domesticated
and settle down to home life.   Witness the thousands of his
kind in the various barnyards of the world.

Our "wild duck" is willing to accommodate himself to circumstances and conditions.   I have seen a flock of home-
reared birds, hatched from wild eggs, that flew about the farm
and to the river, four miles away.   At regular times, regular

as the clock, they never failed to return to the house, waddle up on the porch and into the kitchen, if the door was open. Failing to get into the house they stood about the back door and quacked and coaxed until fed.   On the place of a ranchman in Nebraska who refused to permit the birds shot, they came, hundreds in a flock, to forage in the fattening pens of the cattle, barely keeping from under the feet of the team used in scattering the grain.   Yet, if anyone with a gun attempted to crawl up on them they sprang into the air as one bird, to roar off with frightened and protesting outcries.   In Scotland, perhaps in England also, mallards have been half domesticated, hand-reared, taught to fly from home pens to baited fields, and shot en route.   The English gunners say the mallard is inferior to the pheasant in that he flies too high after being shot at a few times, and the blinds must be relocated daily.   Nevertheless, as many as 3000 mallards have been killed on one estate.

Mallards have a great fondness for timber, timbered lakes, ponds and streams, yet they are equally at home on the prairies.   Formerly they bred everywhere from Florida to an elevation of eight thousand feet in Montana, but we have worried them so much that I suspect most of them are now reared north of parallel 49.   There are, however, many locally bred ducks in Nebraska, North and South Dakota, Minnesota and Wisconsin, and with unmolested water, thousands more should breed in Uncle Sam's domain—drought seasons excepted.

The mallard is a great forager, not confining himself to foods that grow in or fall into the water, being equally liable to dine far inland.   He is fond of peas, corn and kaffir corn, as well as of acorns and the seeds of water-plants.   That his regular breakfast may be spread fifty miles from where he means to take his noonday nap matters little.   From choice, he feeds during the day and roosts at night, but if disturbed will readily reverse the order of things.

One feature of the habits of mallards should be known to all duck shooters, more particularly to all game keepers on club grounds.   Wherever he may be established to remain for any length of time, this duck will find a "hording ground," a place to collect, to rest, visit and play.   At a chosen time, maybe ten in the morning, maybe not until afternoon, depending on how widely they have foraged, all the mallards within a wide range will assemble on this hording spot.   The mallard may be shot while passing or he may be decoyed on his feeding ground, and he will still linger in the neighborhood; but keep away from the place where he hordes.

Sometimes, as when the fowl feeds widely in the daytime, collecting only at night, the hording ground is also the roosting ground.   Under such circumstances the old-time market gunner knew better than to shoot on the roosting waters, for otherwise the birds would be "burnt out" for the season. Therefore such a thing as getting on the roosts, there to shoot until too dark to see, was not tolerated in market gunning. Later, Uncle Sam's Bureau of Biological Survey came along and made the same ruling, under the "regulation" that no shooting was to take place after sunset or before sunrise. This ruling * is right and for the shooter's own good.   Oddly enough, the bulk of the duck killing in England, also on the continent of Europe, takes place in the twilight, therefore is shooting on the roost.   They would kill out all the waterfowl there if they could, but they cannot because the ducks breed

* Unfortunately, while well observed in the United States it is abused in Canada.

in the far North where the population is very sparse and guns are lacking. Nevertheless, the principle of the thing is wrong, and so long as they shoot until it is too dark to see, that is about all the shooting they will have.

A few years ago in midwinter, here in Oklahoma, a pair of duck hunters discovered the hording grounds of the mallards in a wild and isolated section of the Cimarron River. Snow had fallen and lakes were solidly frozen; all the fowls except the mallards and the Canada geese had gone south long since. Duck hunters were taking a fair toll, in the corn-fields, the spring-fed creeks, or by chopping openings in the ice on lakes. But our pair of gunners dug their pits right in the midst of the hording and roosting ground. About two in the afternoon the mallards began to come in. They estimated that 50,000 mallards came into a reach of the river that afternoon! In some flocks there were a hundred birds, in others five hundred. It was snowing a bit, and the fowl showed none of their usual caution but swept over the river bluff from distant fields and piled in. Notwithstanding the bag limit of 25 birds to the gun, our shooters killed 300 mallards by four o'clock, when their ammunition was exhausted. Going to town, 50 miles distant, the nearest place where ammunition was to be had, they laid in a new supply and went back. Not another mallard was shot, not one was seen. Moreover, no more ducks were shot thereabout by anyone that season. Except for the usual cripples, not a wing was flashed on the river or the ponds or the lakes or anywhere.

In the old market shooting days, when America was a virgin territory for the wildfowler, the mallard was *the* duck. Given his choice, as on a great flight, the market gunner would not shoot mixed ducks, but ignored everything except mallards.

His idea of a good bag was to kill one hundred birds a day, not any more and not any less, and nothing but mallards. One hundred birds was enough to fool with—to draw, pack and get off to the commission houses. He knew exactly the price he would get for those birds, while if he mixed a few other fowl with his mallards all would be classed as "mixed" and the price per dozen would be much less.

Our mallard, then, has had plenty of gun education. Cold troubles him little, so long as any open water remains, for he is a field forager. Yet he is the most wary duck of them all. No ordinary blind and bunch of decoys is going to stop a flock of mallards when they have business somewhere else. As he circles to see if anything suspicious develops in a pile of brush, then suddenly breaks ranks, just as well shoot, for he is not coming any closer. He is not a hard bird to hit, once within easy range; the gunner soon learns the greenhead's habit of towering or jumping, and can center him.

The worst thing that the hunter has ever done to the mallard is to use live bird decoys. A well constructed blind, low, made of willows, grass or whatever grows along the shore, backed by a dozen or two of tame mallards, will fool any bunch of wild mallards, or any other ducks. However, after our bird has been fooled a few times he will no longer stoop to his supposed own wild mates, but climbs as he sees them. Very soon all mallards are winging over high in the air, going, gone, and never returning. The reaches of the Cimarron River near where I live were once a great mallard resort. Duck shooters discovered the superiority of live decoys, and coops of them were carried on every car. All up and down the river, blinds not half a mile apart, the shooters waited, with the live decoys swimming about and calling. That was

Live bird photos Nat'l Assn. of Audubon Societies; dead by Charles B. Morss.

Above, bluewing teal, pintail hen and pintail drake. *Below,* mallards, black duck and gadwall.

Black duck toll

a few years ago, because for the last three years the mallards have deserted the river. Except in stormy weather or when a great flight is on, no more mallards are killed at all, and very few are seen. They have learned their lesson and have deserted the river for good. Instead of some of its ineffective regulations, the Bureau of Biological Survey should have strictly barred the use of any live decoys whatever, in any section of the United States.

The mallard is not strictly a cold-weather bird, but he likes frost in the air. He comes north very early in the spring, and will not start for winter quarters much ahead of the ice. Warm weather makes him lazy, and he then will not fly; hence the axiom of the duck hunter that it is useless to go duck shooting in bluebird weather.

THE BLACK DUCK, OR BLACK MALLARD

In the East this bird is called the black duck, while in my shooting days along the Mississippi he usually was referred to as the black mallard. To me he has always appeared to be an off-colored mallard, the change being made somehow in the same manner that domestication affects poultry. Eastern duck shooters maintain stoutly that the black duck is superior in some respects to the greenhead, as in wariness and wisdom; but to me they have always appeared the same bird, barring their coats.

Largely the black duck replaces the greenhead in the East, or east of the Allegheny Mountains and north of the Potomac. I have shot both varieties from one blind on the Okaw River in Illinois, but have never seen a black duck west of Arkansas, though a few have been killed in Oklahoma.

This need not be taken as implying that they are never found west of the Mississippi. However, even along that great flyway they are mere stragglers.

The black duck has been given the Latin name of *Anas obscura*. While the greenhead is known all over the world, the black duck is confined to the indicated very restricted area along our Atlantic Coast. The black fellow breeds in northern New York, the New England states, Ontario, Quebec, Nova Scotia, New Brunswick, Newfoundland, Labrador, and perhaps farther north. He migrates as far south as Florida, yet numbers remain in favorable localities all the way from Maine southward. When fresh water is frozen solid he goes to the seacoast, where, changing his diet, he lives like any other sea duck. Down East gunners say the change in diet makes him taste like a sea-duck, too.

Walter Rich says that New Englanders who know their black ducks separate them into two species, the true black duck and the Hudson Bay duck. The latter is said to be a good bit larger in size, and darker in color, with much heavier streaking on head and neck, brighter yellow of bill, and with a redder tinge of feet and legs. Some New England gunners think that while on their Coast the Hudson Bay duck never goes to fresh water. Its scientific name, given it by William Brewster, of Cambridge, Massachusetts, according to Rich, is *Anas obscura rubripes*.

Scientists maintain that two species of black ducks are found in Florida, also around the Gulf in Louisiana and in south Texas. The supposition is that the true black duck migrates from its breeding grounds south into Florida, and the separate species comes north into Florida and Texas from Central and South America. The southern species is a trifle lighter in color than the black duck of the North, otherwise it is difficult to distinguish one from the other. Black ducks are given a weight of from 2½ to 3½ pounds, while the Hudson Bay variety is said to have reached a weight of 4½ pounds. That is pretty close to the weight of a small goose or brant.

There can be no doubt whatever that the black duck is just as fine a bird as any other mallard. He ought to be given as much credit as the greenhead, and indeed is given a good deal more by Eastern writers. Unfortunately, I am of the West and nearly all my mallard shooting experience has been with the greenhead, so I cannot say whether this is overrating the former bird, which I suspect is true.

The black duck is readily domesticated, and when the time comes that wild ducks are to be hand-reared for shooting, which has long been done in England and is done in a small way on some private shooting reserves in this country, the black duck will be in favor for this. His color is in his favor, for one thing, and he can live right next door to city riot, as he does in New York's parks, without caring much about it.

Not a few Eastern duck shooters would rather make a bag of black ducks than of any other waterfowl whatever. It calls for matching wits and skill with a wise, wary and fast bird. In general, the best sport is had in jumping these fowl on certain favored salt marshes. I am informed that perhaps much the best black duck shooting is had in eastern Ontario and western Quebec, early in the season. At some small shooting clubs on the Ottawa River, whose members live in Montreal and Ottawa, they kill limit bags of twenty-five of these splendid fowl with a regularity unbelievable to a New England gunner. This shooting is over live decoys.

Chapter XIV

PINTAIL, GADWALL AND WIDGEON

THE PINTAIL, OR SPRIGTAIL

THE pintail has too much engine power, too wide a spread of sail, and too little regard for wind and weather to confine himself to any particular part of the world. The Briton says, "By Jove," when he misses this handsome, speedy and tasty duck, the Hollander exclaims, *"Verdamte,"* and the Frenchman *"Sacré bleu."* The Indian of South America knows the long-tailed fellow, and no less the East Indian, the Mongol-Tartar and the Malay. Yet he is a North American bird. More pintails can be found in Saskatchewan, Alberta, and the states immediately south than in all the remaining world.

No member of the duck tribe is better built for speed, nor so well built for it. His racing lines are perfect; from his spitzer-pointed head to his boat-tailed body, no line could be changed. If he had the engine revolutions per minute of the canvasback, shot could not overtake him. Why the naturalists named him *Dafila acuta* instead of compliment-ing his speed and endurance is a mystery. Compared with the short-winged sprinters his wing-beats are slow, but he travels fast and keeps going with literally amazing endurance.

150

In a race from the Arctic Circle to the Tropic of Cancer, without food or water, the pintail would be first with no second.

No other waterfowl so well lends himself to the education and development of the scientific wingshot. The pintail is restless and flies more than other ducks. He is wary, yet boldly takes a chance. He sweeps about the blind in wide circles, once, twice, one circle following the other as though marked in the air, and then he comes in—long neck doubled, legs dangling, wide wings beating to break the fall, his long body striking the water as light as a feather. Disturbed, he climbs out with a tremendous bound that carries him fifty feet into the air.

The pintail is our own best beloved prairie waterfowl. He wings as free and as fast as a March wind in Kansas. He is the most numerous, the most dependable, and the most enticing of all Western ducks. His speed is from 60 to 90 feet a second; his color markings are so distinct as to give a close line on his distance; and his lead can be judged within a foot, though it may be anywhere from one to ten feet. He invariably bounds into the air upon being alarmed, no matter whether rising from the water or winging by, and at the top of his bound the second barrel should catch him.

In migration the pintail wings the highest of all ducks, flock after flock going north at an elevation of from 100 yards to a quarter of a mile. Yet, when localized he may sweep the fields and fan the sand of the river beds. He travels far on a single trek; at night he may be on the Gulf Coast, at sunrise in Oklahoma. In the spring he halts only when he overtakes grim winter, and his flat feet track the snow in many a Kansas field of kaffir corn and wheat. Unmo-

lested, he loses all fear of man in a week or so, and may nest
in the little cane-grown pond just back of the house.

Like the pinnated grouse, the pintail duck is a child of the
prairie.   Alberta and Saskatchewan now owe their reputation as a duck-breeding ground chiefly to the pintail.   Being a bird with the homing instinct of the carrier pigeon, he
returns year after year to nest where he was hatched and to
winter where January found him the year before.   He is a
fowl of regular habits and strong social instincts.   The pintails, or sprigs, as sometimes called, come north on the first
spring thaw, not so much in flocks as in hordes, now flying
high, now pausing for a day or a week.   No other duck has
ventured north, but of a sudden the river is black with pintails, the fields snowy as the birds turn their white breasts
to face us.   Over all the land the "pathfinders" of the waterfowl army are winnowing the wintry air.   I have seen them
rise in such numbers from a cane field as to make an ashen
haze that obscured the timber beyond.   Not another wild
fowl anywhere to be seen.

The pintail is stronger of wing than the mallard, makes
longer continuous flights, is more active and restless.   In
habits this bird is like the Canada goose.   He uses the water,
not to forage in, but as a resting, roosting and play ground,
feeding widely over the surrounding country on green wheat
or in standing corn.   At daybreak, as though at a given sig-
nal, all the birds leave the water to return late in the day, perhaps not until dusk.   Now they decoy readily, come in
persistently.   Extremely gregarious by nature, this fowl
usually decoys freely; get on a pintail flight, sport is sure.

Once on a time, about the year 1911, a couple of us were
on a certain Western river when the pintails began to come

in. By night we had loaded a mule team. We took the birds
into town and gave them away. I remember that one con-
scientious scoundrel wouldn't take a bird unless he could pay
us. We gave him his choice of the lot, and he selected five
ducks for which he gave us a quarter of a dollar! I remember, too, that two of the birds he selected were crosses between
mallard and pintail, the only crosses of this kind that I have
ever seen. I only wish that I had some of those birds now to
shoot at.

THE GADWALL, OR GRAY DUCK

I CANNOT give a complete description of the gadwall, sci-
entifically called *Chaulelasmus streperus*, without competing
with the members of the American Ornithologists' Union.
Best I can do is to tell enough to enable a shooter to recognize
a gadwall if he kills one.

If you happen to shoot a duck from a flock which fly and
look in a general way like mallard hens, then the chances are
that the bird is a gadwall. He looks as large as a mallard, has
the same sail plan, but his body is flatter and he doesn't weigh
so much. The speculum (band on wing) is white instead of
purple, and the breast of the drake is whiter than that of a
mallard hen. The drake's head and neck are a pale yellowish
white, head darker than the neck. Breast all round and
upper parts of the back are bluish black, feathers edged with
white. Lower back dusky, growing black on the rump and
tail coverts. The linings of the wings are white, with white
shafts. The feet are dull orange, with dusky webs; bill
orange blue; iris reddish brown. The female has a general
resemblance to a mallard hen.

The name *streperus* perhaps means noisy or something like

that; the bird is supposed to do a lot of quacking when feeding. His habits are very similar to those of the mallard, he being a fresh-water duck, with a liking for small ponds and small hidden streams. He is not a diver, instead feeding like all the shoal-water tribe, by "tipping up," standing on his head in the water for whatever he can reach. At that he is a little more of a water bird than the pintail or the mallard, not visiting fields so often.

The gadwall decoys readily, not being as suspicious as a mallard or a black duck, instead coming in to the decoys promptly. His quack is hardly to be distinguished from that of the mallard, and he comes to mallard calling. Frightened, he doesn't tower so much as some of the other ducks, hitting a medium grade of getaway, between the spring of a mallard and the dash of a redhead; he climbs and gets away at the same time. In flight he much resembles the mallard, but is less likely to sheer away from danger. If the gadwall wings by at fairly long range and height, he will keep his course regardless of having been shot at, much the same as a canvasback or widgeon. As a table bird he is as good eating as a mallard, though perhaps he does not become so fat and inviting.

The gadwall is one of our finest fresh-water ducks. He too unfortunately is not by any means so plentiful as he used to be. Now and then there is a gadwall flight on, which the duck hunter who happens to be on the river will consider one of his red-letter days. In migration or when shot in the middle states as he travels from his breeding grounds in the North to the Gulf, he usually is in pretty large flocks, not being shot singly or in pairs, as some other species so frequently are, such as pintails or whistlers. Most of the gadwalls were killed off in spring shooting days, because they were pretty tame in the spring, decoyed well, and a magazine shotgun might account for a half dozen birds from a flock.

So far as I have been able to learn, the gadwall is exclusively an American bird.   He was formerly very plentiful on the central duck flight, that is up and down the Mississippi River. A few were shot along the New England coast.   There is from a fair to a good flight from Nebraska across Kansas, Oklahoma and Texas.

THE WIDGEON, OR BALDPATE

ENGLAND and some sections of Europe have a widgeon that differs a little from our bird.   The Latin name of ours is *Mareca americana,* that of the Old World cousin *M. penelope.*   It is not worth while to go into an extended description of the European widgeon as compared with ours, because the chances are a hundred to one that we never shoot one of the foreigners.   However, the European widgeon is better known or has had more written about it than has our own bird.   It is the one duck which affords the pot-shooter of Britain a great amount of sport with his big punt gun carrying a pound to two pounds of shot.   Over there the widgeon is a night feeder, and the punt gunners steal alongshore and shoot into the feeding flocks by moonlight.

Isn't it queer that in Great Britain these birds can hold their own when shot at night, with big guns having 10-foot barrels and carrying from a pound to two pounds of shot, while our ducks are being killed off in good daylight with small-bore guns?   I suppose the answer is decoys.   In the use and de-

velopment of decoys we became too darn smart for our own
good.   English wildfowlers know little of decoys.

By the way, the English spell widgeon without the *d*, which
is the first instance that I have known of their putting one
over on us in the matter of spelling.   What is the use of that
extra *d* in spelling wigeon, anyhow?

Unlike the fowl previously dealt with, the American widgeon
is not a shoal-water duck.   He belongs with the divers.   We
need not give an extended description of the widgeon.   He is
sometimes called the *baldpate*, and there you have the key to
his identification.   Kill a medium-sized duck, the drake having the top of the head so white that he has the appearance
of being bald-headed, and that is a widgeon, and can't be
anything else.   Like a good many bald-headed men, the
widgeon is a handsome fellow notwithstanding.   Without the
flashy coloration of the mallard, he has a beautiful blending
of delicate shades.   He is in fact one of the most handsome
and graceful of all American waterfowl.

As stated of the English bird, the widgeon is mostly a night
feeder.   Note a flock in the daytime, and probably they will
be idling about, alongshore or on the sandbars, sitting in the
sun, preening their feathers, dozing.   Toward night he
starts for his feeding grounds, and if decoys are on the way
he pays no attention to them whatever.   One thing he will
do, however, if flying by the gun: he maintains a straight
course regardless of suspicious appearances or even being
shot at.   I have killed six single birds out of a flock that undertook to pass me within easy range, and the only hiding I did
was to kneel down on the open prairie.

Along the line of their migration, widgeons come and go in
distinct flights; today four out of five birds which fall to the

gun may be the baldpate, tomorrow not one.   As is true of all
the waterfowl which breed away up in the vicinity of Hudson
Bay and winter along the Gulf Coast or below, these birds
migrate in large flocks, and when "traveling" absolutely refuse to notice decoys.   On the other hand when they have
"localized" in the vicinity, and the decoys are rightly placed,
as on rice or celery beds, our fine birds come right in without
any hesitation whatever.   The bulk of the widgeons perhaps
are now killed in the South, on the coast of Texas and Louisiana, and in the East on the rice beds of South Carolina and
Georgia.   The lines of flight are down the Atlantic Coast,
and down the Mississippi River, thence westward to the mountains.   Returning to the breeding grounds in the spring,
many more birds cross the prairie states than do when bent
for winter quarters.

The widgeon is not a very good diver, yet likes his celery.
Therefore he is popularly supposed to follow the canvasbacks
and rob them when they have dived and pulled that plant from
the bottom of the river or the bay.   I have been reading this
story ever since I can remember, way back in Lewis' "American
Game Birds."   I do not know how true it is, but it seems logical
to me that if the widgeon couldn't dive deep enough to help
himself, he might take what came to him, even if another duck
had hold of it.

Of all the ducks I know, none is so readily "burnt out" as
is the widgeon.   Probably this is partly because it is necessary to place the decoys on his feeding grounds, perhaps surrounding a sink-box in open water.   In any event, give him
a hot reception today, and tomorrow the reception may be
there but the ducks won't be.

Our baldpate will not nest in a civilized community, and

I have never yet seen a widgeon's nest or immature birds. He breeds farther north than I have ever been, and I am convinced that it will be some job to entice him away from Canada in the good old summer time. Moreover, I believe that if the time ever comes when waterfowl are pretty well extinct in this country, the widgeon will hold his own to the last.

I remember a time, back in the old spring shooting days when the more ducks we killed the more would return next season, that word reached us that the widgeons were in. Not very far away were two small lakes, perhaps forty acres in each. It was a rainy spring, with plenty of water, and some kind of succulent plant had grown up in our ponds. Two of us went down and we found widgeons all over the ponds, strangely enough feeding in the daytime.

Knowing that if we shot the birds on one pond they probably would go to the other, no more than a quarter mile away, two of us each took a pond. When I shot, the birds came out all over me, paying no attention to the gun at all. They went straight to my companion, who was shooting his ducks at the same time. Back and forth the ducks traded, and a little thing like a smoking gun in the way made no difference. I had recently been reading instructions by Doctor Yorke for killing more than one bird to the shot, by watching when two or more would cross in their flight, and tried it. It worked. In the course of an hour we were out of shells. I do not remember how many cartridges we had nor how many ducks we killed, but it was plenty. That night a warm rain came up from the south and the next day, while there were plenty of spoonbills and teal, no widgeons remained.

Chapter XV

THE TEALS. THE SPOONBILL

THE BLUE-WINGED TEAL

THE wood duck is sometimes called the summer duck, but the blue-winged teal better deserves the title. The wood duck comes north in the early spring, as soon as the ice is gone, and he may linger until late November, but the bluewing will not tolerate ice or snow or even frost. One reason for this is that he is an insect eater or worm eater, most of his living being obtained from shallow ponds, where he feeds upon the small animal life which would eventually become insects or frogs. When chill weather drives these down he flits away to where his favorite diet is still active. Hence the bluewings do not come north until mid-April, and they are all gone in early October.

The Migratory Bird Law has been of great help to the bluewing, and he needs its protecting mantle. He can no longer be shot in the spring, and he leaves for his Southern home before the season opens in the fall. This is well, for while this little waterfowl is an enticing mark, swift of wing, a dainty on the table, he really is too tame for a true game bird.

In the old days when snipe could be shot in the spring, the

bag was commonly mixed, part snipe and part teal, for the
little fowl were all about over the snipe marsh, and they got
up with the snipe.

The bluewing is a most confiding little fellow, no persecution ever causing him to lose trust in man.   Dropping into a
puddle of water beside the road, he keeps right on fishing for
tadpoles as vehicles pass by.   At daybreak he may be in the
stock pond with his tame cousins, and when these are called
to breakfast he merely looks up inquiringly and keeps right
on rustling his own grub.   Later, if the location suits him, he
will be found heading a good flock of tiny paddlers on that
pond, both the old and the young birds knowing everybody
for "home folks."   All over the Western prairies, we have
seen thousands of bluewings nesting within gunshot of a house.

We can never have a perfect game bird in a little fowl that
is not afraid and cannot be made afraid.   Years of persecution should have made him cautious, but no caution is in him.
Flush and shoot into a flock, and in ten minutes the remaining
birds may be right back where their mates were killed.   Shoot
one of a pair, and his mate will circle about until the reluctant
gunner kills her out of pity.   No blinds are needed in bluewing shooting, for this bird will fly right overhead with the
gunner in plain sight; nor will he waver when the barrels are
trained on him.   I am aware of no game bird so helpless except the snipe, which having once eluded the gun wings high
and far, then comes right back to pitch where he escaped
death a minute before.

The bluewing is one of the fastest of all ducks, his speed
being estimated at not less than 100 feet a second.   However,
his small size is deceptive, and I have noticed that a spoonbill
or a pintail can keep right along with a flock of teal when

he wants to. But anyhow, a passing bluewing at 50 yards is an attractive mark—no finer is to be had in wildfowl shooting. Oh, yes, shoot the bluewings; but only in October, when, collected in great flocks preparing for the southern migration, they are circling their summer home in final farewell, whereupon a single shot will send them on their way to the sunny South. If anybody wants to know it, the Latin name of this bird is *Querquedula discors*.

THE GREEN-WINGED TEAL

A barefoot boy with his grandad's gun,
A little red dog to see the fun;
A creek well hid in a prairie glade,
Riffling dark in the sycamore's shade.
Ware, teal, O teal, have a care!

Sunlight gilding the topmost limb,
Mirrored below in the shadows dim;
Stealthy, stealthy, the bare feet creep,
Nor mind the frost where the grass is deep.
Ware, teal, O teal, have a care!

Little ducks feed on with never a care,
Though the jay's sharp cry breaks the morning air;
From back of a bole grim barrels frown,
And the little red dog is crouching down.
Ware, teal, O teal, have a care!

THE green-winged teal is the smallest of all our wild ducks, though it is said the European teal is a trifle smaller. What bob-white quail is to the grouse, the greenwing is to his larger kin. He is very tame, "lies to the gun," is lightning-fast from scratch and a difficult mark. The man who can take a greenwing on his bound will have no trouble whatever with the jump of any other duck.

No easy mark is the greenwing either, when his wings are under him and he is in full speed of flight. His only flight weakness is that he flies in compact bunches, and a big, open gun can rake the flock fore and aft. In the old days of market shooting, the mallard days, this little fowl was quite ignored. So many birds meant so many dollars, if the fowl were canvasbacks or mallards; if teal, maybe only enough to pay the freight. Then the greenwing was a boy's duck. So far as the Mississippi River country is concerned, nine boys in ten learned to shoot ducks by hunting the green-winged teal.

As distinct from the bluewing, which is a pond duck, the greenwing is a bird of the small river and the creek. Hard by where our boy lived was Deep Creek or Bird Creek or Stony Creek, a stream with tree-lined banks, sudden turns and twists, shallows and reaches of deep, quiet water. In the bends, under the brush-lined banks, now hidden by pond lilies, now boldly resting on the open water, teal could always be found in acorn time. Maybe they would be in pairs, maybe in small flocks, maybe a "horde" of them, but the boy knew where they ought to be. And he knew every bend and bank, every clump of tall grass, and every big sycamore from back of which he might make his stalk.

The Indian had nothing on him in stealth. He crept from bend to bend, always approaching a "duck hole" under cover. Now the gray squirrel might bark from a limb overhead or the cottontail sit upright in his path, and he gave them hardly a grunt of contempt. At last he saw the ducks, well out in the open water, a half dozen teal closely bunched. Very slowly he brought his big gun to bear, pulling just under the flock, as he had learned to do when shooting on the water. As the 10-bore roared, two teal only took flight from that bunch; but, alas, from right under the bank below a great flock took wing, climbing, flaring, curving, every little duck taking his own course. The startled lad fired the second barrel into them, without aim and without effect. Then he sat down to wait, if perchance they might come back, which they sometimes did. Anyhow, there were four dead teal idly floating on the still water, and presently he set the gun aside and began pulling off his shoes and his pants.

The greenwing breeds farther north than the bluewing, withstands cold better, and is more of a grain eater. He is frequently found in company with the mallards; that is, both will be in at the same time. Flocks of greenwings will come north very early, and they may linger in spring-fed creeks well after ice has formed. The range of the greenwing extends westward to the Rocky Mountains, beyond which the cinnamon teal begins to displace him. He is a great table bird, as is the bluewing also. The European teal is given a length of 14 inches, and is said to weigh up to 14 ounces. I'd judge that our greenwing weighs about a pound. His Latin name is *Nettion carolinensis*, that of the foreign bird *Anas crecca*.

THE CINNAMON TEAL

THIS is the common teal of the Pacific Coast. I have shot them as far east as western Oklahoma. Any time a man kills a teal in the Rocky Mountains that is obviously not a bluewing or a greenwing, instead a bird with a buff-colored or red breast, that is a cinnamon teal. This little bird is to be found not only on the Pacific Coast, but anywhere in the adjacent mountains, in Colorado, Utah, Arizona, New Mexico, Texas and old Mexico. It is likely to breed on mountain lakes, then migrate southward into Mexico, also down the Rio Grande to the Gulf.

I have not shot many cinnamon teal and know little about them, other than that they appear to behave very much like the other teal. They go in large flocks, fly in compact masses, wing low along the water, and can be "raked" about the same as greenwings, just when they bunch up in making a turn. If jumped, they have more the flight habits of the bluewing than of the greenwing, winging off close to the water, while a greenwing towers, every bird for himself. Like all teal they are a dainty table bird. By the way, a young teal can be fried the same as a young domestic chicken, and is extra-fine eating. This has reference to other teal as well as the cinnamon. Once, a long time ago, when we didn't know much about duck laws or maybe didn't care, two of us were boarding with a South Dakota ranchman. He didn't have meat of any kind, so we made it a point to shoot a mess of young teal now and then, and the good wife fried them for us. I never can forget how good were those fried teal.

THE SPOONBILL, OR SHOVELER

THE English have a spoonbill duck, or shoveler, which is probably the same bird as our *Spatula clypeata*. They call their fowl *Anas clypeata*. There again is the fault in Latin names. Every chump of a naturalist invents a name of his own, and we are supposed to remember them all, and to know which is correct. For another example, in Europe the gadwall is called *Anas strepera,* in this country *Chaulelasmus streperus.* Whether they are the same duck or not, you can't tell from the name; probably somebody found an imaginary difference.

I have included the spoonbill with the teal because, while not in the least alike or of the same size, the shoveler is much like teal in his habits. Both are very tame, and shallow-water pond ducks. Neither comes north until the weather is warm enough to develop insect life in the water. Then the two birds are often found together, and not seldom wing together. If they haven't been shot at too much, you can walk right up on a flock of spoonbills, and if they do conclude to fly, may turn and come right back by the gun. Having decoyed, which they readily do, the shooter may have to climb up in his blind and say, "Shoo-oo!" before they will take wing. Shot at, if they like the place they may be back in twenty minutes.

The spoonbill is a beauty, barring his monstrosity of a bill. Like some women, he would be very attractive if he only had a perfect nose. As it is, that disfiguring bill is a 100-per cent. distinguishing mark. Shoot a duck with a long flat bill that is about two sizes too big for his head, widening at the end, and that is a spoonbill or shoveler, and couldn't be anything else. Notwithstanding this duck is too tame to develop the skill and strategy of the hunter, he is a rapid flyer, demanding no less lead than the best of them. I have seen a single spoonbill leading a bunch of teal in flight, having no apparent trouble in holding his own. In fact, I have seen a spoonbill start well in the rear of a flock of bluewings which he overhauled like a veritable sprinter.

The spoonbill is a real "puddle" duck. If he can find an

acre of water that is from six inches to a foot deep, it is to his precise liking. Then he becomes extremely busy, too busy to apprehend danger. Half the flock will have heads under water at the same time, and the other half will be looking for a good place to "grabble." On the wing, in singles, pairs or flocks, he is looking for a good place to alight, always in shallow water. He is no hermit, instead likes company—company of his own kind or any other kind. When no other ducks will decoy the spoonbill comes in. A man can sit out in front of his blind, smoking his pipe, and the spoonbill will drop in just the same. He doesn't know anything about swerving or dodging and not much about climbing—just pursues the even tenor of his way and takes his chance. Shoot the spoonbill only when you can't get anything else. A bag of them and not much else marks the novice, and if he shoots them on the water the mark ought to be on his back.

When on the wing, the spoonbill is no less showy than the mallard, flashing brilliant colors in deep contrast. Give him a mallard bill and he would be a smaller edition of that fine bird, with coloring more varied and delicate. Except for his bill, he would be the prettiest wild-fowl ever mounted and in a glass case. He is a warm-weather fowl, almost a tropical duck, breeding in Texas, Oklahoma, Kansas, Nebraska, and not going any farther north than he has to in order to find water and room. An old spoonbill hen with young is not much wilder than a barnyard fowl, and will merely paddle idly out of the way. Probably this bird could be very readily domesticated; but it might be troublesome to feed when insect life was gone.

Chapter XVI

THE PRINCIPAL DEEP–WATER DUCKS

The Canvasback, the Redhead, and the Bluebills or Broadbills

See the canvasbacks coming; hear the rush of their flight.
Their strong wings are humming like winds in the night.
See the flash of their pinions like dash of the spray,
When the wild waves break white o'er the dark seaway.

In his coffin-like box the grim wild-fowler lies,
While swift overhead the gray canvasback flies.
See the flash from his muzzle, hear the sound of his gun,
Now float the dead wildfowl with breast to the sun.

THE ducks to which this chapter is devoted all have the same scientific family name, *Aythya;* they are "deep-water" ducks, and all have pretty much the same characteristics. All have heavy, rather short bodies, and comparatively short wings. They are known as diving ducks, generally procuring their food by diving for it. All have their legs set far back, which facilitates diving and swimming but not walking. On shore they stand very erect and do not walk much. They labor when rising, but once on the wing are strong flyers, the very fastest ducks we have. A crippled or winged canvasback, redhead or bluebill will dive if he can, and may not be seen again. It is almost impossible to retrieve a crippled canvasback under some conditions.

In their flight characteristics, all of these ducks are very much alike. Their short, powerful wings beat very fast, and they bore through the air in steady fashion—do not dodge, swerve or tower like the shoal-water ducks of the mallard type. In the interior all are more apt to be found on large lakes. Many are shot over salt water, on coastal bays and wide mouths of tide-water rivers. As a group, they occupy a mid-position between the true fresh-water ducks and the true sea ducks. The redhead is the nearest to an inland fowl, and the bluebill the closest approach to a sea duck.

Any of these fowl can earn a living on the seacoast, but all prefer food that is obtained from fresh water. The redhead is said to forage in the fields as well as on the water, but I have never, myself, seen a redhead in a dry field. The canvasback is noted for his fondness for celery, upon which he becomes very fat, tender and fine in flavor—by epicures held in the highest appreciation of all the wildfowl in the world.

All of these birds are alike in going in large flocks, and they rest in great "beds" or "rafts." I have never known them to be mixed in flight, though at rest there may be canvasbacks, redheads and bluebills in the same raft. Another common characteristic is that all ducks of this family demand hard hitting to bring them down. Further, if it is seen that a bird is winged, to save trouble shoot him again before he strikes the water. There is some humbug about a repeating shotgun being needed to knock over the cripples when shooting these fowl, on account of their diving ability. However, if it is a canvasback, shot from a gunning float, that kind of gun really is needed.

Above, part of a merged flock of lesser snow geese and blue geese, at winter
quarters in the Rainey Wild Life Sanctuary in Louisiana.
Below, canvasback ducks on Belle Isle Lake, in the same sanctuary.

Snow geese, specklebelly or wavey, and brant

THE CANVASBACK

(*Aythya vallisneria*)

THE canvasback is supposed to be the fastest of all the ducks. I do not know anything with wings that can outspeed him unless it is the goshawk. I have seen these hawks overtake a teal with such a burst of speed that it seemed no canvasback could get away. Question is if the hawk could handle the big fowl when he caught it. The canvasback is usually granted a speed of 120 feet a second; which might be merely an estimate. But it is certain that he could not fly slowly if he tried. Apparently he has just one rate of speed, modified a little by the wind, and that is so fast that he commands all attention no matter what other fowl are awing. Worthy too, is he in all ways, of all the attention he gets. No better game falls to the fowler's gun.

The canvasback is strictly a North American bird. No like duck is found elsewhere in the world, nor any duck at all like him or his equal. Moreover, in shooting canvasbacks the American duck shooter of the Chesapeake and the Potomac has developed a style of duck shooting that has no imitators. Since the canvasback will not come to him on shore, he goes to them, "rigging out" a great "stool" of decoys on their feeding "grounds," in the midst of which he hides low in a "sinkbox" or "battery." When a northeaster is in the offing, shooting from a sinkbox is the last word in skilled wildfowling, unequaled for the courage and fortitude demanded, and for skilful use of the gun.

One of the best divers of the deep-water or diving family of waterfowl, the canvasback is distinctly different from the surface feeders in rustling his victuals. Preferably he secures his food by diving and tearing it from the bottom, in water that may be forty feet deep. Wild celery is his favorite diet, and gunning clubs plant it to attract him and the other divers.

In shooting canvasbacks swinging by or passing over, it is safe to add 50 per cent to the lead that catches a mallard or a pintail. But not so if you jump a single or a pair that have swum into your decoys. Since his wings are rather short and his body heavy, he requires time to gain momentum, and is not fast when rising from the water or climbing away from the gun. Like all birds with rapid wing-beat, as previously said his speed is uniform, and once we know where to hold, taking him is no more difficult than shooting slower fowl. Trouble is to get enough canvasback shooting for practice.

The canvasback is our wildfowl of romance. The mere mention of him brings to mind a thousand tales, told by the great duck hunters of the last one hundred years. Enough has been written on how to cook this noble bird to fill a library. To eat him is to acquire not only profound appreciation of his flavor but as well due reverence for his legendary delectability. The American who is inclined to think well of himself, to think well of his shooting, to think well of the game he shoots, may take all proper pride in the great canvasback, for in all the world he has neither a superior nor an equal.

As to the appearance of the bird, if you do not know him, shoot a fowl with a bunty tail, wedge-shaped head and red eyes, and that is a canvasback. The only duck that could be mistaken for a canvasback is the redhead, and his forehead is high and arched. In flight the birds appear black and white or red and white. They do not wing in close order like the small ducks, but require elbow room, the same as geese.

Killed in the air, if the bird is at height and going full speed, our canvasback will keep right on like a baseball hit for a home run. This reminds me of an amusing incident.

We were shooting canvasbacks on Trappers Lake, Minnesota. Our blind was located about seventy yards from shore, and the birds were not decoying, instead going past high, with a wind back of them. The wind and their momentum drove some of the birds we hit clean ashore. Jim, our driver, stood on shore, retrieving some of my birds. I noticed him now and then making a futile attempt to catch them as they fell. He was a ballplayer, so finally I yelled to him to catch one. As it happened, immediately thereafter a flock of "cans" came along, over a hundred feet high, and the second barrel killed pretty well after they passed. I saw Jim set himself for that bird. He held his hands all right, but down he went as flat as a pancake. Waiting only to see that he was getting up, not much hurt, I had Indian enough in me to laugh loud and long. With hands on hips Jim stood and stared at me till I subsided. Then having thus secured my attention he shouted back: "Go to hell and ketch your own!"

THE REDHEAD

(*Aythya americana*)

It has already been indicated that the redhead has the same family name as the canvasback. He is about the same nature of duck, too—plump, inclined to become fat, fast on the wing, but a bit more certain to decoy than the canvasback. The drake is marked much like his larger relative, too; however, being a trifle darker. The females of the redhead and the bluebill look much alike, each having a white bar extending laterally from under the chin to the top of the head between bill and eye. A flight characteristic of the redhead, wherein he differs from the other ducks of this family, is that if high in the air he may descend with such rapidity as to make a loud humming noise that can be heard a half mile. This noise has sometimes warned me that the ducks were coming in when I had not seen them.

In the days of wildfowl abundance along the Mississippi the redhead never was a very common bird; but he always was most highly appreciated. In the early days a duck hunter might kill a hundred mallards and say little about it, but if he bagged a half dozen redheads, that was something to tell about in camp. I remember that when I was a boy in lower Illinois two well-known duck hunters, named Bonneman, knew exactly where to find redheads, always made a bag of these fine fowl, and were the envy of everybody else, myself included. Later I killed a good many redheads myself, and found they had a marked line of travel from the Nebraska lakes south across Kansas, western Oklahoma, the Panhandle of Texas and on to the Gulf. This line of migration was particularly adhered to in the spring, when the birds evidently were taking the nearest route to their breeding grounds. Most of the redheads that I saw in the North bred beyond the Canadian boundary, while numbers of canvasbacks nested in the wild lakes of the sandhill country.

The redhead is a wild-rice bird, and doesn't remain for a great length of time where the rice is not to be found. I am told that he is equally fond of tame rice, and a good many are shot in Arkansas, Texas, Louisiana and along the Atlantic coast in South Carolina and Georgia. I doubt if the redhead of the Atlantic Coast ever comes west or if the western bird is ever seen south of the Potomac.

The redhead is no less fond of celery than is the canvas-back, and is found celery-hunting still in company with the big bird on the Susquehanna flats and on Chesapeake Bay. He is still very common on the Potomac River, even in mid-winter. I happened to be located on the Potomac below Mt. Vernon during the war, and the redhead was one of our most common river birds, driving up and down that stream in tre-mendous flocks sometimes. The Potomac River shooter formerly was very much inclined to use a larger gun than the law permitted, in order to sweep the flocks that refused to decoy. I suspect that he still does that very thing.

Among the lakes of western Minnesota where I have been in summer, the redheads used to become localized, remaining for a month, perhaps longer, in one lake or set of lakes along Red River. Under the circumstances they "traded" about very much like the fresh-water ducks, in small bunches, pairs or even singly. That was a great country for a mixed bag, in the old days when the birds were shot in September, and a good per-centage of redheads always fell to the daily bag. Canvasbacks were shot, too, but usually from a flock of from twenty to forty.

They tell me that when both birds are fattened on celery, nobody can tell a redhead from a canvasback, simply by eat-ing him, and I suspect this is quite true. It is certainly true that the redhead is just about the best bird to eat that falls to the gun in the rice country. In speed on the wing he is second only to the canvasback, and like the latter is very uniform in direction and speed of flight. All of us in my shooting crowd used to know that when a redhead started to come over us he'd come regardless of what happened to him. The redhead has a relative in Europe called the pochard, which is very popular in England.

THE GREATER BLUEBILL
(*Aythya marila*)

THE LESSER BLUEBILL
(*Aythya affinis*)

THE greater and the lesser bluebill are not to be distinguished except by size. The greater bluebill is given a length of from 18 to 20 inches, with wing-spread from 32 to 34 inches. The lesser bluebill is from 15 to 17 inches long, with a wing-spread of 27 to 30 inches. The greater bluebill is the more common bird in the East, the lesser bluebill in the West. On the Atlantic Coast the greater bluebill is usually called the "broadbill," while the lesser bluebill has long been known among many Mississippi Valley duck hunters as the "blackjack." For many years of my younger shooting days I knew this bird only as the blackjack. Both species are sometimes called "scaup ducks," from their habit of eating "scaup" when nothing else is to be found; but the name has a nasty sound, doesn't describe the beautiful bird in any way, and is nothing more than an entirely useless nickname.

The name "blackjack" might be so classed also, but the bird earned a great reputation for himself under it. I once asked an old market gunner which was the most difficult bird to hit and bring down. He studied a moment and said he believed the blackjack flew faster than any other duck, and was the hardest to kill. Certainly he was no easy mark, despite all that was needed was to know his distance and the lead. He did his part by flying just as fast as he knew how, and doing that very thing every time he went by.

Eastern duck shooters are much indebted to the greater bluebill, almost sure to be called the broadbill. When winter comes on and all the other ducks are gone, except sea ducks, with all the rivers and bays frozen solid, the bluebill goes to the sea coast, there to wing in and out from shore to sea. Whatever he may be to eat when living on sea foods, he is a splendid mark, always reliable, affording good duck shooting when otherwise none could be had. He is to the Eastern gunners what mallard is to those of the West. If thoughts of duck shooting come to mind, the Yankee gunner has a vision of broadbills, in great rafts on the sea, or winging low to the water in widespread flocks. He thinks of shooting them from a battery, or he might find a jutting point of rocks alongshore or on an island offshore, there to place his decoys and low blind of seaweed, while the spray broke and ice formed on his gunbarrels.

The broadbill is a Northern bird, breeds in the Hudson Bay country, or equally far north along the coast, and he is apparently reluctant to go any farther south than he has to. Ice and snow have no terrors for him, and shooting is sometimes done in a northeast snowstorm, or among ice cakes, the hunter dressed all in white. Like all the birds of his family, the greater bluebill keeps his course when he starts. Sometimes the shooters line up in their boats, covering some inlet or bay, knowing that if one boat misses a shot the next one will get it; for, whether or no, the ducks are going in or out as their minds may be bent.

The greater bluebill is an inhabitant of Europe as well as of America, but the lesser bluebill is at home only in this country and Canada. This does not signify that the latter bird doesn't migrate south of the United States, for he is said to reach Central and even South America, on his winter migrations. He is moreover, a more southern bird than the broadbill, and may not reach his breeding quarters in Nebraska, the Dakotas and Canada until April. It is quite likely that the broadbill breeds to some extent in Greenland, both those that wing down the New England coast and those that reach the mainland of Europe, the birds simply separating, some going south and east the others south and west. On the other hand, the lesser bluebill is more an inland bird. He collects in beds or rafts, the same as his larger brother, but his rafts will be on fresh-water lakes, not on the sea. He is a very common bird on our Great Lakes, and the man whose shooting is confined to Lake Michigan, for example, will get more lesser bluebills than of all other ducks combined. Twenty-five years ago I myself killed a good many from the long jetties or breakwaters that extend into that lake from Chicago. Oddly enough, the lake shooter didn't know the bluebill as a blackjack, just as the gunner of the lower Mississippi didn't know him as a bluebill. The name blackjack will probably die out with the passing of the last of the old-time market gunners.

All the bluebills are fond of wide open water, and they do not seek protected inlets and ponds like the surface feeding ducks. The waves are never too rough for a bluebill, and in flight he seems to take pleasure in just skimming the waves.

A closely allied species to the bluebill is the ring-necked duck, a bird of the same habits, same family, and very much the same appearance except that he has a ring or collar of deep orange brown or chestnut about his neck. In size the ringneck is midway between the greater and the lesser bluebills. Its Latin name is *Aythya collaris.*

Chapter XVII

DUCKS ORNAMENTAL AND OCCASIONAL

THE WOOD DUCK

THE GOLDENEYE; BARROW'S GOLDENEYE

THE BUFFLEHEAD

THE RUDDY

IN this the last chapter on the ducks we have grouped a number together where they do not belong. Certainly the wood duck deserves a chapter of his own; however, he no longer is considered a game bird, being protected throughout the year. The goldeneye, or whistler, is a good game bird, but is of small importance except along the North Atlantic coast in winter. His cousin, Barrow's goldeneye, a Western bird, is shot on opportunity, though nobody goes duck hunting especially for goldeneyes. The bufflehead is a plump little fellow, and many are shot, too many of them pot-shot. The ruddy belongs with the blue-wing teal, being too tame and unsuspicious for a true game bird.

In addition there are the mergansers, fish-ducks. Old duck hunters have a great contempt for the "sawbills," since they do not smell like wholesome ducks, can't well be eaten, and in market shooting days couldn't be sold. Nevertheless they are fine looking birds and can fly with the best. Nowadays, especially in the East, they are shot for want of better game—just as in the Middle West plenty of shooters are not above killing mudhens, or coots. The American merganser (*Merganser americanus*) is the largest of the three varieties. He weighs up to 4½ pounds, being as large as a brant, with a somewhat goose-like appearance in flying. The second and more common merganser, in the interior, is the red-breasted (*Merganser serrator*), a black-and-white bird, easily identified in flying by his black and white appearance as well as by his sharp saw-toothed bill. He is the bird that the oldtimer won't let you shoot, though he is a most tempting mark as he wings by in big flocks, steady, unafraid, not batting an eye. The hooded merganser we used to call the "topknot" duck, and we knew him very well along the Mississippi long before we recognized him as a merganser. Neither did we know that he wasn't good to eat, for we ate him, and to us he was the same as any other fresh-water fowl. He was liable to be seen in pairs in the spring, as well as in flocks. He is more or less of a woods bird, nesting in trees the same as the wood duck. His Latin name is *Lophodytes cucullatus*, which would indicate that he is only a relative of the true mergansers. All mergansers live pretty much on fish, though the hooded merganser can and does live on a vegetable diet at times, hence becomes quite palatable.

I have had but one opportunity to watch the mergansers at their fishing. A party of us were camped on Sand Creek, in my early Indian Territory days. Our tent was at the head of a reach of water, 40 yards wide, 200 long, and quite deep. I was awakened one morning at daybreak by a commotion on the water. Looking out I saw some kind of diving ducks; most of the time they were under water, now and then one bobbing up.   Fish were breaking water, hundreds of them, some apparently a foot in length.   The ducks had driven all the fish in that pond-hole, evidently, right up to our end, and they were giving those fish a mighty brisk time of it.   A hundred fish were in sight to one duck.   I grabbed my gun and hustled out there, meaning to shoot one of those strange ducks.   Just then an older companion, an old-time duck hunter, got a peep at the mergansers and yelled to me not to shoot.   His voice had another effect, for the whole pond quieted instantly.   No more fish broke water; no ducks appeared on the surface.   In the clear stream I saw darting shadows moving off, looking more like submerged loons or cormorants than anything else, and traveling, I thought, at a mile a minute!   Very shortly, the whole flock, not less than twenty birds, bobbed up as one fowl, struck the water a few flashes and went away.   They arose more like geese than ducks and looked nearly as large as geese.   These were the large American mergansers, or goosanders, as they are sometimes called.

Many years later I missed a chance at the red-breasted merganser that I do not seem able to forget.   We had been in a sand-pit blind from before day until ten o'clock.   Not a shot had we fired, not a duck was to be seen, as we slowly froze stiff.   Of a sudden a great flock of ducks came down the river, not very high, meaning to pass us at fifty yards. I had a new super 12 gun and was keen to try it.   I could see that about six birds headed the bunch, the remainder strung out back.   I meant to rake those six birds with the first barrel just when they got in line.   My gun was up and swinging when my usual old market-gunner companion yelled, "Don't shoot, don't shoot!"   I dropped the gun, thinking that he knew the birds would decoy.   But they never wavered.

My friend explained that they were sawbills and couldn't be eaten.

"Eat, hell!" I said, "I wanted to shoot!"   I went out and took in the decoys.

This reminds me that there are a lot of sea ducks that afford good shooting, and are commonly shot on the Atlantic Coast, but tough eating.   Of these we might mention the old squaw (*Harelda hyemalis*), the harlequin (*Histrionicus histrionicus*), the Labrador duck (*Camptolaemus labradorius*), the American scoter (*Oidemia americana*) the white-winged coot (*Oidemia deglandi*), and the patch-head coot (*Oidemia perspicillata*).   They are among the showiest of all waterfowl and afford good sport, but are not of prime importance to the duck shooter.

THE WOOD DUCK
(*Aix sponsa*)

I DOUBT if there is any other such duck as the wood duck anywhere in the world except on the North American continent.   Indeed, he doesn't appear to have a near relative.   He is the most ornamental of all the duck tribe.   There never was a duck that wasn't handsome, but this fellow is purely a beauty.   He should be domesticated, now that he can no longer be shot as a game bird, and his greatest utility should be as an ornament for parks and private ponds.

All his habits are peculiarly his own.   He much prefers the woods to open waters, and is found, for the most part, on small wooded rivers and creeks clothed with timber, and ponds snug in the forests.   Most of the wood ducks used to be shot by jumping them from streams so narrow that the oaks met overhead. Tramp along such a watercourse and every now and then a flock of wood ducks would take flight from right under the bank, with frightened squeaks. Very often the wood ducks would merely paddle out of the way, bunch up and wait to see if perchance the danger was real. That was the opportunity for the small boy, for the pot-hunter, or for any other scamp who would shoot ducks on the water. Nobody ever did take any pride in a duck shot sitting, if he will be honest with himself, and it is all a simple wasted opportunity—an opportunity that may have cost us time and effort, yet is thrown away. A man had as well hang clay birds on a post, shoot them and then tell how many clays he had broken straight. Pot-hunters have killed off the wood duck, until now we no longer dare shoot him for fear he goes the way of the passenger pigeon.

The wood duck deserves his name, for he builds his nest in a tree, in a hole in a tree if he can find one, and usually he can. The nest may be in a stump or a snag, or, again, it may be up seventy feet or more. The height of his nest doesn't make any difference, because he is as much at home on the limb of a tree as he is on the ground. He can get into a very small hole, only a trifle larger than that used by a flicker, and, oddly enough, he can enter that hole at speed. I have seen them fly at a hole and just dash into it. When a boy, a pretty small boy, I saw a duck coming down the creek, and set myself to take it as it passed. Curiously enough, that duck never did pass, but suddenly curved upward and alighted close to the top of a giant sycamore. This amazed me so much that I wouldn't shoot, thinking that duck must be some kind of bright-colored woodpecker!

The greatest breeding ground of the wood duck was the so called sunk lands of Missouri and Arkansas. I had occasion to take a horseback ride through that region about forty years ago. It was spring, April or May, with the dogwoods in bloom. On every hand the swamps encroached on the corduroy road, extending thence mile after mile on every side. In that twenty-mile ride the wood ducks were never out of sight, pair on pair, unafraid, looking up idly as they paddled about. Thousands and thousands of wood ducks were building in that great swampland forest, and nobody then imagined a time when it would not be so.

I have never in my life seen more than one flight of wood ducks, a flight unaccompanied by any other fowl whatever. That one flight was on Bird Creek in the Indian Territory, in the late eighties. Camped near the creek, I presently learned that starting every evening, without fail, about an hour before sundown, flock after flock of ducks came in, alighting in a sheltered pondhole that was heavily bordered by timber. The flocks came from both up and down the creek, and some of them across country. In the acre or two of water a hundred flocks of ducks might alight within two hours. I kept the camp supplied with ducks day after day, by intercepting the flight some distance from the pond. I can remember yet how noisy and tickled those birds were to get in home after a hard day's work, maybe, up and down the far reaches of river and creek. I killed just six ducks a day, neither more nor less, the shooting lasting about ten days without any apparent diminution in numbers of the birds that came in. Perhaps I killed more wood ducks at that time than during all the rest of my shooting career. When I was a boy my mother sternly forbade the shooting of wood ducks in their mating plumage—she wouldn't permit it any more than she would condone shooting redbirds.

The last wood ducks I shot were on the Verdigris River in Oklahoma, about the year 1906, where the birds were quite plentiful in the early spring. I do not miss the shooting, but do miss the sight of the beautiful birds as they used to be.

THE WHISTLER, OR GOLDENEYE
(*Clangula americana*)

BOTH of this fowl's names are probably descriptive. His wings whistle when he flies, and his iris is a deep golden yellow. In the East the bird is likely to be called the whistler, in the West the goldeneye. In addition, the whistler has a certain amount of crest, erected at will, and the male has a white spot on the side of his head just back of the bill. The general appearance of this bird when on the wing is black-and-white.

Except on the seacoast no special whistler decoys are needed to bring in these birds; they come well to mallard blocks or to live birds, if they decoy at all. Off the New England coast in winter special efforts are made to bag whistlers, decoys being placed about the breakwaters and rocky ledges. The whistler is not like the redhead or the canvasback; he won't fly right over you without batting an eye; if he sees anything suspicious he will break ranks, jump, and tower like a pintail. Also when decoyed he gets away by climbing into the air.

Since spring shooting ended not so many goldeneyes are being killed. In former times these birds always were prominent in the larger lakes of open water. They are not likely to hide in the weeds and rice like mallards or some other kinds of ducks, but will ride out the waves in open water, well out from shore, from which point of safety they will observe the work of the gunner on shore with entire indifference. Take to a boat, though, and your whistler is gone.

One spring on Schoen Lake in the Mississippi bottoms there was a great flight of goldeneyes. Whether the true goldeneye or Barrow's goldeneye I do not now know; it was over forty years ago. The birds packed in the middle of the lake in a great raft, undisturbed by the shooting, but we got on a flyway as the birds came in to join that pack, and had great pass shooting on these fowl. Decoys were useless, the whistlers meaning to join that raft on the open water nearly a mile from shore. More whistlers were killed that week than of all other ducks combined. They looked a bit like "seaducks" and we had misgivings about their edible qualities, but pot-roasted with bacon stuffing they were fine.

BARROW'S GOLDENEYE
(*Clangula islandica*)

Most shooting men won't know the difference between the goldeneye and Barrow's goldeneye. The Barrow's is said to be a trifle larger and the white spot between bill and eye is larger, with rather a crescent shape instead of round. In a general way it might be said that if a goldeneye is killed in the Panhandle of Texas, or anywhere adjacent to the Rocky Mountains—in the mountains too, for the matter of that—it will be the Western species, a Barrow's. This bird is very common on mountain lakes anywhere from Montana to the Rio Grande.

Our Western goldeneyes can withstand a good deal of cold, and are about the last ducks to leave the mountain lakes, remaining until ice forces them to leave. They are so reluctant to leave a lake which they like that bags are made by locating guns at either end of a small lake and driving the birds back and forth. Heavy bags are sometimes made in this way, since, unlike mallards, they appear to forget just what happened to them when they visited a certain point the last time.

I used to amuse myself in New Mexico by taking both a shotgun and a rifle into the blind with me. Sometimes in shooting at a distant raft I'd hit a duck with the rifle, but more likely I'd put the whole pack into flight, and here they'd come, sweeping the water and curving about the shore. Then the pump gun would come into play, and there was havoc among the whistlers when I happened to be right. Without the rifle, nothing at all could have been done with those goldeneyes. In the small Rocky Mountain lakes, not the large ones, perhaps, the whistler is the most common of all ducks, from the time that ice forms until the water is frozen solid.

THE BUFFLEHEAD, OR BUTTERBALL
(Charitonetta albeola)

THIS duck was universally known as the butterball in my Mississippi River duck shooting experience. It was a common lake bird, not very wild, and nearly always in evidence in the spring each year. He could be told a long distance off by his white topknot, and the way he rode the waves, motionless. This little duck appeared to have great ability to "rest" if he wasn't disturbed. A great many of them were eaten by oldtime market hunters, because they were always plump, not to say fat, and they were too small to command much of a price at commission houses.

In habits this bird is much akin to the whistler, and in appearance a good deal like him, except smaller. He is easily distinguished from the whistler, even in flight, because the top of his head is white, rather than having a white spot between eye and bill. Both the whistler and the butterball are somewhat related to the diving ducks, and go under water much more promptly than the shallow-water feeders like the mallards and pintails.

The fault of the little bufflehead, as he used to be known on the Mississippi Valley flight, was that he was too tame to afford the best sport. He might be a different bird on the seacoast, and is said to be.

THE RUDDY
(*Erismatura rubida*)

THE ruddy is widely known. He is as tame as a teal or even worse. Though a fine bird to eat, plump and always fat, he is really somewhat akin to a mudhen, or coot. In rising from the water he may paddle along for some distance, very much as a mudhen does, though when he gets his wings under him he flies strongly. He is a pond duck, like the blue-wing teal, and on being disturbed may simply dive, to bob up again a few yards away. It is a wonder the ruddies were not all killed long ago, though this diving habit may save a bird if he has water enough.

Perhaps also his laziness is of some benefit to him, since he is not a restless bird that keeps winging about until running into danger. Though he will decoy readily enough, the chances are he never even sees decoys, but very contentedly "stays put" wherever he happens to be.

Though he blossoms out in wedding clothes, sometimes, and then has a great white patch from eye to chin, in the fall he is a dun-colored fellow, dark gray, not much different in coloration from a mudhen. His distinguishing mark is a spike tail which he keeps very erect, feathers spread in a row of spikes. If you see a little duck that looks at you curiously, then paddles off with that spike tail flirting back and forth as though it were some kind of propeller, that couldn't be anything except a ruddy.

He can dive without any effort when he feels like it, just dropping beneath the surface, not even ducking his head. This ability is furthered by the ruddy riding the lowest in the water of all ducks. He can dive the most quickly of all ducks, too, but cannot dodge shot like a helldiver.

When ruddies are plentiful enough any tyro can make a bag of ducks, if he can hit things at rest with a shotgun. Even the man who takes his birds legitimately won't have much trouble with little birds that labor slowly into flight. Forbearance is needed. If the little fowl are jumped, let them get their wings under them, and then they probably will swing back within reach of the gun—going fast now and affording a sporting shot.

Chapter XVIII

GEESE

The Canada Goose
Hutchins' Goose
The White-fronted Goose
The Greater Snow Goose
The Brant

THE CANADA GOOSE

THERE are geese and geese in America; we have selected only the important species for descriptions and are confining these to one chapter.

This book is not sufficiently scientific to require explaining the difference between geese and brant—if there is a difference other than size, coloration, feathering, habits, voice, and general appearance.

To the mind of the North American gunner, there is just one goose, the great Canada "honker," just as English fowlers have but the "gray" goose. At the time of writing this I have just yesterday been reading Audubon, but I won't quote our great naturalist anent the Canada goose. Nobody today cares about what he has to say. In Audubon's time people could read leisurely, but today they have too much else to do, so read a bit and break away.   I confess that what I read yesterday I have forgotten today, and at best I could hardly tell a goose from a "shypoke" from reading a naturalist's descriptions.   I do remember that Audubon said a Canada gander weighed 7½ pounds and a goose less; which proved to me that the great bird man must have weighed the skin of a *Branta canadensis* (old Canada honker) after it was stuffed with straw, for I never have seen a Canada goose over two-thirds grown which weighed less than 8 pounds. The heaviest honker that I ever heard of weighed 19 pounds. I never saw him, you understand—but my good friend Uncle Billy Hardin said it was possible.   He had a gander fall on the back of his neck, which the fat man swore weighed a ton and a half.

As befits things North American, our Canada goose is the greatest of his kind, search the world over.   None other is so large, none other so wary and wise, none other affords the man who bags him such depth of satisfaction.   I regard geese and elephants as being in the same class.   They are fairly easy to hit when you get close to them, but mighty hard to close in on, and both are lead carriers.   However, considering his size, the wild goose has it on the elephant.   An elephant couldn't tote seven tons of lead, even on his back, but in my early days, down at Grand Tower, Illinois, I knew a youngster who fired fifty pounds of St. Louis No. 1's and got but one goose!   He maintains to this day that while in war ten pounds of lead may kill a man, it won't feaze a goose unless you get it all into him at one time.

The Canada goose is a military chap, his entire life being absolutely governed by military discipline.   Every company has its captain; guards are mounted as strictly as ever they

were in Indian fighting; on the march ranks are maintained
more uniformly than in the German army, and all maneuvers
are executed with absolute military precision.   It would do
you good to see a flock of geese, all abreast, circling a pit, and
note the speed with which the outer birds "hopped to it" to
keep the line.   In migration the leader gives all orders, and
is never replied to except by some woman goose away back
in the ranks, presumably his wife, and her advice is ignored
in manly fashion.   By the way, it is my belief that the Canada
goose alone has a masculine theory of government, while all
lesser geese are ruled by suffragettes.   Just note how the
brant chatter and gabble and break ranks, and refuse to be
governed by any discipline, military or otherwise.

Perhaps a few words concerning the breeding habits and
breeding grounds of the Canada goose may not be amiss, now
that the Federal law may change his habits more or less,
though to date it has not done so.   When I was a boy they
taught me at school that wild geese nested entirely beyond
the ken of man, in that farthest North which is somewhere
"forninst" the Pole.   Supposedly veracious Arctic travelers
spoke of them as still wending their way northward far beyond habitable regions, across the Arctic Circle's vast expanse
of eternal ice and snow, bound, presumably, for some magically sheltered island in some magically open polar sea.   Today we know more about the Canada, and it is the snow goose
and especially the blue goose * which are supposed to make
the journey to glamorously unknown breeding grounds.

When I got out among real fowl shooters, who knew a good
deal more than they had ever read, I got a different story as

* Recently discovered for the first time to have its summer breeding
grounds on Baffin Island, north of Hudson Bay.

to the breeding grounds of the Canada goose. They told me that originally geese bred everywhere north of the "alligator belt," and that south of this limit, about the latitude of Cairo, Ill., they could not remain during the breeding season because the goslings were eaten by alligators and alligator gars. Mississippi Valley geese, therefore, nested along the big river in an early day anywhere above Cairo, also on the Illinois River, the Missouri, Platte, and all tributary streams of that region.

The farthest south that I have myself seen a goose nest was on the Minnesota River in western Minnesota, but they tell me that a few geese still breed on the upper reaches of the Platte and on the lakes of the sandhill country in Nebraska. Confirming this, I have seen geese winging up and down the Platte in July, and undoubtedly they had nests in that vicinity. Even more than ducks, the goose demands isolation and freedom from disturbance when nesting. This probably will always lead the bulk of them to breed beyond the "grain belt." The Indians have always taken pretty severe toll of young geese, and an old Sioux once told me that the daintiest tidbit that ever tickled Indian palate was a gosling, fat and heavy, just before he was able to fly. It no doubt always will be so, for the geese cannot go so far north as to get beyond the reach of Indians or Eskimos.

The Canada goose weighs from 8 to 12 pounds, occasionally going heavier, for he has great ability to lay on fat when conditions are right. He lives a long time, too, and gets no smaller with age. His distinguishing marks are: size, larger than other geese; black neck and head, barred with white on the cheeks; tail black with the upper tail coverts snowy white. He differs from his lesser relative, the Hutchins' goose only in his size. His appearance when standing is first to be noted, for an old Canada appears to stand a fourth higher than any other goose.   If a goose is killed that weighs considerably under 8 pounds, shorter in the neck than a Canada should be, shorter in total length, with a wing expanse under 60 inches, that is probably a Hutchins' goose.   If it is a matter of argument, to be certain about it count the tail feathers.   The Hutchins' has from 14 to 16 feathers in his tail, the Canada from 18 to 20.

The wild goose has been a fowl of great interest since the beginning of the written story of the Anglo-Saxon race. Gray-goose-feathered shafts were sped by the "merry men" of Robin Hood.   If our fowler has had poetry in him, he inevitably has taken it out on the goose.   Probably all of us always have wanted to fly, always have wanted wings.   The wild goose, winging majestically high and far and never tiring, has been a grand bird of inspiration.

I remember that, when little boys longing for spring and bare feet, we were always on the watch for geese.   Seeing a flock coming, we ran to the house, calling, "Geese! *Geese!*" If my father was about the house he hustled out with an old Spencer rifle and shot at the geese.   That he couldn't kill one, passing over as they did sometimes no more than twice the height of the barn, was a source of great wonder to us. The nearest he ever came to killing a goose was to cut a wing feather from one, which came floating down, to be preserved for a long time.   If the rifleman were not present, then we boys shot arrows up into the flock, now and then thinking we came mighty close, but never touching a goose.

Later I made amends for those misses, and such is the fascination of goose shooting that after a lifetime with the gun I still would rather shoot a Canada goose than any other bird that flies. There is rare music in the cry of a wild goose pack, endless power in the swish of their mighty wings, and their flying wedge transcends all other moving beauty painted against the sky. Let us hope that they never disappear into that unknown void from which no traveler ever returns.

THE HUTCHINS' GOOSE

THIS chap is, as already indicated, much like the Canada goose—so much that for a long time it was not granted the honor of a name of its own. However, being a smaller bird it presumably was under suspicion, until finally the number of feathers in its tail settled the question ornithologically. It became *Branta canadensis hutchinsii*. No goose can grow more or fewer tail feathers at will; that the naturalists know, and such things they depend on for accuracy. How a Canada gander who can't count can avoid selecting a mate that hasn't enough feathers in her tail, I don't know. Maybe it is significant that such a goose is indeed wiser than man.

The best flight of Hutchins' geese is probably from Manitoba across the Dakotas, across Nebraska, down the Platte, and so to the Panhandle of Texas, thence to old Mexico and the Gulf. In my spring shooting days, the Hutchins' geese appeared to come a little later in the spring than the Canadas, or to linger a bit longer when they did come, and many were killed in the green wheat fields. They were, in my opinion, easier to get, even if smaller and therefore presumably harder to hit. Even now, when a man who shoots on the big prairies tells of making a large bag of geese, I am ready to bet they were of the Hutchins' variety. No goose is so smart as the Canada.

Beyond this, anything we may say of goose shooting applies to one variety as well as to another. And any man so fortunately situated that he can regularly bag geese, season after season, can afford to go without a Ford car, a radio, a wrist watch and an outboard motor. If he never sees a moving picture he needn't care a whoop, for he has pictures on the plates of his mind that no camera will ever reproduce. Me! I'd be willing to sleep forever on an old-fashioned feather bed, to dine on mush and milk, and never vote for president, if I could only have all the geese I wanted to shoot.

THE WHITE-FRONTED GOOSE

HERE is a Western goose, sometimes called a "wavy," sometimes a "specklebelly." The distinguishing marks of the whitefront are: head and neck brownish in place of black; white spot is not on the cheeks but just back of the base of the bill, there in a more or less crescent shape, bordered on the side opposite the bill by black; bill is a pale pink with white nail; pink feet. They have a fairly similar goose in Europe called the "pinkfoot." Birds in their first year lack the white spot back of the bill. The length is around 25 inches, a foot shorter than the Canada, compared with which he is only pint size. Called by the ornithologists *Anser albifrons gambeli*.

The whitefronts fly in the same formation as other geese, a V shape when traveling; but they are a good deal more likely to break ranks at little excuse, and gabble a good deal instead of trumpeting. They may come into a field in ranks, and then will break all up before alighting, talking about it all the time. These are more or less a prairie bird, and numbers are shot in Manitoba and the Dakotas, thence south into Louisiana, where they are a common goose.

On their foraging grounds, the whitefronts decoy readily, but they are more wary when passing over water. In their winter quarters they travel about a good deal, breaking up into singles, pairs, and small flocks. They are difficult to call, and I have never seen anyone who could do much at it. When migrating they decoy well on the prairies, but it is best to have fifteen or twenty decoys if possible.

In the West the whitefronts make long flights, usually one jump carrying them from northern Nebraska to the Panhandle * of Texas. Thence they jump to the rice fields of the coast.

This is a common bird on the Pacific Coast, but uncommon on the Atlantic, except in the vicinity of the Carolinas and southward. On the prairies he is usually called a "wavy," owing to the transverse stripes of black and white across his belly. He is a good bird on the table, not becoming as tough with age as a Canada.

THE GREATER SNOW GOOSE

THE greater snow geese are said to breed in the far North, in Alaska and along the shores of the Arctic Ocean. Thence they travel in pretty well marked lines of flight, one down the Pacific Coast and a second east of the Rocky Mountains. They come south a bit earlier than most of the geese, and

---

* The author's somewhat numerous references to the Panhandle of Texas signify mostly a personal leaning toward that locality. There is a vast extent of just as good game country, several times larger, farther south in the Lone Star State.

linger in the spring.   This is one of our fine big geese, weighing up to 8 pounds, sometimes more.   The length is up to 30
inches, with a spread of wings of 5 feet.   They look as large
as a Canada in flight, or on the water, but appear shorter
when standing on the ground.

The distinguishing mark of a white goose is of course his
color.   He is as white as a pelican, and appears as white as
snow, except on the wing displaying black wing-tips.   His
feet are purple, with black nails; his bill is pink with a white
nail.   Not much need to fully describe a snow goose, because you can't mistake him.   He is *Chen hyperborea nivalis.*
A smaller relative is called the lesser snow goose (*Chen hyperborea*), and yet another white relative termed the Ross snow
goose (*Chen rossii*), the smallest of all our geese, which may be
recognized by a slight, wart-like growth at the base of the
upper mandible.   Shoot a white goose that is not much larger
than a big duck, but with a greater expanse of wings, wart
on the base of his bill, and that is a Ross snow goose.   The
difference between the lesser and greater snow geese is mostly
in size.   A white goose weighing in the neighborhood of 8
pounds is a greater, and one around 5½ pounds a lesser snow
goose.   The habits are the same, and why they do not mix
up in their breeding I do not know.   Maybe they have a sub-
stitute for counting tail feathers.

The Canada and most of his near relatives are "land birds."
They feed on land for the most part, going to water of course,
but after drinking and swimming about for a while will take
to the shore to rest and preen their feathers.   Ducks prefer
to rest on the water, and so does the snow goose.   He is a
lake bird and perhaps a sea bird at times.   Reaching a lake
he is likely to take to the middle of it and stay there.   In mi-

gration he is not so liable to be seen in the fields as on the lakes or even on small ponds.

The snow goose is not nearly so wary as a Canada, and can be stalked much more readily. I have crawled up on snow geese many times, usually getting a shot, which doesn't happen so often with Canadas. I have also pushed about in reed- and rice-grown lakes and had good shooting at the snow geese. They rise heavily and slowly, like any other large geese, and unlike Canadas do not become alarmed at suspicious circumstances. For example, if a boat is pushing about, alarming the mallards, and a bunch of Canada geese note that something is scaring the ducks, away they will go; but snow geese will sit tight until they themselves see something wrong.

The snow goose decoys well on the open prairie, but is said not to do so when decoys are placed on the water—particularly on inlets of the sea. Perhaps he has been disturbed too much by coast gunners.

This is the most beautiful of the goose tribe, his appearance being startlingly attractive under some conditions, especially when in flight. In a field of dark green wheat he becomes a great patch of snowy white, and in the slanting rays of the evening sun leaves a lasting impression of wild-life charm that is rare indeed.

THE COMMON BRANT

THE brant is a water bird, and is sometimes called a maritime goose. However, I have seen plenty of brant in Illinois in a time past. No doubt they migrated up and down the Mississippi, from the Great Lakes to the Gulf. I have never seen a brant in the western prairie states.

The English name for the brant is brent, meaning burnt— or burnt goose, from his dark color.   I surmise that the English brent is precisely the same bird as ours, for the Latin name is nearly the same, *A. brenta glaucogaster* for the English or European brent as compared with *Branta bernicla glaucogastra* for ours.   The brant is said to breed all along the northern Atlantic Coast, on Greenland, and across northern Europe.   Probably birds from Greenland diverge, some going to Europe and others coming to this country.

The length of the brant is given at 22 to 24 inches, and his weight around 4 to 4½ pounds.   We used to know the brant at sight in Illinois, because his wings beat faster than those of other geese; he was apt to wing in the irregular order of ducks, and he gabbled instead of honking.   If a 4-pound goose is killed which has a jet black head and neck, small spot of white on the side of the neck well below the head, with short neck and general black appearance on the back, and if the flock from which he came flew now in a goose-like line, now a jumbled pack—that bird is a brant.

Although the brant is a goose and looks like one, in weight and in habits he is very much a duck.   He may alight on land, but as already said his home is on the water.   He feeds on the water, in the shallows alongshore, for he is not a particularly good diver.

Extensive plans are made to bag brant up and down the Atlantic Coast from Maine to Florida.   Permanent blinds are built, decoys are bred for the purpose, and even "tollers" are used, tame birds tossed up in the air when a flock of brant are coming in.   Lucky are the shooters who can locate a shooting pit on ground hard by some bar thrown up by a seaway or channel, where the brant will come to "gravel" at low tide.

Probably the brant affords more sport to the New England gunner than any other goose, as brent shooting is highly regarded in England.

There are other geese and at least one more species of brant, but like a day a book has limitations.   As at best descriptions are pretty dry reading, the reader being any akin to me, and there being neither room nor reason for giving more than the briefest of them, we will pass on to something more interesting.

Chapter XIX

THE TRUMPETER SWAN

TO be consistent, perhaps I should give a lengthy, pseudo-scientific description of the trumpeter swan, since I really know more about swans from reading than from personal experience. The man who knows the least generally can write the most, from what somebody else has said. However, better be inconsistent than insincere.

A full-grown swan, *Cygnus buccinator*, to be technical, is said to be 68 inches from point of bill to tip of tail. His feet and bill are black, with orange trimmings about the mouth; color is pure white, except the young and sometimes older birds may wear a brownish-red cap. His body is longer than broad and wider than deep, and he is heavy, having the queer quality of gaining a pound a rod for every quarter of a mile you have to carry him into camp.

Like the Dutchman's sausage-like dog, anybody would recognize a swan by sight; anyhow, even if he never saw him, from his call. Don't mistake me. The swan doesn't howl. His voice is, to the hunter, the most musical of any wild thing that lives, not excepting the bugling of an elk, the far-reaching call of the crane, the wild honk of the Canada goose, the weird wailing of the curlew or the sweet, plaintive whistle of the prairie plover.

The sight of a great flock of swans coming in and dropping

to the decoys is the most gloriously exalting that any American sportsman will ever see, while the clear, penetrating trumpeting of their voices vibrates on the very heartstrings of the waiting wildfowler.

I am not mentioning the swan by way of giving instructions for shooting him.   The Bureau of Biological Survey has taken him from the list of game birds—very properly, I think, for swans are rare today.   In fact they have been rare for more than a quarter of a century.   In thirty years of pretty steady shooting, when the birds were in season, I killed no more than half a dozen swans.   A market shooting acquaintance who did nothing but shoot during the time from 1880 to 1900, told me that his entire bag of swans did not exceed ten birds.   Another, an Arkansas River market gunner, who had bagged carloads of ducks and geese, declared that never in his life had he shot a swan, nor had an opportunity of doing so.   In the last twenty years in Oklahoma I have not seen a flock of swans, even flying over, and the only flock that I have seen in all that time was in New Mexico, high above the mountains.   Few can find fault with the Government for placing a perpetual closed season on this disappearing fowl.

However, I do not believe that the present rarity of the swan is due in any great measure to American market gunners or other waterfowl shooters.   So far as I know, the birds were never listed as game by commission houses, prices not being quoted on them; neither were they to be compared with even a forty-year-old Canada goose, for as a table bird they were classed, and rightly, with the sandhill crane.   On the other hand, I conclude that numbers may have been slaughtered by the Indians and trappers in Canada.

The Hudson's Bay Company long made a specialty of

swan skins, these having a use similar to fine fur.   Swan's down and eider down once were staple articles of commerce, and I think we can safely charge our northern neighbors with killing off the swans, even though the "swan's down" may in many instances have come off the body of a goose—as "eider down" comes from geese and all sorts of common ducks.   In any event, the action of our Government in prohibiting the killing of swans can have little effect so long as they are shot by the Indians and others in the far North.

The majority of the swans slaughtered for their skins are killed in the spring, when the down, being without pin-feathers, is at its best.   Of course the swan cannot withstand being continually persecuted in nesting time, any more than could the egret or the teal duck, for the matter of that.   No bird can take proper care of itself when busily engaged in mating and nest building.   This is emphatically true where birds are being shot without limit, for commercial purposes.

When I was a boy, swans appeared to be plentiful enough; but they were always on the wing and nobody could tell me where they went.   In after years I found them on the Minnesota lakes, on the ducking grounds about Grand Tower, Illinois, and in the New Madrid marshes.   Swans are now reported as being found on certain lakes in Oregon, and a correspondent recently wrote me that these birds were using not very far from his home in Idaho.   Some winter on the Gulf Coast, some down along the Pacific, and many in old Mexico, probably going thence to South America.   Like the crane, the swan has great powers of flight, winging high, and passing over a great scope of country without stopping.   Having alighted on the water our great birds are slow in getting under way, for it takes time to get their 8-foot wingspread into action. On land they take off like an airship, and in the old days many were killed by dashing in among them before they could get under way.

While the swan is no longer to be considered a target for the gun, yet the position he once occupied entitles him to a place in a book of this kind. I shall, therefore, instead of giving instructions for bagging him, be content to tell a little story of a swan shoot which occurred about forty years ago.

My old market shooting chum, Terry Parsons, got me into it. Terry was shooting that fall on the New Madrid marshes in Missouri. On his invitation, I ran down from St. Louis to join him. When I got there early in December I found the New Madrid marshes alive with hunters, on the river side. For this reason we concluded to run around to the west side, a place more difficult to reach and hence less liable to be shot out. Getting off at the little station of Marston, a few miles from the lake, we had our outfit hauled down to the marsh, here simply a great cypress slash, and went into camp.

We found mallards in untold quantities, together with other ducks, plenty of geese and a few brant. Then, too, there were quail, turkeys, and deer.

After the usual "daylight" shoot, I presently began putting in my time in pursuit of upland game. Terry shot ducks, such being his professional occupation. Shooting mallards in the open holes among the cypress was a simple mechanical proposition. The birds came in through the trees from the east or above the trees, and settled slowly down among the decoys. Fired at, they climbed slowly up and out. Given a couple of automatic shotguns, huge would have been the slaughter, and as it was Terry killed enough.   So many brass shells loaded, so many ducks killed, so many selected and prepared for shipment, so many given away to our neighbors, and the day's work was done.   I tired completely of it after a week, and got Pete Madden to call turkeys for me.

Pete was a typical swamper, lean, sallow, deliberate, a skilled hunter and good rifle shot, but "climatically" lazy, and he had other faults besides.   He kept camp for us without charge, cooked when we happened to be absent, and made heavy inroads on our tobacco, whiskey and bacon, whether we were absent or present.   Pete differed from our neighbors, or his, only in having a wife who refused to become a squaw. She believed in her husband doing the work, and furthermore insisted on his doing it.   Many a morning hunt I had spoiled through Mrs. Madden sending the boy, Tommy, down to camp for his dad to come home and drive up the cows out of the pasture.   The youngster had as well brought them himself, with less rods to travel, but that was not the lady's scheme of things.   Pete constantly threatened revolt, but, except on one memorable occasion I never knew of his doing so.

Ordinarily, Pete's duties should have been shooting eight or ten deer in the fall, enough to last all winter, killing half a dozen acorn-fed wild hogs, a daily mess of squirrels, an occasional wild turkey, and the remainder of his time should have been devoted to trapping and catching mud-cats on a trot-line.   However, besides bringing the cows, Mrs. Madden insisted upon the poor fellow tending ten acres of corn, whether the work gave him the "ager" or not.   Additionally, he had to hoe the cane-patch, make the molasses, get in the pumpkins, cut and hang the tobacco, and dig the "taters."   All things considered, Pete was an overworked and somewhat abused man.

Swans were the last thing we thought of, but Pete came in one night, after a trapping expedition to an island some miles out in the slash, with the statement that he had discovered a swan roost.   He declared that on several different occasions when in the marsh after night he had found the big birds resting in this particular place, fifty acres of deep, open water in the midst of the cypress forest.   His conclusion was that the great fowls came in there every night.   It was a new thing to Pete, the swan never having been there before this particular season.

We were of course anxious for a crack at those swans.   According to our calculations, the wary fowls must have been much disturbed by the constant bombardment to the east, so they were coming in to our cypress slash to roost.   Pete had seen them at night only, but we thought it probable that they began to arrive an hour or two before sundown, as ducks and geese would under like circumstances.

Neither Terry nor I knew much about the swamp, never having been more than a mile or two from shore.   Pete did, though; knew every peculiar tree, fallen log, cane-patch and island.   Consequently Pete must take us out, for otherwise our finding the roost was unlikely.   To be sure, he did his best to send us on our own—told us how to go, with such definite instructions that we could not miss the spot.   We were to point north and a leetle east for a half mile, then east and a leetle north for two miles and a half, thence through a channel between Hickory Island and Water-oak Slash, and northeastward to a big cypress with a dead top; farther on we would find shallow water grown up with fishpole cane; a dugout lane broken through the cane would lead us to open water, when we would be at the swan roost.   The only thing Pete warned us about was not to miss the "water-lane," for if we did and got messed up in the cane, we'd be in trouble "shore as hell," according to Pete.

We were looking for swans and not for trouble, so under pressure we took Pete with us as guide, the three of us going in his 14-foot dugout.   Terry could run a dugout about as well as a native, but I had never acquired any fondness for the treacherous craft.   We made rapid and easy progress, Pete being a dandy hand with a paddle.   Naturally, the nervous little craft was pretty well loaded, with three full-sized men, the guns and shells, so Terry and I sat low and said nothing.   Many things interested me.   The cat-squirrels were everywhere, more at home over the water than on shore, apparently.   We saw a coon, lying asleep in the crotch of a tree, and a gobbler winged by so close that I almost upset the boat in an attempt to grab my gun.   Wood ducks paddled slowly aside, and mallards rose with affrighted squawking, setting the dark forest agleam with their vivid under-coloring. I paid little attention to our course, likewise equally careless was Terry.   What was the use of bothering?   We had Pete with us.

An hour's paddling brought us through the cane and to the open pondhole, where, according to Pete, the swans roosted. It was a pretty bit of hidden water.   On the west the thirty-foot cane stood in a long uneven hedge, a clear wall of green above the dark water.   To the east and north lay the great cypress forest, the whole shore studded with cypress knees, many of the trees were eight feet in diameter and stood 150 feet tall, their roots extending presumably to near where the world began. The water was a clear black-blue, with the waves rolling to such a height as to indicate considerable depth.

We made our way across to the east side, taking position in the top of a giant fallen cypress, a tree lying two thirds out of the water. No better blind could have been desired, the boat being perfectly hidden. Around us the cypress knees dotted the lake, standing from four to eight feet high. I suppose a man might have sat on a cypress knee and not been seen.

We were confident the swans would come in from the east, not only for the reason that the great waterfowl marshes lay in that direction, but for the further reason that we had seen none of the big white birds crossing our shooting grounds to the west.

We smoked and waited. A flock of canvasbacks circled the lake, racing past us saucily, not ten feet from the water, but we refused to be tempted. One hour, two hours passed, and the sun was sitting on the tops of the cypresses, but still no swans. I stretched out on the huge cypress trunk quite content, but the usually patient Terry began to fidget. Swans were out of his line anyhow. I surmise that he got to thinking of the eight dozen mallards at three dollars a dozen which he should have shipped that night. Pete had promptly gone to sleep. Terry aroused him. Let me add that Terry had an active mind and a nimble tongue.

"Pete," he queried, "are you sure them wasn't ghost swans you seen?"

"Naw," expostulated Pete.

"You know, Pete, when a swan dies he always turns into a sperit. People don't git to be ghosts, it's swans. Hain't every ghost that ever was seen a white one, and don't they all have wings?"

"I done seen live swans," protested Pete.

"I have heard that swans have their kingdom-come, too, and it is right here in the Missouri swamps or down about Big Lake. The ghost of every swan killed in the whole world comes right back in here. You know there would be a lot of dead swans, Pete, about over the world. They'd be pretty thick in this swan heaven. Git in the right place, you'd see thousands and thousands of them, floatin' around in the dark and singin'. If it was dark when you saw them swans, and if they was singin', then I bet they was all ghost swans."

Pete was impressed. "Sperits!" he ejaculated. "You hain't got no sperits with you, now? Drat the luck! Course it was dark," he continued, peering anxiously about in the gathering gloom. "Maybe you call it singin', but it sounded more like sojer horns to me. But I don't believe them was no ghosts. One ol' gander tuck a crack at another, and you could a heard the whack forty rod."

"That's no proof they wasn't ghosts, Pete. Don't it stand to reason that no big, fightin' swan ghost ain't goin' to stand no foolin' from any little feisty swan ghost? The little fellers would rule the roost if they did, 'cause a thousand youngsters git killed to one smart old gander. I'll tell you how we can settle it. Did they eat anything? Was they scared of you? Ghost swans never eat, and they ain't no more afraid of a man than a cussin'-mad swamp hog is. Them ghost swans won't get out of your way, and the man that shoots at one of 'em, he never is seen no more. You might 'a' knowed some of 'em that didn't come back, Pete?"

"I shore did! Little Sandy Apperson and old man

Bunse—nobody ever see hair or hide of 'em again, nor their boats nor guns. Tell ye what, fellers, thar's things happen in this worl' that can't be 'counted for!"

A cathead owl set up long, unearthly yells, and the sunset breeze went to wailing in the tops of the near-by cypress. Far off a jack-loon pulled his eerie laugh.

"Say, boys, I'm dry," declared Pete. "This swamp water ain't fittin' to drink nohow. Let's— Hello, look a-there!"

From out of the cane on the farther side came a small dug-out, vigorously paddled by fourteen-year-old Tommy. He crossed straight to us, as though knowing by instinct precisely where we would be. When he got within hailing distance he called: "Pap! Ma'am says you got to come home."

"What fur?"

"She says you got to go to the store for cawfee and snuff— it's all out. And the shotes is gittin' inter the punkin patch, and they ain't no stovewood chopped to git supper, and she says for you to come straight home."

"All right, Tommy, all right. Push up here whur I can git in."

"Look here," I broke in, much annoyed. "We need your father to show us the way out of here in the dark. Why didn't you go to the store yourself? It would have been easier than paddling five miles. We can't let him off!"

"Ma done tole me to go fetch pap, an' I got ter. She'd 'a' taken a stick to me."

"I hate to leave you, boys, but I jist gotter go," Pete apologized. "No trouble 'tall about comin' back," he added. "Go through the canebrake where we did, drap back a ways, hit the channel, bear south till you see the old split-fork cypress and then straight for camp. Ef you don't mind, I'll stop at camp and take me a horn—feelin' mighty agery to-day. Better come with me, fellers," he coaxed, "I wouldn't stay in the dark, I tell ye that!"

"Help yourself, Pete," said Terry grimly. "If we don't get in on time come out for us; you can hear our guns from camp. I knocked off a day to shoot some swans."

"Shore," agreed Pete, and vamosed.

"Now, Terry, see what you have done," I scolded. "We may have a deuce of a time getting out of here."

"Oh, I guess we'll make it," assured Terry. "If the wind holds to the west and the stars shine, and we don't get into a canebrake, we'll land somewhere. Suppose we ought to take his advice and go now."

"No. I haven't killed a swan in two years, and I believe they will be in here to roost, just as Pete said."

Dusk was falling; the shadows of the cypress lengthened across the pond and blended with the water. We had been keeping a close watch without having seen a bird, when suddenly we saw a great flock of swans sitting idly on the water fifty yards from the north shore.

"There they are, Terry. Keep your eyes peeled now. How the devil did they get in without our seeing them?"

Carefully we scanned the tops of the eastern cypress, hoping to see a flight of the great birds bearing down on us. None appeared. Again we turned to the flock on the water, hoping they might drift our way. There now were two distinct flocks, the second nearer us than the first. Scandalous work on the part of two old duck shooters, this letting two bunches of these immense birds come in without being seen. We looked east, looked north, looked south; no swans in the air, neither had those already there sailed about the lake, according to custom, before alighting. Something queer about those swans! For the third time we turned to the birds on the water and were dumbfounded to see still a third flock!

Terry swore softly. "It beats the devil we can't see them come in!"

"Look, Terry, there go your ghost birds!"

Two gunshots above us, a long line of big white fowl, from fifty to a hundred, were swimming easily in single file through the cypress, headed for the lake. Regardless where they came from, it was a fact that they were swimming in, not flying. Gradually the flocks drew together in the middle of the lake, all much at home, all silent.

"Down!" whispered Terry. "Mark back!"

At last we had them! Another long line of birds was coming, the file extending farther into the darkening forest than our eyes could penetrate, the leader swimming straight for our treetop. Usually wary birds, they showed no fear, swimming with strong, easy strokes. They were indeed in a haven where never disturbed—else veritable ghost birds.

We waited in tense eagerness while they came on in the stately array of a swan pageant. The head of the line, detouring past our blind, passed on into open water. They were within fifty feet when Terry gave the word. Powerful wings struck the water like the pounding of hammers as the startled fowl tried to get under way. We were old hands and the shots were simple and sure—four stricken birds fell from a height of not over six feet.

The remainder of the flock took wing back of us, but instead of driving off in the direction they had come, swung out directly by us. The sight of the tremendous birds in their panic-stricken efforts, the pounding of their great wings, the vibrant rush of all that horse-power getting into action, caused me to sit with empty gun; but the veteran market hunter reloaded and fired again, getting two more.

An outcry arose from the several hundred swans already on the lake, which took wing heavily, holding together. Gradually though majestically climbing until fairly launched they circled the pond, sweeping down the west side and around past us. Terry would have shot again, but I made him desist.

"Don't, Terry! Don't shoot any more. We have six now—all the dugout will carry." What we were thinking of to come with Pete, the three of us in that shell, I cannot now imagine.

We picked up our game, the lightest one seemingly weighing thirty pounds, shook the water from their feathers, admired them hunter-fashion, for every one was pure white, and piled them gingerly in the bow of the craft, where they made a great white mass.

"Where do you reckon they came from, Terry?"

"You can search me. The nearest open water that I know about to the east is twenty miles. You don't suppose they swum?"

"Hardly! Must be a lake filled with water weeds where they feed, somewhere in the middle of the cypress swamps. Nobody disturbing them there."

It was quite dark now, the cane bordering the pondhole to the west appearing a black, unbroken palisade yards above our heads. Yet going very carefully, we found the lane and passed through without any particular trouble. It took keen searching to find the narrow pass between the islands, since we were fearful of entering the cane until assured we

had found the precise place. Also, Terry was justly appre-
hensive of running onto a snag or cypress root. But at last,
getting into the channel, we no longer worried about reaching
camp. As we were paddling slowly through the waterway,
the tall cane guarding us on either side, Terry unexpectedly
backed water.

"Listen!"

Pete was coming back! Coming back for us, lit up figur-
atively if not otherwise, and telling the world. We pulled
up to listen.

"Shoot thar cussed haids clean *off!* Ol' woman she says
cawfee en snuff. Cripes a' mighty—plenty whiskey en ter-
baccer. Hain't askeered o' no ol' womern an' no *swans.* Try
an' peck *my* eyes. *Who-ooo-ee!*"

Terry was adjusting the top swan of the pile, which apparently was one too many for the boat.

"Two fool Yanks a-thinkin' I ain't seen no swans. A-tellin'
me them was swan ghos'! Wadda *I* care? Wadda *I* care?
Go' bring 'em boys in. Good ol' boys—we-all goin' to have
'nother *drink!*"

Terry Parsons was an artist with the French harp, or harmonica. Now he put that instrument to a use that I can never
forget, and for which I was long in forgiving him. Whipping
his inseparable favorite from its vest-pocket case, he blew
a long, weird blast.

Pete Madden fell silent; not even a ripple could be heard.
He was somewhere near, immediately ahead. I began to feel
uneasy, knowing that Arkansas swampers were not at all backward about shooting first and asking questions afterward.

"Cut it out, Terry," I warned. "One damned fool is
enough."

"Whe-e-e-e-u-u-uuu," sighed the harmonica once more, cupped in the irrepressible Terry's practised hands.

"*Bang!*" roared Pete Madden's old pumpgun, spitting a jet of flame that told all too vividly where he was, and it was *not* too far away.

"Click, clack, whack! Dang the luck! Out o' shells—whar's my pocket."

"Quit that, Pete!" I yelled. "You drunken fool; you like to hit us!"

"Oho! No, sir! No, sir-ree! Never shot at ye, 'tall! Jist shot off my gun—let ye know—comin' help. No ol' dyin' swan gander's ghos' a-goin' to stop ol' Pete. Let him sing—he c'n bust his biler. Whar's he at? What's that white ye got thar?"

"Go along back to camp—we'll follow you," said Terry. "Charley says you like to sunk us, shootin' in the water right at us like that."

"Follow me, boys. Follow old Pete. Never miss camp if you-all come along behin' me. Stan' up an' paddle so you-all can see whur I be. *Who-ooo-ee! Whooop! Come on, boys! Who-ooo-ee!* Paddle er dugout straight home a-standin' up—thash—"

Splash!

By some miracle we managed to rescue Pete without swamping our dugout or losing his, and he was nearly sober when we got home. Next morning Terry took everything I said to him kindly and with no back talk. When I got through he handed me our last bottle of whiskey. "Give that to Mrs. Madden, Charley. For her ague. Tell her she'll have to forgive us for bein' a little too good to Pete, because he sure did show us a swan hunt."

Chapter XX

HUNTING GEESE

EVERY man is his own boss in his goose shooting, and governs himself by conditions. In a general way it might be said that one man depends on pass shooting, another on the use of decoys on land in the grain fields, another on the use of decoys on the sandbars of a river, or again on some estuary of the seacoast. Some geese decoy best over water, others over land. All of us have stalked geese, on opportunity, thus acquiring more respect for them. Then there is the gunner who relies upon a boat to get him within gunshot, perhaps by sculling a disguised craft, more likely by floating down some river, where the current helps him. Additionally, there is incidental goose shooting; without premeditation or malice aforethought, the duck shooter is going to get an occasional shot at geese. Still further, now and then geese are baited, the same as ducks. Lastly, we have pass shooting, the method most often attempted without tangible results. And when all is said and done, the most killing style of goose shooting is done from pits, surrounded by decoys, on the foraging grounds of the big fowl.

Much of goose stalking might be classed as incidental goose shooting; few men who have deliberately planned a goose hunt would depend on stalking the big birds. Goose stalking is done, but mostly by photographers and riflemen rather than by wingshots.   With a good flat-shooting high-power small-bore rifle, fitted with a low-power telescope sight, the shots being taken at ranges up to 300 yards, sport can be had second only to the most attractive work of the scatter gun. At that, Canada geese are uncertain creatures.   As a rule a flock of geese will allow a man to approach within 150 yards, any time or place.   But, let a man with a rifle walk up to within 200 yards and sit down for a steady shot, and away go the geese!   I have had them take wing at 300 yards, just because I stopped and sat down.

However, I am not advocating the use of a rifle on geese in sections where they can be decoyed; it makes the birds very wild and tends to "burn" them out of the country.   The photographer is doing the best stalking these days.   Charlie Cottar, on the open prairie in northern Alberta, crawled up to within twenty feet of a flock of Canadas resting in the tall grass.   Hamilton Laing, the Canadian naturalist, has done as much.   Such a feat is worthy of all admiration.

Sculling for geese is the recognized method of the British Isles, where most shooters appear to have a constitutional objection to the use of decoys.   English methods have something to recommend them and a good deal that might be condemned.   When a man pits his skill in sculling and his knowledge of the habits of game against the cunning and wariness of such game as geese, the chances are about even, and good sport should result.   Nevertheless, since many of the shots must be at long range, the tendency will be to use larger and larger guns; hence we find the Briton favoring shoulder arms of from 4 to 10 gauge, and apparently even still allowed punt guns throwing up to 2 or 3 pounds of shot!   Again, motorboats have been used, and shrapnel from a small cannon,

". . . there is just one goose, the great Canada 'honker.'"

Photo, above, Nat'l Assn. of Audubon Societies.   Photo, below, Charles B. Morss.

Above, mourning dove.   *Below,* trumpeter swan.

with a range of 300 or 400 yards—which is more in the nature of malicious persecution than anything else.

I am well satisfied to have punt shooting legally prohibited on inland waters, for that matter any other waters. Twenty-five to thirty years ago I saw considerable "big gun" shooting on the Sny, a back-water lake or river cut-off near the mouth of the Illinois River. Beginning at dusk and maintaining the work until after midnight, I once saw a market shooter bag forty geese, the majority of them Canadas. It was a moonlit night and the majority of the fowl were roosting alongshore. It appealed to me as good hunting, then; but we no longer have birds enough to stand such methods, even if the law permitted.

Drifting for geese down a shallow river that is filled with bars and islands where the geese use is a fascinating form of sport. The boat must be disguised to represent a floating log or something else familiar to the birds. There is always the uncertainty as to what the next bend may stage, and an equal uncertainty as to what the geese may do when discovered. Now they fly at the first glimpse of the boat, and again sit in unconcerned indifference until it is right on them. Sometimes they display every phase of goose perplexity and indecision, raising their heads for a better view of the suspicious craft, walking away, bunching together, to again resume their previous occupation. Whenever they turn as one bird, prepare for action, as they mean to fly.

Select a day when the wind is behind you, not only because that may aid the drift, but for the further reason that the fowl should rise against the wind and so come within reach of the gun. The skill of the boatman lies in keeping his craft precisely bow on, and so judging the current that when he relinquishes control of the boat it will float within shooting range.

Geese are very fond of large shallow lakes, that are grown up with reeds, rice, and cane. From preference, they breed in such waters, and there, previous to the southern migration, the sneakboat reaps a harvest. Such waters are full of pond-holes, pockets, cane-openings, and sometimes islands. Take care to push down wind, so that in rising the fowl will circle the boat. Since they often are hemmed in, the shooting is not difficult.

Pushing a sneakboat about for geese is good sport only after the first of October. Unfortunately, a lot of imma-ture fowl are slaughtered in this way on the breeding grounds. Like the young of all birds, the young goose is unsophisti-cated, requiring education before becoming real game. Too many Canadas are killed before they become old enough and wise enough to pit their wits against the gunner's. This shooting is mostly done by natives, for meat.

I recall a lake well up in northwestern Minnesota, where a dozen or more Canadas bred. I knew where the nests were, where the goslings paddled about and fed, where they roosted, and knew where to find them almost any day and any time of the day. When they became old enough to fly to forage, I was well aware of the precise route they would take going to the fields and returning, when they would go and when they would come. Under the circumstance it was no trouble to kill geese. They were not fair game.

As to pass shooting, there is never a man jack of a goose shooter or would-be goose shooter who hasn't attempted to take the big birds in passing. At certain places in certain seasons the honkers are continually passing. We can see them coming and see them going, and the thing is to get under them. Now and then we lie flat to see if they won't come right over us, but more likely make a dash for some fence corner, shock of grain, or tree, in line with the oncoming flight. The trouble about all this is that the geese don't come on. They have mighty good eyes and have seen our preliminary shuffling about from a distance of a full mile. They come on all right and perhaps draw a shot, at a distance of 150 yards high. That doesn't discourage a goose hunter much, particularly a boy, who may put in an entire day chasing about here and there trying to get right under the geese.

Nevertheless, pass shooting is done. At a certain locality on the Red River of Texas, Canada geese spend the winter. Except in high water, the river is a wide bed of sand, with a shallow and narrow current meandering about over the sand-bed. The geese feed widely, often twenty miles from the river, but never fail to return to the bars to roost. If undisturbed they will collect, flock after flock, to roost at one precise spot, night after night. Not only that, but they will leave the river in one direction, winging low over a certain bank. There is no use in trying to make a pit out where the geese roost, because your pit will soon fill with water. It remains then to make a blind and take them as they pass. That is done, taking care to change the location of the blind every few days.

There now remains the subject of shooting over decoys, the common way of taking any species of waterfowl. Let me go on record again as to my opinion of shooting over decoys. I am going to talk at length about decoys, including live decoys, and I'll tell of how to use them as well as I know;

but I am totally opposed to the use of live decoys for any kind
of waterfowl shooting.   I fully believe the time is here when
all live decoys should be strictly prohibited.

Decoys may be either live birds, the favorite decoy of the
seacoast shooter, or stools, generally profile, the preferred
decoy of the Middle West.   As is true of mallards, wild geese
decoy far more readily to live birds than to the best counterfeits.   The great advantage the live ones have over those of
sheet-iron lies in their ability to call.   The gregariousness
of the goose is such that the tethered decoy is just bound to
try to call down every flock that comes in sight.   Bet on it,
too, that he can do a better job of goose talking than the most
expert gunner who ever had the conceit taken out of him.
Let me say here, parenthetically, as closing the chapter on
goose calling, that only one man in a hundred can call ducks
perfectly, and of the skilled duck linguists not more than one
in a hundred is equally effective on geese.   Barring two or
three professional market shooters, I have heard no good
goose calling except what came from a goose's throat.   It follows that wherever geese are plentiful enough to warrant a
good systematic effort to take them, a few live decoys add
greatly to the value of the stool.

Lacking the live decoys or the profiles, makeshifts may be
made to serve.   A very good decoy can be made from a piece
of flat pine, cutting the body to shape, and tacking on neck,
head, and legs—one leg is enough.   Of course the makeshifts
should be painted if they are to serve any length of time.
Canvas sacks, shaped and stuffed with straw, mounted with
head and neck of cardboard will do very well.   In Nebraska,
on a pinch I have cut decoys from prairie sod, a horseweed
with one crooked root serving for neck and head; these worked

on a dark day. I have heard of snow geese being decoyed by newspapers, shaped roughly, held in place by clods, with neck of the usual horseweed. Any decoy is better than none, sometimes, for geese are not very knowing in detecting a fraud until close enough to afford a shot.

The live decoys need not be Canadas, necessarily, for the big fellows will come in nearly as well to brant, wavies, snow geese, or even the gray goose which is bred especially for decoys. However, our Canada is a tough lad and there will hardly be a day of good shooting when one or more will not be winged. If situated to do so, save them for decoys; they tame readily, more readily than any duck. Two of them will save their weight in No. 2 shot, eventually, and they will live longer than you do.

Natural blinds may be used in goose shooting; but, except in wheat and corn fields, where the fowl have become accustomed to the shocks, or in cover of such a nature that a blind cannot be detected by man or bird, don't attempt built-up blinds; dig pits. Inland geese, by the way, are shore birds; consequently nothing is to be gained by putting out decoys in open water, or in the middle of a lake. Not for Canadas. Pits must be sunk alongshore, on the sandbars or in the foraging fields. Two-thirds of the food of a Canada goose is obtained on dry land, which should be taken as a hint in locating a blind. A goose will not remain away from water, to be sure, but nine-tenths of his time is spent on land. Go to him, for he will not come to you.

I have spoken of burning out ducks. Geese can be burned out, too, and at best you need expect only one good day's shooting in any particular spot. If you have made a killing, that one day should be enough. Two hundred geese, using in some field or on a bar, make a great showing. The chances are that in one day's shooting they are all so alarmed that they won't come back. Hence, from necessity, the shooting pit should be changed daily. Or better, make no attempt to bag geese every day, but shoot one day and put in the next two investigating their new feeding and play grounds—gunning again on the third day. For that matter, the birds are no longer plentiful enough anywhere to stand continual pounding without being driven quite out of the neighborhood.

There are two places where the decoys should be placed, ordinarily: in the fields where the fowls resort for food, and on the bars where they come to roost and for water. Which place should be chosen depends on circumstances. Very often the gunner with good judgment may elect to put in one day on the lake or river and the next in the field. Again, he may decide to put in all his time in the wheat or corn, leaving the roost as a place of refuge, to hold the birds. It might happen, too, that he would elect to work the water exclusively, changing blinds from day to day, but leaving the fowl to forage in comfort. Except that the marksman has but a day or two for his outing and doesn't care at all for the man who comes after him, it won't do to harass the fowl continually on both roosting and foraging grounds.

Unlike some species of ducks, or unlike all kinds of ducks at times, the Canadas are pretty apt to feed during the day, sleeping at night like white folks. While as a rule I prefer to take my chances on a river bar or lake shore, yet it sometimes happens that the birds remain in the fields all day, not coming in to roost until after dark and departing at daybreak. Such being the case, taking into due cognizance the law for-

bidding shooting after sunset and before sunrise, we may have
to trace the big fellows to the fields and follow them there.

First as to bar shooting: In placing the decoys, remember
that the geese are going to come up over them against the
wind, and that they will likely pass entirely beyond the decoys
before alighting. Unlike ducks, geese are very much attached to their own flock, rarely caring to absolutely mingle
with strangers on first acquaintance, therefore may elect to
alight a hundred yards beyond the birds that have drawn
them in. They may remain right there, too, thenceforth
acting as a counter attraction to other flocks, quite putting
the shooter's gang out of the running. Therefore, *take your
geese when they come within easy range, and don't wait for
them to hover over the decoys like ducks.* The chances are
that you cannot kill more than a single bird to the shot anyhow—a single takes up too much space in the atmosphere for
that.

A sandbar with a narrow neck of water between it and the
shore is a favorite alighting place for geese. Dig the pit on
shore, and place the decoys on the bar; which, however, should
not be over thirty yards distant. While the intent of the
scheme is to have the birds pass over the open water between
shore and the decoys, the big fellows might pass beyond the
stool and thus be out of range.

It is pretty hard for the novice to judge the distance of
geese; generally they appear to be a third closer than they
are. It is a disagreeable experience to shoot into a flock
which appears to be within forty yards, only to hear the shot
whack into them and see the birds keep right on going, with
only the loss of a feather or two. It is hard to miss a flock of
geese at long range, with small shot, but it is a great deal

harder to kill one of them. Through shooting too soon, the inexperienced gunner is liable to cripple two birds to where he bags one. About the whole of goose shooting lies in preserving coolness, and using good judgment as to when to fire and when to wait. For my own part, I believe I have lost more geese through failure to shoot than because they were out of range.

Just the time of the day that goose shooting will be best on the bars is a matter which depends on local conditions. If the birds are observed flying up and down the river, keeping in midstream, conclude that they are just in from a migration or else preparing to migrate. On the other hand, seeing them crossing the river, back and forth, rely on it that they have become "localized," have acquired fixed local habits. Such habits must be studied. It will likely be learned that, except for two or three hours at some period of the day, it saves patience to remain in camp. The geese may come in to the river as early as ten o'clock, prepared to loiter until well on in the afternoon; or they may be absent until nearly sundown, when full-fed they simply pile down on the bar without hesitation or ceremony. For the late afternoon, it is only needful to find the exact roosting spot and get in there on time, with decoys perfectly placed. Two or three flocks are all that the gunner requires, and four geese is a heavy bag. Fred Kimble used to shoot forty geese in half a day, when we didn't know any better than to do such a thing.

Where the feeding grounds are to their liking, geese, if hunted too much, will simply change from one bar or island to another up or down the river, rarely deserting the country except when forced by stress of weather, failure of food, or constant persecution on the foraging grounds. I knew a flock of what was in the beginning thirteen geese to remain on the South Canadian River all winter, only four of their number being left for the northern migration.

Goose shooting is so difficult to obtain these days that I should not advise strictly keeping off their foraging fields. A bit of observation should tell you where to locate. Get right on the spot where they are in the habit of alighting, for you may note that they drop in at one precise point, day after day, thence traveling to other portions of the field on foot.

Dig the pit narrow and deep; if two men are shooting together, two pits should be dug instead of one. The correct idea is for the man, wearing neutral-tinted clothing, to about fill his pit, so that the geese cannot see anything wrong until the gunner rises to shoot. Do not consider a built-up structure; they will see it and avoid it, never waiting to learn if it is occupied. Of course, take advantage of any natural blind when it is to be had.

In field shooting, place the decoys very close to the blind, some of them right beside it. The wild geese think the counterfeits are feeding, and where one goose finds forage others may, so they will pass right over the pit. Field-shooting geese is the simplest of all goose shooting, especially in stormy weather when they are liable to tumble right down on top of the gun. I have had them come in so close that I was obliged to shoot at their heads in order not to ruin the bodies.

The chances are that the birds will come in rather high, and will make two circles, the second lower than the first, then head straight for the decoys, up wind, perhaps no more than ten feet above the stubble. It is then merely necessary to wait until they are close enough. Give due consideration to the fact that when under full headway a goose can sheer off and tower with a rapidity not second to any duck. Therefore, for the sake of the second barrel or subsequent shots, permit them to "put on brakes," which can be told by the heavy swishing as they beat against a forward momentum. Geese should not be shot head on except when close in, for they will beat back and get away. An incomer at forty yards looks right on top of the gun, but shoot at him and see where the next shot has to be taken. Shot at from the rear, geese alter their course very little.

Wild geese can see at half a mile that a man is red-headed and has but one eye, so don't bob up the red head or look at the birds with one eye. In order to prevent that, an acquaintance of mine carried a looking-glass into the pit. He said that looking into the mirror he could see every maneuver of the big birds, and the only trouble was that they never came near enough to shoot at!

Chapter XXI

GOOSE SHOOTING

GEESE are hard birds for the novice to judge. A Canada is a big bird, and simple human instinct is sure to insist that large flying objects are both close to us and moving slowly. Nothing except long experience and close observation will prevent a hunter from believing that a goose at forty yards is rods nearer than a teal at the same distance. Nothing else can persuade him that the teal is not flying faster. Once the fowl is killed we can tell, and I have killed very few geese that did not appear to fall an unreasonable distance away.

Certain errors of the beginner we might as well assume as highly probable. The goose will loom up so hugely, appear so close, that our eager youngster is going to snap straight at the mark, under the impression that it is so big it cannot be missed. Or he will whack away at the bulk of the flock, fancying the birds are so grouped that failing to hit at least one is out of the question.

Though one cannot measure distance in the air with a tape-measure, I have attempted an estimate of the space between geese, when they were flying in regular formation, finding it from seven to ten feet. Judging feet in the air is a most difficult feat. I have shot at ducks passing high overhead when the birds did not appear over eight inches

long, though they were closer to two feet.   In the same way,
many a Canada has winged above me when he didn't look over
a foot long, being however three feet.   That is what makes
it difficult to judge lead.   Some man will say, "Oh, I lead
him about two feet," when his actual lead was probably six.
In the same way the fowl may seemingly have only wing-
room, when there is actually five feet of space between birds
—too much air and too little goose.

Flock shots happen, of course, when the geese are bunched
and in confusion.   It is best not to chance them; instead,
invariably pick out a bird.   Pick one in the center if you
would make most sure of not feeling like a chump over missing
forty geese at forty yards.

When we are off the mark, what looks like six inches is more
than likely a foot and a half.   I have had this happen to me
so many times that I do not trust apparent inches any more,
and make no kick about missing unless the hold was center.
Elevation, and the twist given a gun as it comes to the shoulder, will throw the pattern off far enough without taking any
chance with the front bead not being in the right place.

The apparent size of the fowl is an indication of how near
he is; yet here is a most deceptive ground for judging range.
A deer that suddenly appears, always looks tremendously
large to me, and so does a Canada goose before he is close
enough to put salt on his tail.   A better guide than size is
feather markings.   When the colors no longer blend, when
the bill can be distinguished from the head, when the white
bar on the cheek is sharp, when the gleam of his eye can be
caught, we may be fairly assured that the big fellow is within
range.

It should be kept in mind that in goose shooting a man can-

not stand up to use his eyes in a normal manner.   He is down
in a pit, head beneath the level of the ground, and he must
stay down.   If under the best conditions a man attempts to
judge distance with one eye closed, he can't do it reliably; but
here he may steal but a glimpse out of the corner of one eye,
and a mistake means no goose, maybe.   An old goose shooter
relies largely on his ears, being able to tell within a few feet
of where the geese are by the whiff of their wings.   Sometimes, when it is unwise to budge a particle, say nothing of
turning up one eye, a good line on the actions of the oncoming
flock may be obtained from the actions of live decoys.   By a
turn of the head, a twist of bodies, an increased excitement,
they will tell precisely where the newcomers are.   I have had
decoys that talked steadily until the wild flock was well within
range, and then fell silent, waiting for the shot which they
well knew was coming.   On pain of losing your chance, don't
turn your face squarely towards geese that are low down and
coming in.   A man's face at ground level is altogether too
suggestive of the gravedigger, anyhow; to wild geese it means
dynamite.   As in all wildfowl shooting, the surest and easiest
shot is the one delivered before the birds are aware of danger.
An old goose hunter told me that it took twice the shock to
kill a goose after he got scared and began fighting to get away.
When he was floating peacefully along, the surprise just half
scared him to death.

Most of the misses with the first shot result from the geese
observing the spring of the marksman from his pit.   They
then have time to tack and climb before the shot reach them.
It is then, too, highly important that the first barrel catch
them napping, for in that case they lose their heads, bunching together, perhaps, instead of escaping in orderly goose

fashion.   Take a position in the pit that you can shoot from, and if that is possible keep it until the first shot is fired.   That doesn't mean bobbing up, then to balance, then to raise the gun, then to take alarm from seeing the birds getting away, then to miss the geese.

And keep two guns out of one pit!

I am not going to say much about lead or where to hold. If the average velocity of the shot over a 50-yard range is 700 feet and speed of flight is 100 feet per second, then the theoretical lead is 21 feet.   All this is complicated by swing, and the fact that a goose doesn't necessarily fly at the same rate all the time.   The whole question is made still more complex by the fact that what one man considers 4 feet at 50 yards another will call 6, and yet another 8.   The way to learn to shoot is to shoot until something is hit, then remember where you held when you hit it.   If you make the same lead for a similar shot and hit again, there you are, and it makes no difference whether you called the lead 10 feet or half of that.

The head, neck, and under the wings are the vulnerable spots on a goose, though if near enough we may drive such a weight of lead through him as to bring him down wherever he may be hit.   I am not one of those who advocate shooting at the head of a goose with fine shot.   Of course, hit him in the head and neck if you can; but generally be satisfied to land on him anywhere—shotguns are built that way.   Like the old darky when questioned about shooting his woodcock on the wing.   Said he "shot 'em on de wing and ebrywhah!"

As in duck shooting, accept it as fixed fact that if firing at a flock of geese, every shot after the first barrel must be sent high.   The exception would be when the birds are well past and driving straight on, when the hold would be low.

However, it is goose logic that if a shotgun is roaring under him, the safest thing is to climb. So get above him, anywhere from a foot to four times that, depending on distance and other things. I think that two misses in three, when the fowl are beating into the wind and rising, are due to under shooting. As a matter of fact, two thirds of all shotgun misses are due to under shooting, no matter what the game.

Before taking up the question of a gun for geese I have a word to say on the subject of shot. The shot pellets do the actual execution; certain sizes are best adapted to the work, and certain bores are best adapted to those missiles. It is a generally recognized truth that the larger the shot the bigger the bore from which they should be fired. I haven't the space to go into this elaborately, and just for the present will accept it as fact that big guns best handle big shot.

The English are great advocates of BB shot for goose shooting, while Americans are almost unanimous in preferring smaller sizes. It should be known, however, that American and English shot do not run evenly in size according to numbers. American BBs contain 56 pellets to the ounce, while the English run 84; Tatham's No. 2 is nearly the same size as the English BB (86 to the ounce). It is apparent, therefore, that when the Briton prefers BB and we like No. 2, we are pretty close together, and for guns large enough to pattern well with big shot, No. 2 is right.

American BBs are hardly to be recommended for any gun smaller than an 8 gauge, or for any load of less than 2½ ounces of shot. We must have patterns up to at least sixty yards, and the largest pellets that are certain to pattern on a goose are No. 2, from that down to No. 3 for open-bored guns and gauges smaller than 12. No other sizes have much to commend them in goose shooting, though of course the big birds have been killed in numbers with all sizes from 7s to buckshot. A single pellet of No. 2 shot has a striking energy of 6.31 foot pounds at 40 yards, while a pellet of No. 6 retains a striking energy of 1.96 pounds.

At last we are coming to the goose gun. Permit me to premise what I have to say with the acknowledgment that anybody is at liberty to differ with me, and the other fellow is just as liable to be right as I am. Moreover, what is sauce for the goose is sauce for the gander—somebody's gander!

I find that from East to West goose guns vary gradually in bore. Our English friends are very partial to powerful arms, heavily-loaded 4 and 8 bores. Coming along to our East Coast, the 8 gauge would be given preference, if the law did not intervene. As it is, the East Coast shooter prefers the modern 10 bore with its powerful load of 1⅝ ounces of shot. I use a 10-pound 10-bore myself, but am perfectly willing to confess that if the law permitted I'd own a big Parker or Greener 8 gauge, with 34-inch barrels, weighing 14 pounds, shooting 2½ ounces of No. 2 shot. That kind of gun will kill single geese at 80 yards, and no gun smaller can be relied upon to do it. However, we have to talk of things as they are, and not as they should be.

In the Mississippi Valley, I suppose that five 12 bores are in use to one of all other gauges. To make amends for the bore, if it is smaller than it should be for geese, most of these guns will be repeaters, automatics and pumps. What the pump gun cannot do beyond 60 yards it sure can under 50, and the result is a killing, opportunity being right. The late Captain du Bray, and his friends, have written alluringly of the 28-gauge on geese in Manitoba, and Texans once claimed that the 24-bore would kill geese all the same as a cannon. All true enough; yet allowance has to be made for the shooter and for shooting conditions.

I have never been able to see the horse sense in a big bore of light weight, or underloaded. Goose guns should be heavy for the bore, and the loads as heavy as it is possible to obtain. Featherweight guns are fine, when the piece has to be carried all day, on foot; but in a goose pit—shucks, a good-sized boy can handle a gun weighing 12 pounds. An 8 gauge will kill geese at 80 yards, when gun is of proper weight, loaded in proportion, but an 8 gauge carrying less than 2 ounces of shot won't do it. In the same way, having things to my liking, not permitted to use an 8, I'd like to have a 10 bore, 34-inch barrels, overbored to about 9 gauge, chambered for $3\frac{1}{4}$-inch cases, load 2 ounces of No. 2 shot, and the piece to weigh 12 pounds. That gun would account for geese at 75 yards.

We have pretty good goose guns now, however, in the 10-pound 10 bore with $1\frac{5}{8}$ ounces, driven at a stiff velocity. In the 12 bores no doubt the so-called long-range and super 12s, chambered for 3-inch cases, throwing $1\frac{3}{8}$ ounces of shot, have a few yards advantage of the standard 12s with $1\frac{1}{4}$ ounces of shot. The big 12s, weighing around 9 pounds, when bored to 80% and better, should account for geese up to 65 yards.

Below the 12, the smaller gauges must be considered make-shift goose guns. Some pretty powerful 16s have been made, mostly by the Parkers. These guns have 32-inch barrels, and weigh $7\frac{1}{2}$ pounds and more. Throwing $1\frac{1}{8}$ ounces of shot, such a gun wouldn't fall far back of a standard 12; but the point is that it couldn't be better than the 12, if so good. In the same way a good 20 bore shooting 1 ounce of shot will kill geese, any time they come under 45 yards; but few of us like to pass up geese under 70 yards.

Once on a time, a long while ago, I was shooting snipe in the spring, on an old, disused irrigation marsh on the Elkhorn River in Nebraska.   In the field were two "wavies."   They refused to leave, and every now and then I got a shot at them, firing six shots, not killing a goose.   The gun was a 28 gauge, and I used No. 4 shot on these geese, but just couldn't kill one.

Maybe I ought to say a word more about repeating shot-guns.   I can shoot or aim such a gun, I believe, just a bit better than I can a double.   I like pump guns, and would be perfectly content in a goose pit with one.   There isn't a thing wrong with a pump gun, except that the novice is nearly certain to prefer the repeater, automatic or pump, and he makes sorry work with it by shooting into flocks and crippling birds that he never should have shot at.*   This is not the fault of the gun; but the man with three to six shots at his command is nearly sure to rattle them all off, and devil take the consequence.   In the hands of an expert, who knows when to shoot and when to withhold his fire, the repeater is a splendid gun.

Summing up goose guns and goose loads, I might say that if we had no size of shot for geese other than No. 2, we should be just as well off.   The 10 bore handles No. 2 shot better than any 12 or any gun smaller than a 10.   More powerful 10 bores could be built than any we now have, but a 10 throwing 1⅝ ounces of shot is a pretty good goose gun, capable of killing geese up to 70 yards at least.

* And except besides, that an expert with a repeater can kill three, four or five geese where an expert with a double gun kills two.

Chapter XXII

GOOSE HUNTING STORIES

A LONG time ago, down in Alabama on the Tombigbee
River, where I was quail-shooting one winter, the field
hands kept coming to me with tales of a flock of geese which
roosted on an island near the shore. I found this was true.
The geese were always on that little island at daybreak in the
morning, though how they got there and where they came
from nobody knew.

I might have made a bag of geese right there with a shotgun, because the island was within reach, and when the birds
flew they came out over the west bank, usually not over twenty
feet high, and I had an old hammer-model pump gun which
was good for geese. It looked possible to make a killing with
the shotgun, but having lately come into possession of a
single-shot .25/25 rifle, and having thinned out the buzzards
and hawks, I was bent on trying this gun on geese. My
rifle, a Stevens, had a set trigger and was mounted with a
Mogg 10-power scope. If I ever crossed the hairs on a
goose and touched the trigger, that goose was mine; for not
only was that particular rifle just right for the job, but I
had not long past been a *schützenfest* enthusiast of standing
in St. Louis, where the *scheutzer* boys were good.

The river was no more than a quarter of a mile from the
house, but I had to go some distance downstream. I got out

before daylight, and crawled the last hundred yards, which brought me to the bank of the river right opposite the geese. Raising up, I could see them as dim black objects, all sitting in the grass, not even a guard out. The only thing that disturbed me was that a little fringe of rushes was right between me and the geese, and I must shoot sitting to avoid starting the geese. I expected to find an opening to shoot through when it became lighter.

By and by it became lighter, and I could see the geese, fairly massed—a good forty of them, I thought. I had never before been so close to undisturbed Canada geese, and decided to take a look at them through the glass. Before, I couldn't see the geese very plainly, because cane and rush stalks intervened, and I didn't dare to raise my head above them. Sitting flat, elbow resting on knees, a secure rest, I trained the 'scope on that flock of Canadas. Never before had I seen such a sight! Magically the fringe of rushes had all disappeared; there wasn't a thing in the way. Rank on rank the geese sat before me, the nearest great honker looking no more than three rifle lengths away. I could have laid the crossed hairs on his eye. I could have shot off his head without the slightest difficulty—so it seemed.

Back of him were other geese in line, and knowing the power of my rifle, I thought I'd shoot through about three of them. So I laid the crossed hairs on the butt of his wing and touched the trigger.

Up went the geese! Such a fuss they made. They came right over my head, not fifteen feet high. I tried to reload and get in another shot, but couldn't manage it.

The next thing was to look for the dead geese. But you already know the rest; there were no dead geese.

It was the rottenest shot that I ever had made. Investigation developed that my bullet had clipped twigs within three feet of the muzzle. I could see that from my position it was bound to be so. But again sighting through the 'scope the remaining twigs were gone.

I went back to the house and told Joseph A. Graham, who was with me, that a telescope could see right through brush and never see it at all. He was skeptical, in fact didn't believe it. According to him, I'd simply developed buck-fever.

It was not until years after that I learned the reason. Compared with the human eye, the telescope has a great big pupil. With the 'scope you of course can't see through an object, as I told Mr. Graham had happened; but the rays of light come into the 'scope all around a small object, thence are deflected to a center, and near small objects inside the focus appear as mere shadows, if seen at all. The lesson I got was that if the eye sees objects in front of a rifle which may deflect the bullet, never mind what the telescope says, the obstructions are there.*

WILD AND WOOLLY GOOSE HUNTERS

UNCLE BILLY HARDIN was a confirmed Platte River goose shooter of my acquaintance, always ready to affirm that no other stream at all compared with the Platte. In this I quite agreed with him; but I coaxed him down on the South Canadian in Oklahoma one spring, and this too was a long time ago.

Billy was a good shot, good goose shot and good any other

---

* As only sighting through the rifle's bore itself might show. It should be remembered that the telescope is mounted considerably higher than the bore.

sort of shot.   One time, in an inter-city pigeon match between
St. Louis and Omaha, Billy belonged to the Omaha team.
It was in the old live-bird shooting days.   Contestants from
the two teams were paired off, and the St. Louis plan for win-
ning the match was for every man to hold his individual opponent even, or go him one better.

Jimmy Haggerty was the best known shot on the St. Louis
team, and he rejoiced exceedingly and noisily that luck had
drawn him against a little, sawed-off, moon-faced, moon-eyed,
gray-headed bit of a fat man.   As the race progressed, the
grin died from the face of the Mound City expert; he killed
24 straight, and then, because Uncle Billy wouldn't crack, he
did so himself, losing the last bird.   Billy got his 25, of which
he took 17 with the first barrel, and he had to get the last bird
in order to win the match for his home team.   That was Uncle
Billy.   He was besides more than a good shot, being a cunning
cook, a grand trencherman, a hale fellow, with humor spring-
fed and proof against drouths.

As aforesaid, Billy had to be coaxed from his beloved Platte.
It couldn't have been done except the geese were wintering on
the South Canadian and hadn't yet reached the Nebraska
stream.   He had heard of the Canadian, its perpetual gales,
its sand-storms, its sudden and unaccountable rises, ending
sport, its treacherous quicksands into which the unwary goose
shooter might find the going down easier than the coming up.
Nevertheless, in March his Platte was still ice-bound while
the sun surely glowed mellowly on the southern river, and
goose shooting was goose shooting.

We made our headquarters at Fay, Okla., four miles from
the river, and the section boss, a friend of mine, took us down
on his handcar—sink-box, tent, lunch, coffee-pot, supplies,

decoys, shells, all complete. Billy had no intention of going without his coffee, and he meant that very day to fry the breast of a goose for lunch. He made the coffee, but didn't fry the goose, for a good reason.

We sunk our box on a bar, adjacent to a shallow and narrow current, some 200 yards below a large island, covered with swamp willows and sagebrush. Everything complete, two dozen profile decoys properly placed, and a foot-high hedge of sagebrush about the box, we got in and waited. Going down, we had seen plenty of geese, passing high overhead on their way to feeding grounds, but when we got to the river, while droppings and tracks were everywhere, no geese were in sight. We didn't worry at first, for the section man said they would come in about ten o'clock.

It was a clear spring morning. That is, it should have been clear, for not a cloud was in sight, there was not a hint of moisture in the air. But the sun was dim, red and far, for the whole world was so filled with moving sand as to make a thick, gray haze, pelting us in gusts and waves. Off down the river, we could see those waves coming, rolling up twenty feet high, thick and white. Then it struck us missile-like, with a spiteful, drizzling hum, pouring into the box, banking up against our hedge, peppering down our backs, and getting into Uncle Billy's Greener gun, whereat he abused it savagely. And no geese came—not one.

"What did I tell you!" growled Billy. "No goose is fool enough to stay in a place like this; if he tried to drink the water, he'd get so ballasted with sand that he couldn't wiggle his tail, let alone fly. Why, we couldn't shoot through air like this—stop the shot in fifty feet. Besides, there won't be any water here pretty soon—all covered by a couple of feet of sand. We're a half foot deeper in the ground now than when we came here this morning."

"Guess you are right about the water being covered with sand, Billy. They tell me that the river, which appears to have only a couple of feet of water in it, is really fifty feet deep. Straight down under us the current is running so swift that a Mississippi River steamboat couldn't breast it. They say that the sand drifting into it has raised this false or upper bed of the river a hundred and fifty feet above where it once flowed, and that it is now running a hundred and fifty feet higher than the level of the land just over those hills. Why doesn't the river get out? It can't, because as the river bed rises, the hills hemming it in rise also through sand blowing out of the river and forming ridges. Scientists say that in the course of another hundred thousand years the bed of this river will be a thousand feet above the level of the adjacent country. Then some day she'll spring a leak through her wall of sand and there will be lakes all over western Oklahoma.—Gosh, I'd like to see the day—think of the ducks and geese we'd have!"

"If you keep on livin' here in Oklahoma the state will soon have a reputation for liars not second to California."

"All right, Uncle Billy, but a man's got to have some imagination to appreciate this country," I told him. "You'll find it helps your shooting, too."

"Imagination, hell! Help my shooting! I can beat you right now this minute—show me some geese!"

However, I couldn't show him any geese. Along about noon, not having secured a shot, we retreated to the brushy shelter of the island, and with difficulty started a fire. I had a jug of water, but Uncle Billy had a theory that river water made odds the best coffee, so he hunted a place on the lee shore, where the water was fairly clear, and filled his pot. I didn't think it wise to tell him that the stream contained salt, alkali, sulphur, copperas, alum and the devil knew what besides. Billy made that coffee with the greatest care and gave me the first cup, waiting anxiously for the verdict.

"Best coffee I ever tasted, Billy," I declared, carefully emptying my cup where it wouldn't do any harm.

"Of course, of course, son. Did you ever know me to make a poor cup of coffee? Brought this coffee from Omaha. Couldn't trust 'em to have my blend down here. *Now what in Sam Hill is the matter with this coffee?*

"You damned old scoundrel," he roared at me. "You put something in it! You'd swaller poison to get a laugh on somebody else. Think I've eaten so much alkali that I can't taste any more?"

Uncle Billy glared most belligerently, as he emptied the pot of coffee. "Gimme that jug o' clear water," he barked. "Hell's fire is too good for you, a-bringin' me to such a pizen hole as this."

After a while, having fed well and the day being warm enough, we covered our heads from the sand and had a snooze. Uncle Billy, his face muffled in a vast bandanna which I had brought for the purpose, declared me the equal of "any dirty Arab."

At four o'clock the first geese came in. Very unexpectedly, to me, they came, not from the fields but from up the river. All were talking, and as it turned out this must have been about some goose happening where they came from. I believe that I saw more geese in the next hour than I ever had seen anywhere in a whole day. Some of them decoyed, more did not.

They were spread across the whole width of the river; there was never a minute when geese were not in sight, above us, below, to either side. They flew low, didn't seem to see us, and we had an average of a shot a minute.

Billy was in his glory. Shells were popped in and empties snapped out, while the big Greener roared steadily. No geese were retrieved, for they either fell on the sand or, striking the shallow water floated but a few yards downstream. Presently, when we must have had thirty geese, I stopped and lit a pipe. There was no bag limit in those days, but even a dozen brace is an awful pile of geese.

Uncle Billy's pink face was a study as he stared at me, his blue eyes blazing.

"Why don't you shoot, you chump? Never see a time like this in your fool life again. I have been shooting geese for forty years and I never did. Here, gimme your gun!"

"Billy, hadn't we better quit and get ashore?" I asked.

"Quit and get ashore! What d'ye mean? Ain't we ashore now? Afraid we can't carry them across—is that it? You got quicksand on your mind now?"

"No, Billy; but the section foreman told me that he had orders to watch the bridge. They wired him that there was sudden water, a big rain, way up the river some place. I've been figuring that's what's the matter with the geese—driven out up the river."

"Get down, son! Please git down and give me a chance, if you won't shoot yourself. Load your gun for me! Forty of 'em, if a goose."

"Hear that? Hear it, Billy! That's sudden water coming! Never mind the geese! Come on!"

I grabbed Billy's gun, as he stood up to look for what

I heard, still doubting me. I legged it as hard as I could for the island, leaving geese, decoys, shells, everything. Billy followed.

Up the long reach which swept around the south side of the island I saw a wave of water coming which seemed to be six feet high, its top foam-crested. From bank to bank three quarters of a mile wide, tumbling and roaring as it came, needless to say the look of that Canadian River "rise" lives in my memory still. It scared me pink.

We got to the island before the water came; then, safe for the present, watched it sweep on. In less than a minute there was eight feet of water where our pit had been. All our geese were gone—decoys and all. Between us and the shore, no great distance, the current rolled a deep, angry red; I later learned that the head or bore traveled fifteen miles an hour. The river continued to rise and soon would submerge our island. It was less than a hundred yards to the north bank, but we never could make it swimming.

"Bang! Bang!" roared Billy's gun, at my elbow. Unseen by me, a bunch of geese had attempted to alight on the shore of our diminishing island. Billy had killed a brace. "Mark west," he shouted, "here come more!"

I was too worried to notice him further, though I heard him shout again. Our predicament had been noted by the section gang at the bridge a half mile up, and they were launching something. It turned out to be a great piece of bridge timber, which they intended floating down to us.

The gang waded out, pushing and guiding the twenty-foot length of the fifteen-inch-square timber. By and by when they could no longer wade, the big boss mounted the timber. Guiding it and somehow keeping right side up, by kicking

with one foot and the other, he headed for the point of our
island.   He came on very fast and I saw that despite his efforts the timber would sweep past.   Shucking my boots, I
gave Billy my gun and went out to meet the boss.   Together
we managed to bring the timber close enough for Billy to
mount it with the two guns.   My boots were abandoned along
with Uncle Billy's geese.

Now we headed for the north bank, the great log tossing in
the current like a bronco.   One of us swimming at the bow
and the other the stern, we kept gradually working across, the
water now and then breaking over our heads.   How Uncle
Billy kept on top I never knew.   It was a fight for life with
the chances about even that we lost a man or two.   We had
only a hundred yards to gain, but the river bank swung northward, and with the heavy wind against the current we had a
sea to deal with the like of which I never had imagined possible.   If I had before been scared pink I now must have
been the color of a peeled potato.

"Hold on, fellows!   Here they come!   Charley, take your
damn gun off my lap!"

Slam bang! barked the Greener.

I caught my gun sliding into deep water, and the grinning
section boss steadied the log while the old goose-shooting fool
recovered his balance.

We caught the dead goose as it came drifting down, and with
huge satisfaction Uncle Billy shouted:

"Gentlemen of the jury, your Uncle Billy said fried goose
breast for supper tonight, and fried goose breast she is.
Eggnog too if there's any clean water—left in—hey, steady
there, you'll get me wet!"

A quarter of a mile on down we struck an eddy which helped

us inshore.   If you have never tried swimming with a shot-gun in one hand and a 15 x 15 timber in the other, take it from me that an eddy is a wonderful gift of nature.   When I crawled up the muddy, slippery bank of the Canadian in my sock feet and poured the red water out of my gun, I think if I had been one of those hide-away Oklahoma newcomers and needed to start my life over again I'd have changed my name to Eddy Timber.

And now, as I look back down the years, I pine for the great Canadas, long since gone for the most part from the South Canadian, and for dear old Uncle Billy Hardin, himself but a tender memory.

Chapter XXIII

DUCK SHOOTING OVER DECOYS

DECOYS are an invention of the devil or of his near relative, the American market shooter—anyhow they are of American origin. Very rightly our English cousin will have none of them. He considers them un-British and unsportsmanlike, to be classed merely as "Yankee tricks." The stanch Englishman is a sportsman or nothing. His ethics are rock-foundationed, not to say hidebound. Rather than entice the birds by an unworthy device, which originated, moreover, outside of his own country, he prefers to crawl forty rods to get a pot shot—stalking the fowl, he calls it. However, out in the "colonies" he too can stoop to using decoys after a fashion; shoot with him and you'll very likely wonder if he hasn't been at it all his life and holds a master's degree as a wing shot.

Undeniably, however, decoys lead to the death of a lot of ducks, and if I were interested solely in seeing that the wild-fowl were not hurt, I should absolutely forbid their use. Next I should prohibit the possession of automatic shotguns, pumpguns, doublebarrels, singlebarrels, and breechloaders of all kinds; additionally, I should forbid fall shooting as well as spring shooting, in every state except Texas, which is right handy to me. Also, I would make the bag limit one hundred birds a season and the license fee $100 a year—nobody exempt from the provisions of this law except game wardens, being myself a game warden. I would give the game warden $100 for every violator of the law he managed to catch; and wouldn't put the depredator in a comfortable jail or let him pay a fine, but force him to sit ten days on a river in a sand-pit in January, without his gun and without his bottle, wading the icy stream for exercise. And I would guarantee results.

As I have said before, it is not my business here to tell how to keep the ducks from being shot, but how to shoot them. The telling is not altogether to my liking, for I do not believe in the birds being killed—other than the few some friends and I shoot.

First find your ducks. Blinds are useless, decoys are useless, duck calls are useless, guns are useless, unless you know where the ducks are. The birds are somewhere, remember. Good authorities have estimated that there is in the United States one wild duck for every man, woman and child. But don't let any state fool you into the belief that she has *your* duck and charge you $25 for shooting it, unless you know the duck is there. Reminds me of the classical notice tacked on a tree: *"Shooters are welcome on this place. Kill all the birds you like. Come to the house for dinner when you hear the bell ring."* As originally applied, there wasn't a head of game on the place; there wasn't any house; there wasn't any bell, and there wasn't any dinner.

Granted you know where your duck is, the next thing is to get him within reach of the gun. That means decoys properly placed, a blind rightly constructed, and a duck call in tune. The veteran duck shot knows something besides aligning his gun, if you will believe me. On a certain Western river, twenty-five years ago, two market gunners killed 7000

ducks in two weeks' time.   In the meantime the local hunters,
and they could shoot, too, killed anywhere from ten to fifty
birds apiece.   One party planned artfully, executed skilfully,
knew duck habits, knew the entire game—the others shot haphazard, as most of us do.

PLANNING A CAMPAIGN

A GOOD general depends for his success upon his plan of
battle; this being based on what the other fellow ought reason-
ably to do.   Duck shooting is no less a contest of wits.   The
wild birds are not coming into our trap if they know it is there.
We are not going to outwit them if they know more of men's
habits than we do of the habits of ducks.   Waterfowl have
general habits and local habits, habits peculiar to some species
and habits common to all.   Who knows all about ducks, anyhow?   How many can tell by the manner of a wildfowl's
flight when he is preparing to migrate, when he has just come
in from a 300-mile flight, when he is casting about lazily in
search of playmates, when he is on his way to foraging grounds
and when he is returning?   How many nowadays can even tell
what kind of duck they see flying by?   Our duck may have
become localized, knowing every bunch of cattails, or he may
be a newcomer and "green" in his new surroundings.   Do we
always know when he is looking for a place to alight, or when
nothing short of a stroke of lightning could prevent him
from going about his business?   Of course, here and there a
hunter knows all about ducks; which is more than I do.   Suffice it to say it is utterly futile to attempt to prescribe actions
for given situations.   The best that can be done is to give
some general principles.

California, Illinois and Long Island wildfowlers of the best gunning waters

"Wherever wild ducks resort there will usually be found some native growth which will serve perfectly for you to hide in, as a blind."

Circumstances alter cases in duck hunting the same as in other matters. There are places and times, now more rare than twenty-five years ago, when anybody could kill ducks. I have in mind a small lake in South Dakota where a few thousand webfeet were hatched and reared, to be reinforced in early October by other thousands coming down from the north. Desiring a duck shoot, the hunter drove up to the sunny side of a haystack, hitched his team at the side of the stack where the hay appeared to be sweetest and finest, pulled the boat he had hidden thereabout out into an open waterway and lazily pushed out a few rods.

There was not a minute of any time from daylight until dark when ducks were not in sight. Wild rice grew in one end of the lake, and a great patch of blackened smartweed filled a long slough that led out of it; tall cane grew everywhere, with reaches and ponds and passages of open water. Push the boat into a clump of rank cane to hold it steady; not much need to hide it, because the birds would fly low and be atop of you before they knew it. Have enough open water in front to drop the ducks into, making retrieving easy. Pull off your coat and place it over the ammunition box for a seat— soon be too hot for a coat. Light your pipe, and when a duck or a pair of ducks or a flock of ducks come along, flying just right to fall precisely where you wanted them when killed, why, shoot!

If satisfied with passing birds, no decoys were needed. If desirous of making the work easy, with flocks of pintails and mallards beating the air and hovering above the blocks, then throw out a few decoys. No need to be in a hurry, no need to worry; you couldn't shoot all of the ducks anyhow, no, no!

In the old days I have shot until threatened with a gun-

headache, whereupon I'd lie down in the boat and let 'em fly. Such was duck shooting in the Northwest thirty years ago, when there was no more necessity for planning a duck campaign than there is to search for a fighting Irishman in a "shindy." But thirty years is more than a quarter of a century—today we have better guns, a hundred times as many shooters, and I suppose a hundred times less fowl to shoot at.

A well-planned duck campaign in these days implies such a scheme of action that a proper bag can be made day after day *without burning the ducks out.* Just keep that in mind; the birds are not to be burnt out, if there is any way to avoid it and still make a bag.

Generally the fowl will mass up somewhere to roost, coming in from a little before sundown until after dark, leaving at daybreak. They will decoy on the roosting ground beyond a doubt—pile in on top of the gunner faster than he can load, despite all he can do to keep them out; even if the shooter stands up as bold as a soldier walking guard, they will drop in, showing no sense about it whatever. This for a night or two—and then they will all be gone. Moreover, they will be gone from their feeding ground, gone from their playground, gone from the neighborhood, burnt out. If the sport is to last, keep off the roost, and don't fire a shot before daylight or one after sundown. If you have not had fair success, if it is the last day or two of the hunt, if you have no regard for the man who is to follow, then go on the roosting ground and take your toll—such is the way of the world anyhow. Knowingly and wilfully burning ducks out is a simple, unadulterated form of hoggishness.

Not only should ducks be allowed to roost in peace, but

they should be privileged to feed without molestation. A wild duck has a natural and extreme regard for a well-filled crop. The world in which to forage is beneath his wings; why should he remain with you and go hungry day after day in order to give you a chance to kill him? Be sure he won't do it.

I remember when two of us, youngsters, were shooting on the Minnesota River, at a place where the stream had broadened and enlarged into a lake. By and by we discovered that the mallards and pintails, not the other ducks, left the water about two o'clock in the afternoon, all going to some great stubble-fields about four miles away. We thought it a wise scheme to go to those fields, dig pits and wait for the ducks. The first day we made a big bag, the second day a small one, the third day none, and the fourth we went back to the lake, only to find it deserted as well. We had ruined the shooting by getting on the foraging ground, and as I have previously reiterated that happens many times.

It is true that there are exceptional localities, pin-oak slashes where the mallards live, wild rice lakes, smartweed sloughs, shallow ponds where the bluewings and shovelers "grabble"—places on which we must shoot right on the roosting and feeding ground because the birds remain there all through the day and night. But the rule of keeping off the roosting and the feeding grounds holds good nevertheless.

Where are we to shoot, then? Well, somewhere in the vicinity there probably will be well-hidden ponds or lakes that are not easily invaded without wings. There, filled to the necks, satisfied, lazy, the ducks will come to rest and to play, to preen their feathers and satisfy their gregarious instincts. Go there to shoot and tell no one of your find.

By shifting the blind now and then from one end of the pond
to the other, from one lake to another, fine sport can be had
day after day as long as the season lasts.

The same scheme won't always work on every particular
ground. On a certain island-dotted, shallow, sand-barred
river, the ducks were using by the million (we will say million,
because the word is short and easy to write), coming in mostly
at night and going out early in the morning. Ten miles away
was a great flat, known as the Drummond Marsh—the foraging ground. Three miles from the river lay Indian Lake, a
wooded, willow-fringed, brush-hidden swamp, rather off the
line of flight from river to feeding ground. From twelve
o'clock until evening the mallards plumped into Indian Lake,
where we were waiting for them.

By and by something went wrong. We found the ducks
already on the lake when we got there at noon, and, shot at,
they all went off together. Presently we discovered the reason. Hunters were overrunning the Drummond Marshes,
and the birds had changed from day feeding to night feeding.
Thereafter they left the foraging ground very early and came
into our lake long before we were ready for them. By getting
into our blinds at peep o' day, we had just as good shooting as
before.

Again on this river, in migrating time, late fall, no shooting was to be had except on the sandbars. A redhead flight
was on, the birds flying nowhere except down the middle of the
river. They came in low, tired from an all night's flight
ahead of ice and snow. So anxious were they to rest, so
quick to drop in among the decoys, it was difficult to keep them
from alighting. When a flock went on south they never came
back. But more flocks followed, and for three days it was

nothing but redheads, with a few canvasbacks and bluebills. Ice formed on the still reaches, the north wind whistled and drove the sand into our faces, and, notwithstanding the ducks were pouring in, we frequently had to quit and race up and down the bar to keep from literally freezing. Naturally, there was no danger of burning those ducks out, because they wouldn't stay anyhow.

Whatever the plan, be sure there is knowledge and reason back of it. Don't shoot after night or before daybreak; not only because it is against the law but because it is a fool thing to do. Let the birds roost in peace and feed in comfort. And don't shoot every day from one blind. Don't burn out the birds in Oklahoma, because the fowl we get here are only too well aware of the great state of Texas lying before them to the south. We Oklahomans don't owe the Texas boys anything, anyhow. You see, in Texas the fowl can't be burnt out so easily, not only having generally more water but being there for the winter.

Inland states generally prohibit the use of sink-boxes. Some forbid artificial blinds of any kind, and others outlaw any blind that is built away from the shore. Whatever the law of the state, even where artificial blinds of any kind are termed illegal, it is rare that a clear definition is given as to precisely what does constitute an artificial blind. Certainly, where ducks are shot over decoys it is necessary for the gunner to hide behind something, and if blinds other than those afforded by nature were absolutely forbidden, it would quite do away with shooting on open rivers and the bare shores of lakes.

I am therefore going to take it for granted that the wildfowler is permitted to build his blind after his own liking, in accordance with the needs of the place and time. Likewise, we are of course discussing shooting on unrestricted water and without the services of guides or pushers. This blind may vary from a few rushes, cane, or wild rice bent over the boat to the permanent structures erected in the Gulf of Mexico, with a locker for the lunch-basket, a rack for an extra gun, a crate for the dog, and a swivel chair neatly cushioned. In France, I am told, still more elaborate blinds are built, in the cliffs along the seashore—rooms dug into the earth, having peep-holes commanding the water, and space inside for cooking, eating and sleeping. On an island in the Tennessee River, below Muscle Shoals, a man made a blind by tunneling from a landing place under a forty-foot bank until he came out under the floor of a little shack. This blind was kept heavily baited with corn for the geese, and that man killed more geese than forty ordinary goose hunters. In New England's ponds there are many permanent blinds, with a shanty and an elaborate decoy pen in conjunction—regular traps, called shooting stands.

The diving ducks, canvasbacks, redheads and broadbills must generally be shot over deep water, from a floating battery on the tidewater bay or river estuary, from shore blinds sunk far below tideline, and from sink-boxes and pole blinds on the lakes. I have never been in a battery, and do not mean to give second-hand information. Sink-boxes, other than the battery type, are usually fixed to piling, driven deep and strong enough to withstand storms, the top just above water level. I have shot from them, both in deep water and in shallow—also in quicksand which would not bear having pits dug. In every instance I have found the sink-box a killing device, and a devilish uncomfortable one to shoot from. It

savors too much of professionalism, either market hunter or
professional guide, to receive much consideration here.   The
same objection applies to all permanent blinds, of which I
know there are many.   They are rarely the work of the man
who shoots from them; I have in mind especially the deep,
plank-lined hides in which four or five men can shoot standing
erect, that salt-water baymen guides use.   Blinds, from my
point of view, are the simple hiding places which a man can
throw together in a few minutes.

Wherever wild ducks resort there will usually be found
some native growth which will serve perfectly for you to
hide in, as a blind.   It may be elbow brush, sage, rushes,
cane, wild rice, swamp willows, weeds, cattails.   Whatever
plant grows rankly in the vicinity, being at the same time of
a nature to afford a partial hiding place of itself, use that and
little else.   Many successful blinds are built of green cedar
boughs; but shooters who have never seen them believe in them
with difficulty.   Study the surrounding vegetation, and do
your best to imitate dense spots with which the fowl are quite
familiar.   Don't make a blind of wood in a grass country,
or of grass where nothing but timber grows.   One hunter
tells of using an old hollow, water-tight stump, which nature
had placed in the open water of a Texas lake, the hole in the
top of the stump being big enough to take in the fat man,
all but his head which was covered with—a Texas hat.   The
snag served its purpose admirably, because there were other
similar stumps all about; but had it been placed where trees
did not grow, it would have been about as effective as a United
States regimental flag.   Shooting from stumps, also from
muskrat houses, even piles of brush, is both successful and
common in some localities.   Stump blinds are common on

overflow waters, such as the famous Reelfoot Lake. Grass blinds are the blinds of the equally famous timberless marshes, such as the great old-time marshes in the vicinity of Toledo, Ohio, and Detroit, Michigan.

Don't make the blind too big, don't make it too opaque, don't make it conspicuous in any way. Remember, if your clothing is suitable, if it blends and you know how to keep still, the ducks will not see you, but they surely will see the blind, and may regard it as nothing short of a scarecrow. Any blind, however skilfully built, is worthless unless it fits the surroundings. Be very sure to leave those surroundings intact—broken reeds, trampled cane, the white butts where twigs were cut, anything that couldn't possibly have grown in that shape, is as bad as a white tent with smoke coming from a stove-pipe.

Don't make a blind that is a corking good hiding place but which you cannot shoot from without making perceptible movements. Neither should you so hide yourself that you cannot have a clear view, at least in the directions from which the birds are expected to come. Set the blind with due appreciation of the wind and water; duly considering where the ducks are coming from, where they will circle, where they will turn, where they will "hover," where alight and where the dead birds will fall—no use in dropping birds in the current of a swift river or in cane so dense that they cannot be retrieved. Two guns in a blind are one too many; if need be, have two blinds but a few feet apart.

When the birds show an inclination to shy from the stand, there may be something wrong with it, but more probably it has simply been used too much. So change to some other point—if you can! Unless it is likely that someone else will unwelcomely come in and take possession of it, do not destroy an old blind; leave it there for the ducks to become accustomed to—the very best blind is the one the ducks have tested many times and found innocent.   Finally, don't build your blind on another man's line of flight, unless you can lick him.

Wear any kind of clothing except black or white.   If you must wear a black coat, hang it on top of the blind and stay in camp playing penny ante.   Yellow canvas will do in a dead-grass blind and nowhere else.   Batteries or sink-boxes are usually painted the color of the water (the bottom has a lot to say about the color) and the clothing should be a greenish drab instead of the dead-grass brown that is commonly sold.   For another thing, the average hunting coat will turn dark when wet—quite dark; which is a bad fault, sometimes. There is a mackintosh union-suit rig, developed for use in the navy during the World War, which is excellent for use in bad weather.   It does not readily turn color.

There is more in keeping still than there is in being dressed correctly.   In fact, the first essential as to dress is the necessary protection for warmth and proper freedom of movement so you won't be hampered in shooting.   As to this, the hunting friend whose helpful editing has a great deal to do with the preparation of this book is one of those who are not tied down by convention, and he, so he says, has demonstrated that broadbills can be shot from a battery by a very indifferent shot wearing a very long and very black raincoat. He also says that there apparently is no law in the broadbill statutes that forbids a guide to wear a muskrat cap of inky hue, and wave it to successfully attract passing flocks.

Chapter XXIV

DUCK HUNTING EQUIPMENT

Decoys

AS to decoys, much might be written, but less will do. Decoys may be live birds—mallards or gray ducks, tamed or bred in domestication—or painted wooden blocks or even dead fowl "set up."

Live decoys are odds the most effective and far the most troublesome. The mallard is wise, suspicious and wary; where he has been much hammered over the blocks he can no longer be fooled by make-believe birds. He may circle them again and again, perhaps coming close enough to afford passing shots, but he will not "hover" for the shot that might be taken with a rifle; not unless he sees living fowl beneath him.

In fact, so far as the mallard alone is concerned, a half dozen tethered members of his own breed are worth fifty counterfeits made of wood. Perhaps there is a persistent caller or two among the live decoys, perhaps an old hen will have the habit of raising her wings to give them a vigorous flap, or a greenhead may be persistent in tilting up to see how close he can come to reaching the bottom. Always your bunch of live decoys will be doing something unbearably enticing. When all other conditions are in your favor, down come the wild birds, fairly piling over one another to be the first in the

water. Of course the whistling lead has every opportunity
to mow through the mass, and I never have seen a duck hunter
who wouldn't shoot into the thickest part of a flock descending
tail-first.

It is the custom of duck shooters to use live decoys in con-
nection with blocks, say eight to a dozen live to two dozen in-
animate.   The size of the display is what attracts the travelers, and, on nearer view, the live birds, peaceful, contented,
welcoming, prove irresistible.

Live decoys are troublesome to handle, hence their restricted use. Keeping and transporting them affords its
own problems, and, arrived at the blind, they must be tethered,
at least some of them, to prevent their immediately leaving,
straying, playing hooky, drifting away or getting into the
wrong position for the game.

A good scheme with live decoys, especially where they are
not all tethered, is to bait a hole; take them out hungry,
whereupon they will tip up and fish for their breakfast—all
of which looks proper and right from a duck's-eye view.
When practicable, place your group of living birds a trifle
to one side of the blocks, leaving room enough between for
the wild birds to alight.   Keep in mind that a duck drops
in against the wind, and if he doesn't set his wings and "win-
nows" somewhere within fifty to seventy-five feet of the gun,
either the decoys are wrongly placed or else it's the blind.

For mallards alone, on typical mallard ground, small pond-
holes, oak slashes, timbered lakes—places where the vision of
the fowls has a restricted sweep—a half-dozen live decoys are
all that is needed, omitting the blocks.

Pintails, gadwalls, widgeon, and all varieties of teal, decoy
well to blocks.   Any of these birds will come to mallards, and,

owing to the bright colors of the drakes, mallard decoys are
very conspicuous.   Still, it is the common practice when shooting mixed ducks to use a mixed stool—some mallards, a bunch
of pintails or group of teal; even mudhens help to make the
place look natural and unsuspicious.

The number of the decoys will be governed by the nature of
the ground, as noted, and in some degree by the species of
ducks to be shot.   Mallards, teal, and shovelers do not care
particularly for a crowd, but on the contrary, pintails, redheads and bluebills are sure to be drawn to the biggest mass
of fowl in sight—with the deep-water ducks, where they are
packing and rafting, it is just useless to make a small display of decoys.   Generally speaking there is little danger
of having too many.   The market shooter was rarely satisfied to have less than a hundred blocks, and his example is
worth following.

In selecting a spot for the blind and putting out the decoys, other things being equal, choose a site where the wind
ruffles the water, which will cause the blocks to bob about
with the appearance of life.   The prettiest working bunch of
wood that I have ever seen was on a river where the current
would carry the decoys downstream until fetched up by the
cord and brought back by an eddy.   Under these conditions,
blocks are hard to distinguish from living fowl.

Whether or not the bunch of decoys is to be reinforced by
dead birds "set up" depends much on the water—it must be
practically dead water.   If waves are running, the motion
necessarily affects anything afloat, and the dead birds hanging
rigid and still will arouse suspicion and do more harm than
good.   Keep the dead birds in the blind unless the water is
quiet and shallow—shallow it must be of course, since the head

of the dead bird is held on a forked stick or impaled on a bent wire which must be thrust into the bottom.

Decoying deep-water ducks is a horse of another color. The man who undertakes it must make extensive preparation or employ a professional guide. Generally he must pin to the guide, who has a complete outfit and is all set for business. The birds come in best on open water, usually when rafting after feeding. Birds that mean to pack are looking for a raft already formed, not a small flock. The sink-box or battery man must make a tremendous showing of stool or he will appear a mere speck on the wide water. One hundred floaters are about the minimum for really efficient work, and five hundred the right number. But just try to find the guide and his helper who will rig you out with even a hundred! Use canvasbacks or an allied species—bluebills are good and easily painted.

On salt water, due attention to wind and tide is necessary if the shooter is not to be caught at a disadvantage. If shooting from box or battery, so place the stool that birds will come in from the front and pass or drop to the left—I need hardly give reason to the man who has lain in a coffin-like box, and had to sit up with heels as high as seat and swing his gun to the right.

Having but a few decoys and no help in placing them and retrieving the dead fowl, the gunner had better keep off the open water—nothing can be done on open sea water without careful planning, a lot of paraphernalia, and, I may say again, a guide. In boats alone the minimum is a motor boat, a big dory or bank skiff, and a battery. The latter has to be carried to and from the rigging-out place atop the skiff—all two good men can do to put it there.

DUCK CALLS

Ducks will decoy without the use of a call.   More ducks by all odds are scared away by faulty calling than are ever drawn in by the expert use of a duck-call.   The man who doesn't know how to use a call is better off if he leaves it at home.   At most, the inexpert should be content with one or two quacks, scarcely loud enough to reach the ears of the birds, and, whatever the further temptation, quit right there.   All the novice can expect to do with his caller is to attract the attention of the flock to his decoys, and very often a slight whistle will do as well as a quack.

Nevertheless, if the gunner is an expert caller he will find his accomplishment of the greatest assistance.   Some men have a natural ear for tones, are very observant, and rapidly pick up duck calling.   Nature has not done so much for the mass of us; about nine men in ten never learn to call effectively, and the tenth, barring the exceptional man noted, learns only after much study and many a shot lost through failures and false notes.   By and large, it is the old story of having plenty of opportunity to practice, just as a man learns to shoot by practice and in no other way.

To the veteran wildfowler, ducks speak a variable language, not so much inflected as English, to be sure, but far from a meaningless "*Quack, quack, quack.*"   About the biggest fool thing a shooter can do—probably will do for all that—is to sound the alarm note of the mallard just when the big fellows are threatening to come in.   That call is equivalent to saying: "Get to hell out of here!   Danger!   Fly for your lives! Death is within fifty yards of this spot, ducks, you get me! *Squawk, squawk, squawk!*"

Duck language is as hard to acquire as any other foreign language. Go at it systematically and at least know what you are trying to say before you say it—to the ducks. Tom Turpin of Memphis, Tenn., not only makes a good duck call, but has reproduced duck language on a phonograph disc, with interjections in his own Tennessee tongue explaining what the calls mean; better get that. Learn the loud, protesting notes of an old mallard hen, provoked at the sight of a flock of ducks threatening to ignore her invitation; get the running, satisfied chuckle when she sees the wild birds waver and turn; get the blended, vociferous greeting, sometimes extended by a feeding flock to mates passing overhead; get the dining-room chatter of birds that are merely discussing their dinner; lastly, learn the bass quack of the mallard, the tenor of the pintail, the minor notes of the widgeon—every species of waterfowl has its own "brogue"; be sure to learn the difference, if you can, and then don't talk Dutch to an Irishman.

Keeping in mind that the most of us never learn to call ducks at all but merely to frighten them, it is evident that we take up duck literature before learning the primer. In the beginning, try your duck calling on the tame fowls in the barnyard. Should they reply, turning their heads knowingly to see the whereabouts of their wild relatives, you are making progress. Now if so lucky as to be able to do so, go to a pond near the home of a keen shooting country boy, secrete yourself and call. If the lad grabs a gun and starts for the pond, consider that you are "getting there." But if he fetches a derisive yell, grin and bear it—go off and practice some more.

Granted you can pass the test of the tame mallards and the

country boy, next experiment with the wild birds. Steal within long range of a bunch of mallards, resting close to shore, and begin calling. If the big fellows softly answer, congratulate yourself, but if they let out a startled squawk, and all their wings beat the water as one (chances are they do that), you may as well continue to practice, but not on a flock that is wheeling to the decoys. At last try your art on a bunch that are actually swinging about the blind, undecided as to whether or not to drop in. If the call works on them, you belong to the class of the elect.

No matter what your skill, remember that calling is easily overdone, while the man who thinks he can call but cannot is in precisely the same boat with thousands of young women who feel that their mission in life is grand opera. A good test of your calling ability and apt judgment is to go out with some veteran duck shot, one bent on making his limit that morning; he being content with your performance, convinced that you are bettering his chances rather than injuring them, pat yourself and lay aside the duck call—you are its master. It is a safe bet, though, that the old crab will advise you to go slow with the squawker.

Lastly, develop your calling knowledge with regard to the different species of wildfowl, if you can. If you are able to imitate but the mallard, his voice may be effective with several species, since pintails, spoonbills, gadwalls and teal come in to mallards about as readily as to their own kind. The deep-water fowl, however, do not care to mix with the shallow-water birds, and, with them only their own dialect carries weight. The bluebill is a great talker even when on the wing, but canvasbacks and redheads are comparatively silent. Don't talk too much to such taciturn fowl, that will merely be annoyed by it. The chatter of the widgeon is hard to imitate, though effective when rightly done. Good calling will frequently cause a flock of these birds to swing over the blind when they have no intention of alighting—curiosity leads to their undoing. Pintails should not be talked at too much—never after they make the first turn. Should the passing flock show indecision, some of them wheeling, others going on, give a low, running call and then keep still—you can do no more. The very best caller is an old mallard hen which stands on her tail, gives her wings a vigorous flap, and then scolds the flock vociferously for its foolish suspicion.

DUCK GUNS

No DOUBT plenty of ducks have been killed and many more will be with any kind of gun the hunter happens to own. The regulation trap gun is an especially good "fowling-piece" because of its weight, the heavy charge it carries, the evenness of its pattern, and the long straight stock. For me, individually, the trap gun in a pump or a selfloader is a duck gun, for that reason needing no change whatever; but I am quite aware that others take no privilege in disagreeing. In any event, this discussion is to be devoted entirely to duck guns—weapons of unusual weight, shooting maximum charges for the bore, built, choked and chambered expressly for wildfowl shooting. Guns for long-range duck shooting, pass shooting, jumping the birds, taking travelers, imply powerful weapons, 10-bore or 12. Eyebrows will rise when I say the 8-gauge would be exactly adapted to the work were we privileged to use it; nevertheless, such is the fact. Finally, I'll have to include cursory mention of such small bores as have been given preference in one section of the country or another.

Down southwest, in the land of sage, sedge and cactus, a colony of duck shooters some years ago pinned their faith to a 24-bore; this was in the days of Colonel Guessaz and Mark Dyer. Doubtless some of those guns are still working—with hand loads, as always. Again, sometimes from California, often from Alberta, and once from Arkansas, came vigorous pleas for the 28-bore. The late Captain duBray, for many years the lone traveling salesman of Parker Brothers, was the father of the 28-bore gun in America, and the little arm misses him. All pleas for a very small duck gun are pretty in sentiment and appealing to the imagination, but are not to be taken seriously unless the small guns have some magical quality.

The smallest gun which I would concede as having merit as a duck gun would be a Parker-style 20, which implies an arm with 32-inch barrels, weighing 7 pounds or more, and handling a full ounce of shot. Such a gun will kill ducks up to a full 45 yards, and ought readily to account for every-thing that actually decoys. There is just one reason why the heavy 20-bore should not be selected for duck shooting, and that is the larger bores are better. A man may become wedded to small bores, but if he is still open to reason he ought to be able to convince himself, for a good example, that an 8-gauge throwing 2½ ounces of shot really is a more powerful weapon.

The 16-gauge is the best all-'round gun made, but not the best weapon intended exclusively for ducks. I have had two 16-bore guns that served very well in duck shooting. The first one was built at a time when I thought I'd quit shooting any gun larger than a 16. It had 32-inch barrels, bored to shoot exceedingly close, chambered for 3-inch shells, was never fired except with hand loads, and used charges up to 3¼ drams of powder and 1⅛ ounces of shot. This was, in effect, a 12-bore gun, and would kill ducks up to 60 yards, now and then. This was the best-shooting 16-bore that I have ever shot. It was an Ithaca, but Mark Dyer had a similar gun in a Parker that appeared equally effective. My present 16, which is used on ducks, doves and prairie chickens, also serving well on Mexican blue quail, has 30-inch barrels, both full choke, raised ventilated rib, beavertail, fore-end, cheekpiece, single trigger, soft-rubber butt, and the gun weighs 7½ pounds, being shot exclusively with progressive loads and 1⅛ ounces of shot. It is the best dove gun that I have, and doves are just as hard to kill at long range as ducks. Incidentally, this is a fine trap gun, shooting better than 80% patterns at 40 yards, 7½ shot. With it I have broken ten birds straight at 30 yards rise, regulation trapping. This is another Ithaca.

Now we are coming to duck guns which were not in common use a dozen years ago. These are 12-bores, as typified by the Super Fox, a heavy arm with 32-inch barrels, chambered for 3-inch cases, loaded with a stiff charge of progressive powder and 1⅜ ounces of shot. I have shot these guns extensively, as made by Fox, Parker and Smith. No better long-range guns in 12-bore ever have been made, in my opinion. Probably the most noted of these guns is one built on a Fox action by Bert Becker for Nash Buckingham. This gun has Whitworth barrels, 34 inches long, and the arm weighs close to 10 pounds. This gun is said to kill single ducks regularly at 70 yards, and is all that can ever be expected of a 12-gauge, unless something unexpected develops

in shotgun boring.   One of these guns weighing 8½ pounds
is heavy enough for the average man.

I have a Super Fox, and never have had any fault to find
with it whatever.   Nevertheless, I am more likely to be caught
in a duck blind with just an ordinary trap model pump gun.
The pump gun has done things for me that no double ever
could.   Memories create the trouble, perhaps.   I can always
remember hot corners, when the ducks climbed out and fell
one, two, three, four, five, as regularly as the ticking of a
clock.   Only last fall a flock of widgeon winged by me, and
I killed six, the last one at 60 yards.   The bag limit in Oklahoma is ten ducks, and right there I had six, but I'll remember
those six long after ordinary bags are forgotten.

For me, the pump gun is a better arm than the automatic.
It doesn't shoot any better, and of course it is not quite so
fast, but I hit better with it.   It took me a long time to dope
out the reason.   Finally I learned that my second shot from
an automatic and subsequent shots were liable to go high.
The recoil had apparently kicked my cheek loose from contact with the comb, and the next shot was fired before I had
settled my cheek back in place again.   With a pump gun
every shot is an individual shot, and my cheek goes right back
in place while the gun is being pumped.   A double gun is
likely to use me the same as the automatic, the second shot
going high on a straightway bird, notwithstanding I could
see the muzzle of the gun right on him.   Therefore for me
the pump gun is right for second barrel shooting and for all
the shots which may follow.

The 10-bore is a real duck gun, a waterfowl gun, and not
good for anything else whatever.   This was true as well in
the old days before 1900 and is no less true today, though

there was an interval between 1900 and 1924 when 10-bore guns threatened to become obsolete.   Only 12-bore charges were to be had for the 10, and people could see no horse sense in carrying a 10-pound 10-bore gun to shoot a charge adapted to the 12.   Now we have very powerful 10-gauge loads, heavy charges of progressive powders and 1⅝ ounces of shot. No 12 is going to equal one of these big 10's—never can be made to do so.   The very acme of duck shooting is a big 10, taking ducks in pass shooting only, no decoys, taking anything that wings by under 75 yards.   One duck dropped stone-dead at 75 yards is worth ten bagged under 30 yards.

This gun is built for scientific duck shooting, not for big bags, and I might say the same for the 8-gauge.   The big 8-bore, rightly used, is not a duck killer, and I have never agreed with the Bureau of Biological Survey in their forbidding its use.   Over decoys, a repeating shotgun will bag twice as many birds as an 8 double, but the few birds brought down by the big gun, at distances up to 80 yards, have a value never estimated by numbers.   Of course the 10-bore serves the same purpose, even though the range is restricted by five yards or more.   Strangely enough, I have never done much duck shooting with an 8-gauge, even in the days when this bore was legal.   However, I tried one out thoroughly, discovering that with 2 ounces of shot, even shot as large as Number 3, single birds could be struck with great regularity up to 80 yards.   If I were only allowed 20 ducks in a season, I'd like to shoot them all with an 8-gauge gun, no duck under 75 yards.

The 10-bore is now merely coming back to its own.   We had in the big 10 many years ago, black-powder days, just as good guns as we have now, though we loaded the brass shells

ourselves.   About the year 1889, George Gray and I killed
179 deep-water ducks in one afternoon, canvasbacks, redheads and bluebills, no other kinds.   I shot a big Westley
Richards weighing 12 pounds, loaded with 5 drams of powder
and 1½ ounces of No. 5 shot.   Gray had a similar gun in an
L. C. Smith.   Nobody could make such a bag today or ever
again, though we have the guns once more.

Notwithstanding all that I have said, notwithstanding all
that others have said, notwithstanding that the gun for the
scientific duck shot is a double gun with a powerful load, yet
the most popular duck gun has been, is, and will be the repeating shotgun.   There is a reason.   To the man who has
grown old and maybe stale in the shooting game, there is nothing so exhilarating as the lightninglike action of a repeating
shotgun, trying to effectively deliver its six shots in the space
of two seconds, ducks falling with a regular thud, thud, the
first barely striking the water ere the last shot is fired.   There
are few moments in the life of a gunner comparable to a great
flock of mallards hovering over the decoys, then towering a
hundred feet straight into the air, followed by the fire of a
repeating shotgun.

As to duck shot, only three sizes are really needed, Nos.
6, 5 and 4.   Considering all the gauges from .410 to 10-bore,
no other sizes are really required.   Which to use depends on
the gun.   No. 4 shot are right for the 10-bore, and for the
long range, 3-inch chambered 12s.   With less shot than 1⅜
ounces, No. 5 is best, and for all loads of less than 1¼ ounces,
No. 6 shot will do everything that the gun is capable of ac-
complishing.   We can all get finicky, if we want to, and use
No. 7½ in the small bores, or 7s, or 3s in the 10, but in the
end we shall probably admit that little has been gained.

In duck shooting it is well to select some good, stiff load, thoroughly tried out on the pattern plate and on game—then stick to it. Most of my own misses, probably those of others as well, are due to faulty elevation. Having become accustomed to a certain load, knowing its elevation as fired from your gun, it doesn't pay to change to even a more powerful load, which may change the elevation, kicking the charge over the top of the bird or throwing it under. Changes in elevation are why we cannot shoot two guns equally well, even when both are stocked alike.

Chapter XXV

DUCK SHOOTING HINTS THAT HELP

MANY of the shots over decoys are easy enough to keep the novice on good terms with his vanity. The duck hunter who is in no sense a wing shot can yet lam away in the thick of flocks and kill some birds. The flock shooter, granted some judgment as to when to turn loose, should be able to bag one bird with ten shells. In the old days, Abe Kleinman, on a wager, killed ninety ducks with a hundred cartridges; but there are no Kleinmans any more, unless possibly on the Louisiana coast.

The ordinary duck shooter who occasionally puts in a day with the webfeet does well to kill with one shell in four; a handy man with his gun might account for 40 per cent. of the birds shot at. The market gunner of other days whose misses exceeded 40 per cent. had missed both the ducks and his calling. If I can give hints here that may assist the help-seeking 10 per cent. man to bag 25 per cent., or the 25 per cent. man to reach 40, that is about as well as I could hope to do, without condensing a whole book on wing shooting into one chapter.

To begin with, it must be taken for granted that the shooter has mechanical command of his gun, can point it where he means the charge to go, that he understands swing and knows how to time his trigger to that swing. And as to swing, let me interject here that when I first wrote this chapter, which I am

272

now revising, all my duck shooting was done by covering
the bird from the rear, swinging past him to the lead and
firing while the gun was still moving—carrying through, it
is called.   That still is the correct manner of duck shooting
on passing birds, but I got tired of it.

Covering the mark, swinging by it to the lead, carrying
through, all took too much nerve force out of me when I got
old and lazy, so I learned to kill ducks by a simple upward
sweep of the barrels, at an angle to the flight.   Intercepting,
it might be called.   And I soon learned that with this latter
method results were about as good as with a deliberate swing,
and the shot only took half as much out of me, so that I was
more ready for still other shots, fired rapidly.   The use of
pump guns would have forced angle interception on me anyhow, for in my case as with most others the pump gun is nearly
always pulled down in functioning, and then has to be raised
to intercept the next bird.

Pass shooting, or shooting birds in full flight which have
no intention of alighting, is much a matter of cleverly esti-
mating distance and speed of flight, together with a full knowledge of where to hold, of theoretical lead as modified by the
marksman's own particular shooting technique.   What is
shooting technique?   The dickens!   I just can't write of wing
shooting here; there is too much to say.

I mean to discuss the behavior of ducks under fire, partly
for the reason that while this is common knowledge among
duck hunters, yet little has been written that could help the
man who doesn't already know.   Every species of duck behaves after his kind when coming in to decoys, and this I must
dwell upon briefly.   Further, every shooter has his strength
and his weakness as a wing shot—some marksmen are safe on

towering birds, some on incomers, some on fowl passing to the right, and some on those going to the left. The axiom of the duck hunter should be: Know thyself and favor thy game leg when thou canst.

No two species of ducks come in to the decoys in precisely the same way, no two behave precisely alike when shot at, no two have exactly the same rate of speed. One kind of fowl may drop straight from the clouds on humming wings, while another kind may cup his wings and float down like a bit of thistle. One variety will not decoy except when flying low, and then he plumps in, while a second very determinedly circles the blind and investigates before he will stop. Certain of the birds have the invariable habit of towering as they go out, while just as regularly a different breed skims the water. A flock of mallards breaks ranks and "flares" when shot at, while a canvasback simply "tears the air" on a predestined course, tears the air so you can hear it closing in behind him, same as when lightning cuts a swath. Don't laugh—just you look and listen instead of shooting, sometime, then laugh if you can!

All wing shooting, in its essence, involves a clear calculation of what the mark will do next, maybe a tenth of a second or a hundredth of a second later. We must be able to foresee what is to be the next maneuver, and where the bird will be when the shot have traveled their route—otherwise we simply shoot where he isn't. It follows that the chief study of the wing shot, next to himself and his gun, is the flight habits of the particular bird he is hunting. He who is unable to tell what a frightened fowl will do before it happens has just one chance. If he keeps his eyes open and uses his head he generally can tell what he should have done when it is too late, so far as that duck is concerned. He can do better next time.

Expecting the decoying fowl to jump at the sound of the first barrel, the gunner presumably carries his fired gun high with a view to intercepting the flight.   But if the bird he has his eye on belongs to the non-towering variety, it drives off along the water at a two-miles-a-minute gait, and the shooter is liable to find his best efforts to redeem the blunder are just no good.   Experience and observation lead me to conclude that some account of how the different varieties of waterfowl come in to the decoys, how they behave under fire, and how they go out, will benefit the youngster who is willing to learn.   How the birds get away has always exercised me most, for about four out of five shots must be pulled while the birds are trying to escape.   I will take up the decoying maneuvers and the "under fire" actions of the different species of ducks in turn, beginning with the mallard, *the* wild duck of them all.

When in a decoying humor the mallard usually flies very high, the highest of any member of the duck family—usually from 100 to 150 feet.   Spying the decoys, he may come straight in, cup his wings and "settle," but this only when he has not been molested in that vicinity.   Ordinarily he circles the blind once and perhaps oftener.   His first circle is apt to be wide, keeping just beyond the danger line.   It is while the big fellows are making this first turn that the novice is apt to "spill his fat," for the birds are so large that they appear to be within range when still full 70 yards out.   A premature shot, and the shooter has acquired more experience than he has mallards.

His first preliminary survey being satisfactory, the green-head now drops lower, shortens his turns, lessens his speed, and proceeds to circle the blind again.   Now the flock is within easy range, may pass right over the blind not 40 feet

high; beware they do not see the bristles rise on your neck!
The shooter with but two barrels or he who takes pride in his
holding, can take his shots now.   But remember that an old
duck "sharp" likes to make a complete success of an under-
taking.   He has started in to make the flock decoy, and the
last thing in his mind is wilfully balking himself.   Remember, too, that when the birds have made a second turn, inside
and lower than the first, they mean to alight—will, unless a
gun moves, a hat bobs, or something else is wrong.

The "hover" shot culminates the plans of the shooter and
ends the maneuvers of the birds.   Turning against the wind
on their last swing, the fowl will cup their wings, beat the air
and begin to settle into the open spot left among the decoys
for that purpose.   The instant they check their forward
movement and draw together, their wide-spread, gently fan-
ning wings seemingly filling all the space, is the time to select
the most compact group and shoot.   Don't let them get too
close to the water, for as they near it they will flare out, every
individual duck selecting his own lighting place.   Moreover, a duck dropping in with more or less rapidity is a harder
shot than when he is standing motionless in the air.   Of
course,* never let a bird alight unless he does it when you
are not looking; it is just as reprehensible to shoot a decoyed duck on the water as it is to pot quail over the point
of a dog.

The foregoing applies only when the birds actually come
in, and mallards do not always come in.   Of all the waterfowl
I know, barring possibly the Canada goose, the mallard is the
most likely to decide not to take any chances.   When he has

* Some sportsmen systematically permit black ducks or mallards to
alight, then immediately jumping them and taking them on the rise.

made two circles, each as high and as wide as the other, or if the second is higher than the first or if a single duck lets out a quack and jumps, any time during the swing, pull into them when they come within range; they are suspicious and the chances are they'll never drop to your decoys.

The highly observant and widely experienced duck shooter (guide or market gunner), can usually foretell on the first swing of the fowl whether or not they will eventually stop, but the rank and file of us must use the best judgment we have. Being in doubt as to whether or not the ducks mean to hover, it is wise to give them the benefit of the doubt and wait. It is not quite so trying to lose a shot by over-caution as it is to "spoil a killing" by a futile shot when the birds are out of range.

When mallards are "opened on" as they drop in, they climb for safety, being the most expert, rapid and perpendicular climbers of all the duck family. They are quite likely to go a hundred feet nearly straight into the air— nearly but not quite, for they invariably bear away from the gun. In this they are wiser than the other towering species, some of which are liable to break back right over the gun. It is said that the mallard can climb a hundred feet in less than two seconds, at the same time moving from twenty to thirty yards farther out. Which is well enough, for a pump gun can be fired six times in two seconds. The one idea of our mallard, though, seems to be to climb so high and so fast that the shot cannot reach him. If the marksman is poky, there's a good chance he does it.

About now somebody is sure to want to know where to hold on those climbing mallards. I can't tell him anything very pertinent, not knowing the distance the birds may be from

the blind, the strength of the wind, or the smartness of the
shooter's swing.   One thing, hold a foot to two feet higher
than looks necessary, and have the gun climbing with the
bird.   Granted that the gun opens up when the fowl are hovering within twenty-five yards of the blind, one foot above
should catch the second bird, and from then on greater lead
might have to be given.   Occasionally, if we are shooting
a repeating shotgun, about the last bird needs no lead above,
for he has reached the highest point he means to go and for
the fraction of an instant "hangs" in the air before bearing
away.   Get in front of his bill and let go.

Having made the safe 100 per cent. hover shot, don't fire
at the lowest bird, but take the top one, which will be the first
to escape, and then fire succeeding shots as the birds climb
to the level of the gun.   A good shot should kill his birds
like climbing a ladder, every succeeding shot a step twenty
feet higher.   However, I am reminded to add that, while
I said I intended to tell how to kill ducks, the honest way
to do it is to shoot only a pair of birds from a flock, and take
them in passing.

The pintail is quite like the mallard in his decoying actions,
though not so suspicious nor so shrewd a fowl.   Meaning to
alight, it is rare that pintails circle the blind more than once,
and they may simply pass by, turn into the wind and alight.
Usually, when in decoying mood or at any time except when
traveling or migrating, the long-tail fowls wing lower than
mallards, flying no higher than need be to clear obstructions.
When circling the blind they may not be fifty feet up, and they
may be no more than ten feet high when they set their wings
to drop in.   Like mallards, they never dash into the water,
but break the fall with gently beating pinions.

As is true of the mallard, the decoying pintail climbs for life at the first shot, and the man who jumps up to shoot will find the birds too quick for him. The pintail's eyes are keen, and if there is any preliminary movement in the blind he will jump above the first shot. With this in mind, make it a practice to fire the first shot before rising. The pintail has the same vertical climb as the mallard, and has the appearance of going straighter up, for he points his head directly skyward, while the mallard may bounce up back first.

When shot into as they hover, a flock of pintails split up and flare more than mallards; they may take every direction, some of them coming right over the blind. The holding is practically the same as that for the greenheads, but they do not tower so high, rarely reaching seventy-five feet before sheering off. The flock will have reached maximum height before five shots can be fired, and as they begin bearing off, still rising, the missing begins. Two seconds after the first shot is fired the pintails will be out of range, and after the third shot the holding will have to be both high and ahead.

When a big bunch of pintails set their wings within twenty-five yards of a good duck shot, he will often get a bird with every barrel, and may kill two or three with the first barrel, if they happen to "jam" when hovering. A fair marksman should bag three or four ducks, and less than three is considered poor work. The pintail cannot carry off as many shot as a mallard, but shots are often at long range, where the demand is for a good-shooting gun.

Another duck which has the habit of climbing out of danger rather than going away is the greenwing teal, the miniature mallard. He wings lower than the mallard or the pintail, often in large flocks, and has the fatal habit of bunching in a

compact mass as he turns or as he sets his wings to drop in.
The poise above the decoys is of very short duration and the
birds flare as they take the water.   The crucial moment must
be taken if more than one duck is to drop to the shot.   Being
fired into, the greenwing proves himself a sprinting climber.
Fairly darting upward as though fired from a big-bore, bell-
muzzled scatter gun, every little chap is for himself now, and
the fowler's gun must work like a machine if many are to be
secured.   Fact is, a greenwing on his bound is one of the hardest shots in duck shooting.   He has other habits though that
make amends.   He rarely climbs more than forty feet, after
which he curves away, perhaps making a half turn which
brings him or keeps him within reach of the gun when otherwise he'd have been out of danger.

Many open on greenwings as soon as they are within fair
range, for this bird is extremely liable to pass right over the
decoys and then keep straight on about his business.   Unlike
the big ducks, he doesn't require much room to tack in, either;
he may come down wind like a rocket, make a half hitch to get
the wind under him, and be down before you can bat an eye.
So watch him like a hawk and do not let him alight—by far
the easiest shot is before he hits the water.   The greenwing
is one of the easiest of all ducks for the professional to bag
and one of the hardest for the tyro.   What he did yesterday,
however, he does tomorrow, and it can be learned.

The widgeon behaves a good deal like the pintail when
decoying, being a little more erratic and a trifle harder to
bring in.   He drops harder into the water, too, frequently
making a long, low swing at racing speed, not setting his
wings until just before he hits the water.   Frequently the
first shot will be fired when the birds are not three feet high,

but it is well to take them just before they alight, because they mass more or less.   Being shot at, the powerful widgeon makes one terrific leap upward, where he hangs an instant like a prairie chicken, and then bears away for a horizontal flight. The two easy shots are while he is descending and just as he reaches the top of his bound.   Afterwards you have to hold for him, on a going-away bird, because he never means to swing back.

Personally, I never hesitate to take widgeons any time they come within twenty-five or thirty yards—when passing, not waiting for any hover shot.   Under such circumstances they flare but a trifle, have only a slight jump or none, and the gun need only follow the flight with a lead slightly greater than for a mallard.

The gray duck or gadwall is the nearest akin to the widgeon in his decoying habits.   He doesn't bound so high or so straight up when he goes out, and in alighting may just turn and plump in like a bluewing.   To my shame, I must confess that I like to practice wing shooting on the gadwalls—simply turn a pump gun loose and let it run, same as a corn sheller, as they go by.

A spoonbill is too silly for the shooter to aptly judge what he will do next.   He may come in a hundred feet high and then drop straight down, after his lopsided fashion, first one wing depressed and then the other.   Perhaps when halfway to the water he will catch himself and dash off—reason unknown, for after escaping he may come right back again! Anyway you take him, he is a slow bird over the decoys, and is likely to get hurt if the chap in the blind can shoot.   When passing at top speed he is no less difficult a mark than the mallard or the widgeon.   As a matter of fact, the shoveler is

too tame for any decent sporting bird.   He will permit the
gun to walk right up on him, and if not killed on the rise is
likely to make a half circle around the gunner so as to make
the kill certain.

Now we come to birds with a different style of flight and
a different style of decoying—the bluewing teal, the canvasback, redhead, bluebill, and others which we haven't space to
mention.   Taking the bluewing first, here is a bird that does
little hovering over decoys.   He comes in low and drops into
the water without warning, the whole flock in a bunch.   That
leads to a lot of slaughter if a man is scoundrel enough to
shoot the little fowl on the water.   Flushed, he goes out like
a quail, straight away, slightly rising.   As I have said elsewhere, the bluewing is another bird that can't be made wary,
even with much slaughter.

The bluewing has a very strong attachment to his flock.
This trait leads to certain characteristic actions when the
small fowl is under fire, or is flushed.   When a passing bevy of
teal is fired at, they waver very little and then instantly "close
ranks," and when going out all seem bent on following their
leader; such birds as have started in the wrong direction
quickly curve back to rejoin their comrades, running a further
jeopardy.   The flush of a flock of bluewings is very similar
to that of a bevy of quail, except the ducks head in for a
flock formation, while every little quail keeps his own course
to safety.

As a matter of good sport, bluewings should not be jumped
and should not be shot over decoys.   They are just too tame
and there is no sport in it.   However, shooting them passing,
taking them up to sixty yards, the holding has to be good, for
this is one of the fastest of all ducks.   Thomas Alexander

estimated that with a gale back of him the bluewing could get up a speed of 150 miles an hour. I do not quite believe that, but can't prove that Mr. Alexander was either wrong or right. When shooting in North Dakota in a forty-mile breeze, with the teal flying fifty feet high, I have made an allowance of what I considered fifteen feet at forty yards, and when hit the birds went right along like a well-batted ball, striking the water sixty yards from where they were killed. This kind of work, and taking canvasbacks under like conditions, is the most fascinating of wing shooting.

A canvasback on open water flies low, a bluebill higher, and a redhead may wing high or fan the water. Usually when a bunch of these deep-water ducks see the decoys, they wing directly for them, pass directly over the stool, to swing and alight outside and beyond the blocks. This applies particularly to shore blinds. About nine times in ten the birds will hit the water so far out that little can be done with them. Their intention appears to be alighting outside the decoys, then swimming in to investigate. It follows that when it is canvasbacks, no hover shot is to be expected; you must take them as they come within range. Many a hunter has sat with open mouth, staring after a flock of the big white and dun racers, that had come swooping down over his decoys and then went swooping out again, never batting an eye.

Partially making amends for their behavior over decoys, is the fact that either the canvasback or the redhead is hard to turn. You may open up on him as soon as he gets within range and he will keep his course right by the gun, no matter if the shooter is now on his feet. A canvasback may be met by fire when forty yards off and coming in, but will not alter his line and may pass right on over the gun. No mallard would do anything like *that!*   Get your mallard in close and you have him, but if three shots are to be fired at a canvasback no more than one will be sent after him as he goes away.

With the deep-water ducks, as with all others at times, not being able to take them as they tower, we must rely upon straight duck shooting, judgment of speed, angle, and range. All the deep-water ducks fly uniformly fast; unlike mallards and pintails, which often loiter about at half speed.   Either the canvasback, the bluebill or the redhead is capable of flying a hundred feet a second, and he is nearly always doing that very thing, particularly the canvasback.   These compact birds, with their rather short and rapidly beating wings, have apparently one gear ratio only and that is high.

The lead on a canvasback at sixty yards, granting him a rate of a hundred feet a second, would be over twenty feet. The lead can be learned by experience only, and it is no use to tell a man to lead twenty feet, because he won't know what twenty feet looks like, up in the air.   That is why advice as to lead is largely useless.   What looks to one man like twenty feet appears to another to be only ten feet or eight.   I can recall holding on a straight-away quail at forty yards, saying mentally as I fired, "Three inches to one side."   The quail went on unhurt, and yet I knew very well that I had at least a twenty-four-inch spread of pattern at the distance.   My three inches must in reality have been twelve inches.   Again I have tried rolling my gun at moderate ranges, in order to give the shot lead without an opening between gun and bird. A man can so roll his piece to left and right as to give a lead of two feet at forty yards.   This rolling of course throws the eye to one side or the other of the center at the breech, and when done unconsciously is one of the faults that have to be considered in wing shooting.   Again a rapid swing can materially reduce lead, and not knowing anything of a man's shooting style it is of course not much use to tell him what his lead should be.   If you could convince him that the lead must be ten feet, and to him the lead that killed appeared to be no more than five feet, that man had better continue to say that he led five feet, and let it go at that.

Which is the easier shot, a canvasback passing at a hundred feet a second or a mallard towering at fifty feet a second, is much a matter of the special skill of the gunner.   One man is deadly on a towering bird, another on an incomer, a third on a passing mark, and a very few on fowl that have passed and are going away.   As a general principle, for the average gunner all fresh-water ducks should be allowed to set their wings and hover before a shot is fired over decoys, but a deep-water duck is to be tripped whenever he gets close enough.   A canvasback winging above the decoys gets out of range in half the time of a mallard, but his shooting is more of a mechanical problem, and he has little ability to duck, dodge, or swerve.

In most instances the accomplished shooter of fresh-water ducks is an expert on towering and incoming birds, while the deep-water man has greater skill on passing shots at long range.   I think the mean distance at which canvasbacks are killed is a full fifty feet beyond the average range at which mallards are dropped, while the bluewing is the webfooted quail and falls nearest the gun.   Were I shooting bluebills, redheads and canvasbacks, or sea ducks of any kind, a 10-bore gun would go into the battery with me.

Chapter XXVI

HITTING OR MISSING QUAIL

WHILE this chapter has the same heading that I used sixteen years ago when I first wrote the subject up as a magazine article, the text has been changed radically. That indicates the value of the advice one can give, for right now I wouldn't follow the old prescription. Mostly it is the guns that I once used which would not be tolerated now. Thirty-five years ago I used a full-choked 20-bore gun for four successive seasons; twenty-five years ago I shot a full-choked 28-bore for several successive seasons; fifteen years ago I was shooting a 20-bore, modified in one barrel and full choke in the other. Now I have come to improved cylinder boring in any quail gun, no matter the gauge, and if the second barrel was improved cylinder that would be just as well. My latest quail gun is an autoloader, cylinder bored. I do not like straight cylinders at that, and the chances are time will find me putting a bit of choke into that barrel. Our big barrel makers mean it when they say cylinder, but my cylinder is improved or choked a little.

Now about hitting or missing quail. It is easier to hit quail than it is to miss them, and the hitting deals far more gently with a man's egotism. I find that when a man kills he has a good opinion of himself, regardless of whether he shot a pattern a yard wide at 20 yards, or only twelve inches

wide. Hitting leads to hitting, that is proverbial, and after
a man hits often enough he comes to believe that missing is
just a rare accident, and that kind of accident doesn't
happen often. Hence hitting birds is the common order of
things, and missing them is inexplicable. Therefore all the
reader has to do, if he would bag 90 per cent. of his quail, is to
follow my directions closely, bearing in mind that they say
no man who ever wrote a book on horsemanship could really
ride a horse.

Here is what I said about quail shooting fifteen years ago.
I wouldn't say it again, because I can't shoot as well as I could
then, and I have begun to be skeptical as to whether I ever
could or not:

"The writer is not one of the people who consider the
quail 'dead easy,' and he has been shooting them pretty
consistently for thirty years. I have done some pretty good
work, too, in my time, and, remembering the hits and forget-
ting the misses, I might be tempted to pronounce quail shooting a simple performance. I can recall one afternoon about
twenty years ago when I killed 23 birds straight, using a shell
to the bird. Two years ago I bagged 22 birds with a box
of twenty-five shells. The season just passed, I killed all the
birds shot at in an afternoon, ten, with a full choked 20-bore
gun, using the second barrel but once to stop a cripple. I
kept a record of shooting during the month of December
(1914), and found that I averaged just under 70 per cent."

That will do for that, if I haven't already said too much.
Dempsey could fight in his day and I could shoot, but today
neither of us wants to bite off more than he can chew. I can
now miss quail a plenty, and for that matter probably I always
could. No living bird can rattle me so quickly and so ab-

solutely as the bob-white quail, and there are occasions, which recur entirely too often, when I am willing to swear that I can't shoot the bird, never did know how, and never will learn.

I have devoted twice as much time to quail as I have to any other bird, and yet I rarely walk in front of a dog to flush with the absolute and calm conviction that a kill is certain. The little brown scamps can always keep me guessing and they do it, which means that I get a lot of kick out of quail shooting. Getting that kick is what has kept me quail-shooting with unalloyed pleasure this many a year.

Human nature is just queer anyhow. I once became ambitious to see how small would be the smallest groups I could shoot with a rifle at 100 yards. Procuring a long and heavy-barrelled rifle, the best 'scope sight that money could buy, constructing a rest that left nothing to chance, loading my own shells and weighing the powder, I finally shot several 1-inch groups. That settled that rifle. I could not ask more of it, yet I laid it aside and finally sold it. So long as the sight of a deer in the woods tends to give a man buck-ague, deer shooting is a noble sport, but let him shoot deer until the sight of one affects him about as much as does the old brindle cow's calf, and he had as well quit deer hunting. Plenty of men have to go to Africa in order to get a kick out of big-game shooting, whereupon the kick comes from the fear of fang and talon. As for me, I get a kick out of quail shooting because I am afraid I'll miss them.

When a prairie chicken or a snipe gets up within a few yards, the settled conviction previous to shooting is that he will be killed. It is different with a quail—at least until he is on the wing and I note his flight. The ground may be open, level, cover just high enough so that we might assume the

bird would fly off straight and true, yet, while endeavoring
to walk the bevy up we hear a rush of wings directly behind
us—and the birds are in the air and so too are we.   Most of
those birds are going away nicely, ought to be easy, but we
get our eye on a cantankerous little scoundrel that has headed
right over us and not ten feet high.   Having made a half
turn already, we make it right back again now, get our legs
all tangled up, body out of balance, and miss.   When the gun
has been emptied, one belated rascal gets up at our feet and
wings steadily off about four feet high.   The combination of
misses that missed and misses when we couldn't shoot gives us
the kick.   If anything further is needed, a companion with
a horse laugh will furnish it.   Brush shooting, too—man
alive!—if there is a tree in sight I can always hit it!

Attempting to analyze the causes of missing, I'd say that
the first is a wrong style of shooting, together with the difficulty that most of us have in altering our style to suit the
occasion.   The quail is as much a bird of the woods as he
is of the open fields, and, taking the season through, I believe
about half the birds will be killed in the open and half in the
brush.   The style of shooting which will prove very effective
in a ragweed field won't do for a jackoak thicket or second-
growth pine.   Most of us have fixed shooting habits, a system
of aiming that is more or less mechanical, and half the time
Bob White doesn't fly like a clay pigeon.   He doesn't himself
know what he is going to do next, and we become more or less
"rattled" because we don't know either.

In my time I have had a score of good quail shots tell me,
"The only trouble with you is that you shoot too quick," and
as many others have told me, "You are too darned slow for
these birds in the woods."   Just so!   What is too fast for

one bird is too slow for another, and every man has shooting habits.   So emphatically is this true that our quail shooter gets a reputation for being a good brush shot or a good shot in the open, but rarely displays equal skill under both conditions.   In the woods a bird may wing across an opening, fairly riding the air on level keel, for a fraction of a second. One man will slam into it, no trouble at all, but another fellow would slam into the limbs of a tree, just too late; no trouble at all either!   On the next occasion the snap shot drives in *Bang, bang,* while the bevy is still performing preliminary gymnastics.   He does the missing, while a little later his deliberate companion has no trouble in making his double.

I have seen two good, all-'round quail shots.   One man was called "Dutch Fred," and the other "Irish Jim," both market hunters.   Jim had learned to shoot in the Old Country, and had his own ideas about giving the game "fair play."   With a rabbit or with a quail in the open, he wouldn't shoot until beast or bird had covered just thirty yards, or was thirty yards from the gun.   Then he killed—rabbit, woodcock, quail, snipe, duck, it didn't make any difference to Jim.   He could and did alter his style in the woods.   "Dutch Fred" had only one style, which was to shoot as quickly as the devil would let him.   He used an old Winchester lever-action 10-bore with a short cylinder barrel, and I have seen him kill quail after quail within forty feet of the gun.   Timber didn't seem to bother him—he didn't see the trees and he didn't hit 'em. What he did today he did tomorrow, and every time that I saw him shoot.   He was too quick for a quail, and Jim was too accurate.   I do not know whether either of them got much kick out of shooting, but both got birds for Tony Faust, the restaurant man, in St. Louis in the old days.

The styles of shooting, so far as gun movements are concerned, are the rough snap, the delayed snap, and the rapid
swing. Which is the best? That depends on the bird. The
rough snap, commonly called snap shooting, is to pull trigger
as the butt hits the shoulder, varying the gun neither up,
down, nor sidewise after the piece comes up. Suppose you
can see that the piece is not pointed right—well, you don't
take time to see that. If you did it would be a delayed-
snap. Instructions for snap shooting say, keep the eyes
focused on the bird, forget the gun, bring it up though as
fast as human arms can work, and shoot where you look; down
goes the bird because you were looking right at him. Maybe
so; unless the bird did something unexpected while the gun
was coming up. The crack snap shot is lightning-fast in his
gun handling, but I doubt if any man can bring his piece from
"ready" to shoulder in less than twenty-five feet of quail
flight, after the bird has his wings under him. Will the bird
be precisely where the mind anticipated when orders were
given about where the piece was to be pointed? Maybe, and
maybe the bird will be three feet from where he should have
been. Snap shots are predicted, the aim being the culmina-
tion of a movement, and that movement culminates in where
the bird ought to be, and maybe is—he is often enough for us
to land on him sometimes. Upon the whole, though, that kind
of snap shooting is to be done in the woods where we have time
for no other aim.

The delayed snap means getting the gun up to the shoulder
as before, but don't fire until the relation of bird to gun is
plainly seen by the eye. Now the gun may be pointed a foot,
two feet, three feet, perhaps more from the bird, but it won't
take as long to shift the piece and cover the mark as it did to

raise the butt to the shoulder; hence the delayed snap is a short, accurate movement, that would not miss, except for all those reasons that lead every wing shot to missing sometimes.   I used to know a crack duck shot.   He shot a pump gun and kept his cheek glued to the stock as he shot.   He used to tell me, much mystified, that if he ever missed the first bird he'd miss all the others, or if he missed with the first shot, he'd "shore" miss with the second.   George didn't know the reason, but he was either cross-firing to right or left, or his cheek was so placed as to spoil his elevation.   We may point the front end of the piece exactly right, but if the rear end is out of place, there you are.   Having the breech end right is a matter of gun-fit, but gun-fit accomplishes little if you don't put the butt to the right place on the shoulder and the cheek to the right place on the comb.   You can't shoot unless you can shoot, and a correct system merely makes practice more immediately helpful.   Another reason for missing is that you get the gun up and see that it lacks two feet of covering the mark; you start the piece to cover that two feet, but, unfortunately, you also start the trigger pressure, and by the time the muzzle covers one foot of the two, *Bang!* goes the gun.   Only the second barrel will save you now. Nevertheless and notwithstanding, the correct method of quail shooting is the delayed snap.

The above being true, or more or less true, why not use the delayed snap all the time?   Well, seven in ten shots in the course of a day ought to be fired with the delayed snap. There are reasons why all of them cannot be.   First, we have the rough snap in the woods, no other chance if we shoot at all. Again, what is to be done when the bird gets up directly in front and the shot is fired at a 90° angle from where the quail

broke cover?   When the quail jumps in front of us the natural impulse and the impulse sure to be followed is to try to
throw the gun on him.   If he is curving about he won't be
there when the gun comes up, far from it.   Now what is to
be done?   Well, if the shooter is just a human sort of man
he will follow after that bird, trying to overtake it and shoot
it.   That is a simple form of a rapid-swing.   The farther
the gun is from the bird the faster that swing will be, and that
is what causes most of the misses in a rapid swing.   Plenty
of men use the rapid swing altogether in quail shooting and it
works.   What I have against it is that it takes more nerve
force out of a man than the delayed snap.   At that, a percentage of our shots will always have to be directed by the rapid
swing, and all of them may be.

Our style of handling the gun, optically, is of some importance.   The old style of shotgun aiming—which I believe is
about obsolete—is to close one eye and sight with the other.
The second style is binocular or two-eye aiming.   The third
style is to simply point the gun, both eyes open, but never seeing the muzzle or knowing where it is pointed, except by
results.

One-eye aiming is quite useless in the brush.   This method
implies that when the piece is brought to shooting position,
it is checked long enough to permit the one eye to be closed
and the other to find and focus on the front sight or the barrels, whatever the shooter is accustomed to seeing.   Two objects at different distances are rarely seen plainly, and when
we have found the gun-sight the next thing is to find the bird.
When you do see him with that one eye, now focused on the
sight, it will be dimly, and he will look far away.   I had an
old friend who used to complain that when he had found his

sight he couldn't see the bird any more at all.   That's that, and is the result of closing one eye, so keep both open.

When two eyes are open the mark is not darkened; there is no effort to see the sight, and in fact the best way to shoot with both eyes open is never to see the gun at all.   Hitting where we wish, without seeing sights or the gun, is merely a matter of gun-fit and mechanical training.   When we hit a nail on the head, we watch the nail and not the hammer.   If we tried to watch the hammer and not the nail we all know what would happen.   Also, if we tried to change our hammer to one with a longer handle or a crooked handle, we know what would happen.   In my quail shooting I haven't the least remembrance of seeing the gun, and if I do see it I'll miss the bird.

A season or two ago, when one of the gun companies was building a duck gun for me, the head of the firm insisted on fitting the rib with Lyman front and rear shotgun sights, declaring that these would lead to more accurate work.   I told him that I'd never see those sights, and I never did.   Somebody else told me that I really saw the sights, but not consciously.   By way of testing this I placed a sight a third of an inch in diameter on the muzzle—and I never saw that either. I doubt if I could see a goose egg on the muzzle of the gun, except when it began to darken the target.

Quail shooting, as a rule, doesn't require extraordinary judgment as to lead or where to hold; neither is extremely accurate aiming demanded, especially with modified choke or open-bored guns.   The birds usually rise close to the gun, are shot at very moderate ranges, and, except on crossing shots, the lead will rarely exceed two feet, being from that down to "fair on."   About any of us can tell where a shot ought to be sent, but the trouble is to send it there, that is with mechanical execution.   Quail have to be walked up, and no man can tell where the little fowl will break cover, nor which way he will go.   Remember, then, that the gunner is walking, and more than likely the bird will spring unexpectedly as to place and time.   Shooting with the wrong leg in front and the body out of balance, doesn't mean hitting anything.   Therefore, maybe in the brief space of less than a second, the shooter has to whip his legs into position, to whip his gun into position, to whip his piece into a steady swing which must not be either too fast or too slow—all of which comes under the head of mechanical execution.   Do you get your cheek to the precise place on the comb, after making a half turn, that you would have placed it when standing perfectly balanced and shooting to the front?   If you do not, you fail in mechanical execution.

All this is a different thing, believe me, from taking a clay bird from the trap, body perfectly poised, gun at cheek, knowing just where the bird will spring and what he will do. It is also a far more difficult proposition, mechanically, than any description of waterfowl work.   Hence we have good duck shots who are poor on quail, and a darn big lot of good trap shots who are good on neither quail nor ducks.

The great secret of missing quail, what makes the bird really hard, is the long "aiming swing."   A man can jerk his piece or move it as fast as he likes, up to the time that movement must be governed by the trigger pull.   The farther the gun muzzle moves while aim is being taken, the greater the strain on the shooter, and the faster the muzzle of the gun moves the greater the probability of missing.   I have tried this out thoroughly, time and again, on a stationary mark, and whenever the muzzle movement exceeds a certain rate of speed, then the mark can't be hit except by accident. Swing the gun fast enough and its muzzle will make a haze in the air, like the wings of a flying duck that the camera is not fast enough to stop. Under the conditions a quail couldn't be hit were he standing still in the air. Men of very rapid perception and the greatest quickness and certainty of nerve action can govern a faster swing than other men, and this difference marks and separates the natural snap shot from the natural deliberate shot. Nature has as much to do with making a man a snap shot or the reverse as she has with making him a sprinter or a weight thrower.

Now, coming down to applied science, we find that during the time necessary to make a lightning snap the bird will fly forty feet from where he breaks cover. I have seen snap shots fired when a quail was not over twenty-five feet from the gun, but this was when he was either climbing or swinging about. In a delayed snap, the bird will cover forty-five to fifty feet, and in a rapid swing from fifty to sixty feet. In the woods where there are little openings but a few feet across, why, snap; it's your only chance. If the openings are wider, if you can see that the bird will remain in sight long enough, steady yourself and make the delayed snap—it will account for two birds to one taken without aim.

At last we are coming to the birds that are missed through errors in judgment as to where the pattern ought to be placed. Not a great many birds are missed for this reason, but some of them are. The first of these is the rising bird, which to the man back of the gun appears to be flying level. Stand off to one side and it could be perceived that the bird was steadily climbing. Shoot directly at one of these fellows and the result will be an inexplicable miss. Make it a rule to shoot high on all birds that have not towered, and are going away above the level of the gun.

The towering bird which rises to a certain height and then drops away is another story.   Shoot above him and you will miss by two feet.   Hold under him as you would at a going-away duck that has passed overhead.   It is harder to take a dropping bird than it is to take one rising, because the trigger pull must be timed to both the descending flight and the rising movement of the gun.   Pull quick now or the gun will get above him.

A lot of missing is due to hilly and irregular ground.   A bird flushed on the side of a hill or under a hill will generally go up and over it.   Get on him and over him before he reaches the top of that hill, if you can, for if you don't he will drop away so quickly as to become unhittable.   Misses are for two reasons—the bird drops like a rocket, and he curves away to one side or the other.

Catch incomers before they get too close.   A bird within fifteen or twenty feet of the gun, passing overhead, is an impossible mark—same old reason, too fast movement of the gun.   The passing bird must be led, led more than almost any other mark, because the little bird is so small that the distance between gun muzzle and mark in aiming looks greater than it actually is.   Ten feet in front is only five lengths of a big duck, but it is closer to twenty lengths of a quail.   Rarely is the allowance in front of a quail too much.

Some quail at distances of thirty yards and beyond are going to be missed by their dodging the pattern, after the trigger has been pulled to a perfect aim—doing this in the eighth of a second it takes the shot to reach them.   A larger percentage are missed between thought and action.   It takes two or three feet in the flight of a quail to make the hammer strike after the mind says the trigger is pulled.   During this interval, if the bird is so minded, he can duck, jump or swerve; whereupon if the pattern is no more than fifteen inches wide, there you are and there goes the quail!   In the brush another large percentage of quail are missed through the charge striking trees; for the man who can see a tree when the bird is in plain sight is no quail shot.   A bird in the woods climbs, then shoots for an opening which he may not have seen until on the wing.   The gun shoots for the opening, too, but the quail hits it and the gun does not.

The dodging, jumping, climbing and ducking of a quail are what make the open-bored gun necessary.   The little inaccuracies of holding, the small errors in judgment, the minor things that are unforeseen, make it imperative that we have some leeway in pattern.   The full-choked gun shoots mighty close and misses, the improved cylinder shoots no closer and kills.   At best, no man lives or ever has lived or ever will live who can kill all the birds shot at.   If any man ever tells you about someone he knows who never misses, don't call him a liar; just think it over and you'll understand that he either knows nothing about it or else his champion actually never does miss a quail—because he never takes the risk of shooting at them.

Chapter *XXVII*

HUNTING DOG AND HORSE

THERE are perhaps very few hunters in this country who believe in the Hindu theory that after death the soul of a man is reincarnated in an animal. For one, I grant some men might become lions, some cats, some wolves, others sheep, but never a man have I seen that was of sweet enough nature to become an ordinary little cur dog. An unspoiled child and a dog are somewhat akin, but a man has lived too long, and life has made him callous and selfish. As a penalty for his privileges, a man loses confidence in nature and human nature; he bristles sourly at all of his kind. Yet if he retains the love of a dog, or if he still loves a good dog, there is hope for him. The man who hates dogs or whom dogs hate, I have never understood—never have wanted to understand. He is not of my people.

In the shooting history of any man who has shot much is a long chapter to be devoted to his dogs, for they would be in the beginning of the story and in the end. It is well, then, to mention the dog here, together with the game, with the shooting horse and with the gun, if only for sentimental reasons. Truly, the wise and faithful dog, the thoroughbred horse, the straight-shooting gun, the swift-flying birds, are all inseparable.

I believe that many will agree with me that half the pleas-

ure of quail shooting comes from the unalloyed happiness of
the dog, working perhaps for his own pleasure, but far more
for that of his master.   Unlike waterfowl shooting or big-
game hunting, there is no tiresome waiting, nor are there any
colorless intermissions, where a merry and industrious dog
has the field.   His delight in his work, his obedience and will-
ingness, his wonderful nose, his wisdom in meeting the wiles
of the game with doggy intelligence, are all a source of endless
entertainment.   I have never yet reckoned a day lost where I
followed my dog through wood and thicket, across the stubble
and over the hills.   My game bag might be light or heavy, and
that would be forgotten presently, but the day would be
printed on the film of memory.

All in all, it has seemed to me that in conclusion of this
book it might be most appropriate for me to tell the story of a
man, his horse, his dogs and their last quail hunt of the season.
It was the last quail hunt forever for one of the dogs, which
died the following spring.   In fact, this little tale may also
be taken as a tribute to his memory.

Buster was and is a gaited saddlehorse—fox trot, pace,
running walk, canter, it was all the same to Buster.   A man
mounted on him, however old he might be, would have his
youth renewed, would feel that he was as good a man as ever
he had been, would see life as he had seen it, maybe forty years
before.   Buster was birdshy, his only fault.   Shooting off
his back he didn't mind, but the minute birds or a bird broke
cover, he pivoted on his hind legs, and the shot could not be
taken.   Neither could he be turned loose with the reins
dropped over his head, because he'd run away for home as sure
as fate.

Bobby was a true fox terrier.   He knew all the things a

If you happen to like any color so long as it is red. Irish setter and Irish water spaniel. They may be hard to see but they're never hard to look at.

Typical of Middle West wildfowling. A glimpse of the famous Illinois River, a noonday return on a camp hunt, and an Illinois River duck club's clubhouse.

terrier ought to know, had learned all the things that a terrier naturally ought to know, and would do nothing that a terrier didn't like.   He chased all the rabbits on the course, treed all the squirrels, caught all the vermin, retrieved all the game, land or water, taking it away from the other dogs.   He wasn't afraid of anything and never obeyed anybody.   He came to our house shortly after the war, as a stray, and was adopted by the little girl, taking his place behind the stove, and there he stayed.   He flushed every bird that was pointed by the setter, and if left at home, for this reason, escaping within an hour or two, was certain to take the track of Buster and find us.

Cute was just a trained white setter in his fourth year on game, much shot over and highly reliable.   He had few faults, when taken out alone, but when Monty and Bobby went along, Cute knew it was just a go-as-you-please holiday, —and he led in the mischief of chasing rabbits and coyotes, even deer, barked the loudest of them all at a treed squirrel.

As to the third dog, Monty, he that was the first to pass on, I must say more; and I find I shall after all have to disclose the identity of the man in this hunt.

My son was in the Forestry Service in Montana, located at a "lookout" cabin, thirty miles out in the mountains, all alone, so he sent for a sheep dog puppy, and got Monty at four months old.   He followed the boy out to his mountain home and the two lived there together for the next four months, seeing perhaps half a dozen people.   The little dog learned to hunt deer and elk and bear.   He would grasp a fallen deer, hold on like a bulldog, growl and shake.   On one occasion he and his master followed a wounded grizzly thirty miles back into unknown mountains, in snow a foot deep.   The bear had been knocked down twice, but the rifle lacked power and the grizzly kept going, though he had frequently lain down in the snow until the hunters approached.   The dog would have dashed ahead on the trail, but the boy wouldn't let him, knowing it would be the death of his dog.   When night came upon them high up in the mountains, it started to snow, covering up the tracks.   The boy cut a great mass of pine brush and piled it on the lee side of a big log.   He and the dog crawled under it, and the snow drifted over them.   The next day they traveled by compass, from morning until after dark, getting home and into bed too tired to eat, though nothing had been eaten since breakfast of the day before.   Naturally the dog and his master were thereafter greater pals than ever.

At the end of that year the boy transferred to the Border Patrol, and the dog was sent to me.   When he reached me, though young, he was a well-grown dog, weighing sixty to seventy pounds, and nobody could tell him from a great gray wolf.   Whatever the ancestry of the so-called German police dog, Monty had taken after the wolf, not a sneaking wolf, but a bold one, a wolf that should have been a killer, not afraid of anything whatever.   No man could put a hand on him, except the man he recognized as his master, and he never showed the least friendliness toward any other member of the family.   He charged any dog that approached him, on sight, a grim-visaged, heavy-shouldered, straight-charging wolf, that meant to kill as he struck.   No dog ever met that charge more than once, for the steel jaws would crush a leg or cut through a shoulder.

On the way to the shooting grounds I passed the house of a neighbor who owned a pack of hounds which took a deal of pleasure in coming out to the road to thrash the bird dogs.

They charged up to Monty just once—thereafter the whole pack would turn tail to escape under the porch when they saw him coming.

Monty knew nothing of cattle when he came to me—knew nothing except wild game, which was his meat. Before I knew what to expect, he drove into a bunch of cattle, caught a young steer by the hind leg and threw him. Probably he would have killed the beast except that I was near. I punished him and scolded him—more scolding than anything— and started him off for home. On my way in some time later, a poor forlorn sheep dog came crouching up to me from where he had lain in the tall grass, making what apologies he could, and asking that I take him back. I picked him up and hugged him and gave him a shake, the caress he liked best. Put down, he circled around me, yelping his delight. I never punished him again, and he never disturbed cattle again. He was the most biddable dog that I ever have known, a king only to be taught what was wanted of him.

By and by the quail season opened, and Monty was so sorrowful about being left at home when the horse and the gun and the setter started, that I just had to take him along and teach him something about quail hunting. He never made any protest when told he had to stay at home, but as I rode off would place his paws on the window sill and stand watching me go. He would remain so, if permitted, until I returned. I couldn't stand that, so except when I had company, Monty went along. He learned to back the setter, after a fashion, also learned to stop on birds, after his fashion, and he always would stop and stand to order, so we got along nicely. He had a good nose, hunted with high head, and drew on his game with a stiff, low crouch. He found birds, but his greatest delight was rabbits, and I never had the heart to break him of rabbit chasing, or coyote chasing, though I did stop him from running deer.

It was to be the last quail hunt of the season. Though close to midwinter, it was a mild and mellow autumn day, for winter hadn't really begun in Oklahoma. No wind blew, the sun was warm, and the shadows were dark on the yellow grass. The crows massed on the green wheat, and the bluejays were busy in the jackoaks. I tied a sheepskin-lined coat back of the saddle, for this day was a "weather-breeder," but rode in my shirtsleeves.

This day was to be a treat for the dogs—all of them. I had been shooting in company, and that meant Bobby and Monty had to stay at home. Now they were keen about it, with Monty jumping playfully at the horse's head, while Bobby jumped and turned wrong end to. Cute galloped away with reckless abandon, flag feathering merrily.

In a level expanse of meadow Cute drew to a point. Monty saw him and drew up slowly, a step at a time. Bobby went in as fast as his short, keen legs would carry him. I put Buster at a stiff gallop, and went in too. We all knew that it was a jack. In went Bobby and off went the rabbit, the terrier close after him, Monty next, with Cute and I coming hard. Bobby yelped, Cute yelped, Monty said nothing, and I "whooped," riding close up, for Buster was a quarter horse and couldn't be left behind in a short race. The rabbit escaped into a weed-patch, with Monty trying to hit off the trail. We were all feeling as fit as a fiddle, and the afternoon had begun well.

Down an old sand-trail, we came to an abandoned house, among the jacks, the house tumbled down, hedged by a dense growth of locusts two acres in extent. Cute had gone on about his business of finding quail, but Bobby and Monty were with me, poking about among the thickets, searching for whatever might turn up. Into the locusts they went and out came a bevy of quail, a bevy that I thought contained thirty birds. Buster pivoted on his hind-legs, with some excuse, for birds were all over him. Out came Monty and Bob, Bob yelping. They followed the birds into a dense jackoak thicket, where that particular bevy always went, and presently Bobby started barking, at a treed bird, with Monty trying to climb the tree. I got off and deliberately tied the horse, knowing that the setter was still in that thicket, and must be holding a point on some birds that hadn't flushed. Sure enough, a lingering cock bird came out. I hit him so hard that he was driven out of his course. Cute raised up among the locusts not forty feet away. Monty came up to see what was going on, but Bobby kept up his barking and I suspected a treed squirrel instead of a quail.

Monty went back to Bob, while Cute and I went on down the trail. Before long the two dogs came up, Monty carefully following the tracks of the horse, but Bobby knowing well where we were. A red squirrel flashed across the road, a fine bit of color in the somber woods. The dogs all saw him, and he was hard put to it to reach an oak, where I saw his tail waver and flash as he went into a hole. Bob barked and Monty climbed six feet into the tree and fell out.

Farther on the jays were having some kind of noisy dispute, in the jackoaks, towering above the trees and dropping back. I suspected a deer, but a great horned owl flew out as Cute went in to investigate; the old fellow was followed hard by twenty jays.

Cute began feathering on game, and Bobby saw him.

Monty was acting strangely. Drawing slowly up the hill on the opposite side of the road, a step at a time, ears pitched forward, tail stiff, hair slightly roached, creeping up on his prey —deer, I knew.

I rode just back of the big sheep dog, and when we reached the top of the hill, from a jackoak swale beneath, where the grass grew tall, where the shadows were deep and dark, great white birds began to flash out, bobbing up and down. I sat my horse and counted eleven of them, nothing but whitetails. Then a great buck hit an opening, rocking along gently, horns agleam. I sighted on him and said to myself, "Dead deer if I'd had a rifle." Monty looked up at me questioningly —this new master was different from the old one in Montana, who would surely have killed one of those deer.

I didn't want to torment the dog with the fresh scent of those deer, so turned away for the Thompson fields in the rear of the old house-place. One quail came sailing by us, and after him Bobby and Cute. In the old forty-acre field, away off in the distance, I saw the white dog standing, facing up the hill, rigid, head and tail high, a picture dog. No finer place could be found for a double, if I could beat Bobby. I didn't dare to hit a gallop, for the terrier would have understood. Seeing a bush handy, I jumped off, fast work now, and began tying the horse. Monty passed back of the setter and stood to order. Bobby didn't stand to order or for any other reason, but ran directly in, missed the birds, made two or three quick swings, and away went my chance for a double. No use to worry about it, that was what I expected when I took the terrier. The birds had gone into the timber, no more than seventy yards away, and I followed on foot—might accidentally get a shot or two.

Cute was standing in the edge of the timber, with Bob well down in the woods, out of sight. Monty was busy about a brush-pile, looking into it, wagging his tail. I flushed the setter's bird and killed; went to Monty, kicked on the brush, drove out a bird and dropped him. It was a winged bird, as it happened, but Monty saw it fall, and I knew that bird couldn't get away. The bird was a runner, but the sheep dog never hurried, following the track as relentless as fate, presently to come back with a cock quail, head held high, parading about me, talking deep in his throat. I pulled off the head of the quail and gave it to the dog to eat, talking of what a fine quail dog he was. Bobby came running back to see what the shooting was about, flushing and driving by me a half dozen birds, of which I killed one. Bobby retrieved it, after giving it his customary bite.

Mounting, I led off into the depth of the woods. The dogs needed water, and I knew where there was a well and a tank. Getting any more birds didn't matter in the least. We had quail at home, hanging in the pantry. Pointing birds didn't matter, chasing birds didn't matter, hitting them didn't matter, nor did missing them—this was a day of pure enjoyment, with never a worry in the whole world. Presently we came to an open glade, long and narrow. The white dog stood. Monty and Bob were out of sight. From the direction they had gone, a bevy came, winging in close formation, flying low. Cute's birds were flushed by the sound of wings, and went off after the first bevy. With these two flights of quail not yet out of sight, still a third bevy broke from the tall sedge and followed—all gone off in the same direction, headed for a swale grown up in sumac bushes a couple of feet high.

Of a sudden the shooting fever came over me. This was

an opportunity that must not be missed.   Stopping the dogs from following the birds, I looked about for a place to tie Buster, since I had lost that horse before.   High in a tree near by was a great hawk's nest, half as large as a barrel, and I tied him to that tree.   I could always find that hawk's nest, I thought.

The birds had apparently gone into the sumac swale. They ought to lie close in there and give me fine shooting as they topped the brush, which was not over three feet high.

Down we went and were into the thick of it immediately. Monty made game, and I stopped him.   The setter came up to back, Bobby came up to flush, and out went the birds, one at a time, until half a dozen had gone.   I killed a pair, not a double but one at a time.   Monty retrieved one and Bobby the other.   Monty moved up and held his point.   Scent must have been good this late in the evening, for the sheep dog never had stood so many birds before.   Cute was moving from point to point.   I shot the wolf-dog's bird first, knowing that he wouldn't hold if the gun cracked, while the setter would. Bobby was a busy terrier, trying to flush all the birds pointed, which he did.   That bothered me not at all, for they all got up within range, a bird every minute.   The game-carrier was getting heavy, this day when I didn't need birds.   It was a hot corner, the best shooting I'd had all the season.

Presently a dozen or so quail had gone over a ridge into a neighboring draw, and we went after them.   Later a half dozen had crossed a second ridge, to be followed.   The shadows suddenly blended, for the sun, already low, had gone behind clouds.   The white dog found again, and I killed; followed two birds, for a double.   The last bird was apparently winged, at a range I had no business to shoot, but nothing

could be missed this day.   That bird had struck the top of
a ridge, and I knew he'd prove a runner.   Monty struck the
trail of the cripple, and in the gathering darkness passed out
of sight, his gray and black colors blending, as they always
did in the dark.   Within a few minutes Bobby left me, going
up the hill, and then I heard a threatening growl.   I knew
what that meant—the sheep dog had the bird and he didn't
intend to give it up.   He came in with the quail, talking to
himself and to me, chuckling.   I picked him up with his bird
and gave him a shake, whereat he paraded about when re-
leased.   It was the last bird of the season, and I didn't know
whether I had exceeded the bag limit or not, and don't know
to this day.

It was time to find the horse and get away for home.   I
knew we had passed over two ridges, and the thing was to
retrace our steps.   Presently it was quite dark.   The wind
was humming in the tops of the jacks, a northwest wind.   I
couldn't find the hawk's nest, nor the horse.   In half an hour
I didn't know where I was, and hadn't the least idea which
way to go.   I went with the wind, thinking the horse must be
southeast of me.   At last it was evident that the more I wan-
dered about the farther off I'd get.   It was getting cold and
I wanted my sheepskin coat.   Among other things which
would occur to a lost man was regret that a human lacked the
instinct of a dog.   Those dogs were following me about in
the utmost confidence that I knew exactly where I was going,
and that I'd get out when I got ready.   In all probability
every one of them knew precisely the direction of home, and
precisely where Buster was, but if we stayed out all night
that didn't make any difference to the dogs.

A fire was started on the lee side of a fallen tree.   That fire lit up the woods, was warming and cheerful. I had no intention of leaving it until daylight. I knew that by facing partly into the wind, I could find my way out and get home, but my good horse was patiently waiting where I had tied him, and he knew I'd stay with him. An occasional flake of snow fell into the fire. The tops of the trees swung and groaned complainingly. I shucked the coat of a quail, held it over the fire until it was done and ate it—ate four of them, and then gave Monty three, Cute two, and Bobby one. The tired dogs curled up in the leaves, where the log broke the wind.

Of a sudden came the wailing of coyotes, to the west, not far away, attracted by the scent of the broiling quail. There was a quavering appeal in the lonely howling of the little beasts, and a certain hoarse, threatening rasp. Monty got to his feet, walked out to the limits of the firelight, sat down, and gave vent to such a howl as no coyote had ever heard since the days of the lobo. I had never myself heard such a howl—deep, threatening, making the very air vibrate. Monty came up to me, wagging his tail, but the hair on his back stood up. We heard no more of the little wolves, but listening, I heard the whinny of a horse.

We had no trouble in finding Buster, a hundred yards away, for the howling of the wolves had made him restless. I got into my heavy coat; then, having put out the fire, I rode off in the direction I thought right, and presently struck the old sand trail, and down it for home. Bobby took the lead as he always did, Cute to one side, and Monty directly behind the horse. It was snowing now, a dense, fine snow, but Buster held the trail and went along briskly for home.

The first thing to do was to bed down and feed the horse, Monty going along, as he always did. In the house we stirred up the fire and added great oak logs. The coffee-pot was put on, and a huge roast of beef and sweet potatoes warmed up. A corn pone was put in the oven to heat, and we found an apple pie. The folks were off on a Christmas visit, and we had the whole house to ourselves, the dogs and I.

Soon we were all eating, for the dogs would eat supper with me that night. Monty got a chunk of roast beef, Cute a slice, and Bobby his bit. We were all just as hungry as though we hadn't eaten those quail in the woods. How much meat there was in that roast I do not know—enough to last me three days, it had been thought. We ate it all that night, and all the potatoes and all the cornbread and the apple pie. Each dog got a piece of pie, and each ate his piece with due politeness.

The meal finished, I gave Cute an old coat back of the stove, Monty an old coat beside my chair, while Bobby curled up in his padded basket. I tried to read, but the sheer comfort of the house, after the cold we had endured, was too much for me. I pulled up a chair on which to rest my feet, put a cushion under my head, and lighted a pipe. The storm rattled the windows, shook the house, wailing and howling. I put more wood in the stove and shut off the draft. Bobby dreamed of chasing jackrabbits and barked in his sleep; Cute whimpered, but Monty was quiescent, after his kind—his the deep sleep of a well-fed wolf. The rattle and rush and roar of the blizzard blended into a lullaby, appropriate contribution of Mother Nature to croon and rock her children to sleep.

Thus the reader may perhaps fancy bidding Good-bye to us, the tired Oldtimer asleep in his easy chair, surrounded by his good dogs, snug in the glowing warmth that is the epitome of life, snoring all four cheek by jowl with the bitter blizzard that is death.

All life is composed of contrasts. No man can take a pride in his hitting unless he has also missed; no man can enjoy riches unless he has also seen poverty; no man can enjoy eating who has not known hunger. No man can enjoy blithe summer who has not also known grim winter; and no man can enjoy the height of happiness who has not also known the depth of sorrow. And so it is now in the spirit of the peace and the strength and the happiness of a day closed as was our day just told of that I turn down the light that is this book. It is written out of not forty but a full fifty years of shooting experience, in which as a shooting man—for I have never really been anything else—I suppose I have tasted the full gamut of ups and downs. In poverty or in wealth, in comfort or in hardship, in good weather or in foul, the Oldtimer wishes you well, with many happy days when the mallards tower or the bonny brown quail break from the ragweed field.